THE GAY MARRIAGE GENERATI

The Gay Marriage Generation

How the LGBTQ Movement Transformed American Culture

Peter Hart-Brinson

NEW YORK UNIVERSITY PRESS

New York

NEW YORK UNIVERSITY PRESS
New York
www.nyupress.org

References to Internet websites (URLs) were accurate at the time of writing. Neither the author nor New York University Press is responsible for URLs that may have expired or changed since the manuscript was prepared.

Library of Congress Cataloging-in-Publication Data
Names: Hart-Brinson, Peter, author.
Title: The gay marriage generation : how the LGBTQ movement transformed American culture / Peter Hart-Brinson.
Description: New York : New York University Press, [2018] | Includes bibliographical references and index.
Identifiers: LCCN 2018012204 | ISBN 9781479800513 (cl : alk. paper) | ISBN 9781479826230 (pb : alk. paper)
Subjects: LCSH: Gays—United States—Public opinion. | Gay rights—United States. | Same sex marriage—United States.
Classification: LCC HQ76.3.U5 H37 2018 | DDC 323.3/2640973—dc23
LC record available at https://lccn.loc.gov/2018012204

New York University Press books are printed on acid-free paper, and their binding materials are chosen for strength and durability. We strive to use environmentally responsible suppliers and materials to the greatest extent possible in publishing our books.

Manufactured in the United States of America

10 9 8 7 6 5 4 3 2 1

Also available as an ebook

CONTENTS

Introduction: From Nonsense to Common Sense in
a Generation   1

1. Imagining Generations and Social Change   11

2. Contesting Homosexuality's Imagination, 1945–2015   36

3. The Evolution of Public Opinion about Gay Marriage   72

4. Young and Old in the Cross Fire of the Culture Wars   96

5. The Imagination and Attribution of Homosexuality   129

6. The Imaginary Marriage Consensus   163

7. Narratives of Attitude Change and Resistant Subcultures   189

Conclusion: Moving beyond Generational Mythology   213

Acknowledgments   229

*Appendix: Studying Public Opinion with Qualitative
Interview Methods*   231

Notes   243

Bibliography   267

Index   285

About the Author   293

Introduction

From Nonsense to Common Sense in a Generation

On Friday, June 26, 2015, the US Supreme Court legalized gay marriage in all fifty states. In the controversial five to four decision (*Obergefell v. Hodges*), the Court not only ruled that same-sex couples are protected by the Due Process Clause of the Fourteenth Amendment and that they cannot be denied the right to marry, but also sounded a ringing endorsement of marriage as an institution that should be open to all, gay or straight. That night, to celebrate the resounding victory for lesbians and gays, the White House was bathed in rainbow-hued floodlights as if draped by a glowing, translucent pride flag.

The image was—and still is—breathtaking. For both supporters and opponents, it was a powerful symbol for everything that transpired— though it carried drastically different meanings. Speaking of the hundreds of supporters who gathered outside the White House that night, President Obama described the lighting as symbol of validation: "To see people gathered in an evening outside and on a beautiful summer night, and to feel whole, and to feel accepted, and to feel that they had a right to love, that was pretty cool."[1] By contrast, to the more than 133,000 religious conservatives who shared Reverend Franklin Graham's post on Facebook, it was a symbol of how much America had lost its moral compass: "God is the one who gave the rainbow.... Only those who are found righteous will be able to escape His judgment."[2]

To me, there was no better symbol of how quickly and dramatically the United States had changed. The ruling capped a titanic shift in public opinion, virtually unprecedented in modern polling.[3] In 1996, when President Bill Clinton signed the Defense of Marriage Act (DOMA) defining marriage as a legal union between one man and one woman, only 27 percent of Americans supported gay marriage. Over the next nineteen years, support for gay marriage grew by 30 percentage points—a big change for any political issue, let alone one involving such intimate matters as gender, sexuality, and religion.[4]

The shift looks even more dramatic if we travel back to 1988. That year, for the first time, researchers at the National Opinion Research Center asked Americans how they felt about gay marriage; only 11.7 percent supported it. How low is that number? It falls squarely in the range of conspiracy theories and congressional approval ratings: about 6 percent of Americans believe the Apollo moon landing was staged, 11 percent of voters believe the US government allowed 9/11 to happen, and 14 percent of voters believe in Bigfoot.[5] At the time of the Supreme Court ruling, 17 percent of Americans approved of Congress.[6]

In other words, back in 1988, the idea of gay marriage was *nonsense*. The idea was more or less equally ridiculous to young and old, liberal and conservative, religious and secular. Andrew Sullivan, one of the earliest public advocates for gay marriage, notes just how absurd the idea seemed at the time:

> I remember one of the first TV debates I had on the then-strange question of civil marriage for gay couples. It was Crossfire, as I recall, and Gary Bauer's response to my rather earnest argument . . . was laughter. "This is the loopiest idea ever to come down the pike," he joked. "Why are we even discussing it?"[7]

Twenty-seven years later, the "loopiest idea ever" became the law of the land.

How did this happen? How did gay marriage become accepted? And not just accepted, but enthusiastically embraced by the sitting president and a majority of the population? These are the questions this book answers. I tell the story of how what was once nonsense became common sense—how in the space of a single generation, the institution of marriage was revised in a fundamental way. In the process, we will address some more fundamental questions, beyond the case of gay marriage. How does social change happen? What are generations, and how are they made? Where do our worldviews come from, and how do we express them?

The Gay Marriage Generation?

Although gay marriage was not legalized in the United States by popular vote or legislative act, public opinion still affected the Supreme Court's decision to legalize it. Writing for the majority, Justice Kennedy devotes a full paragraph to explaining why he thinks there had been ample democratic debate on the issue, which "led to an enhanced understanding of the issue—an understanding reflected in the arguments now presented for resolution as a matter of constitutional law."[8] Had public opinion not evolved so much since 1996, the Supreme Court would not have heard the arguments that it did.

In an especially evocative passage, Kennedy writes, "changed understandings of marriage are characteristic of a Nation where new dimensions of freedom become apparent to new generations."[9] In one short sentence, Kennedy invokes three powerful ideas: that sexuality and one's choice of intimate partners are matters of personal freedom, that our understandings of marriage have changed, and that the emergence of new generations is part of the change. Kennedy implies that *time* was implicated in the Supreme Court's decision to legalize gay marriage because young people led the population as a whole to rethink its views on homosexuality and to remedy the injustice of excluding same-sex couples from marriage.

Over the course of this book, we will examine all of these issues, but the point about generations deserves special attention. Many Americans—especially those who lived through the battle over gay marriage—may already have an intuitive sense that generational change is a key part of the story. When I began studying gay marriage in 2006, commentators and public opinion analysts already had determined that the two key indicators of generational change were present: young people were more supportive than their elders, and public support for gay marriage was gradually growing. Whenever we see this pattern in public opinion data, there is a good chance that generational change is the cause.

So, is there a gay marriage generation, and was it the cause of the change? These simple questions turn out to be surprisingly complicated. To start out with, we have to clarify what we mean by "generation." Strictly speaking, social scientists use the term to refer to relations of kinship descent (grandparents to parents, parents to children, and so on). By contrast, a *cohort* is a group of people who experience the same event at the same time (e.g., people born during the Baby Boom, people who graduate from high school the same year). Hence, most social scientists would call the gay marriage generation the "gay marriage cohort."[10]

But even if we allow ourselves to use the term *generation* casually to mean cohort, there are still other issues to resolve. Sometimes we use *generation* to refer to broad cohort groupings that roughly divide a society's entire population (think Baby Boomers, who were followed by Generation X, who were followed by Millennials, and so on). At other times, we use the term to refer to specific groups who come of age during a particular historical event or phenomenon (think of youth during the Great Depression or the Vietnam War). The idea of a gay marriage generation belongs in this category, and this is not a trivial point. As we will see in Chapter 1, these two kinds of cohorts-as-generations come from different theories and imply radically different things about how generational change happens.[11]

Beyond the difference between cohort and generation, we also need to distinguish between cohort replacement and generational change. *Cohort replacement* is the inexorable process of population turnover—the continual remaking of the population through births and deaths. Sociologist Norman Ryder memorably called cohort replacement the "demographic metabolism" of society because young people, through birth, continually supply the society with new energy to keep it going, while old people, through death, continually leave the social body, their energy spent.[12] Until we stop having babies and learn how to cheat death, cohort replacement is inevitable.

To the extent that the young cohorts entering the population differ systematically from older cohorts leaving it, we can speak of *generational change*. To some extent, generational change also seems inevitable because it is hard to imagine young cohorts *not* differing from their elder counterparts; but many things don't change with cohort replacement because forces like parental socialization and religion reproduce old norms and values in the young. Essential to the study of generational change is therefore the study of how and why young cohorts develop attitudes or behaviors that differ from those of their elders.

If Justice Kennedy is right that a new generation (read: generational change) caused public opinion to shift in favor of legalizing gay marriage, then we must both count the numbers of people who changed and explain why they changed. We have to determine how much of the change came from cohort replacement, how much of it came from people changing their minds, and what would have caused either of those changes to happen in the first place. In Chapter 3, I provide a quantitative estimate of *how much* change in public opinion about gay marriage happened due to cohort replacement, but the real questions that this book answers have to do with *how* and *why* generational change happened: How and why do young people develop different attitudes about objects of profound social importance, like marriage and sexuality? How do historical forces cause generations to emerge, and why are some affected but not others?

Many readers may already have decent answers to these questions because we all intuitively know something about generational change. We all know about youth rebellion and about the potential significance of experiencing world-historic events firsthand. We are aware that our biographical experiences while we are "coming of age"—typically during late adolescence or early adulthood—shape our worldviews in enduring ways. We remember where we were on 9/11 or when we heard about President Kennedy's assassination, and we have all been caricatured as Millennials or Generation X or something else.

Generational theory is this body of thought concerning the intersection of history, biography, and social change: it blends the study of the demographic metabolism with the study of the cultural and psychological processes that make cohorts think and act differently from one another. As it turns out, generational theory is as alluring and evocative as it is puzzling and stubborn. We intuit that there is a kernel of truth to the generational labels but know that they are still stereotypes. We know that our formative years really were formative but that our attitudes and beliefs are not set in stone; we change as we age. It's intuitively obvious that our biographical experience of history shapes us, but we are hard-pressed to specify exactly how.

Generational theory was the underlying academic interest that drove me out into the fields of northern Illinois to interview college students and their parents about gay marriage in 2008–2009. Although it is much more common in the social sciences to study generational change by quantitatively measuring cohort replacement (for reasons explained in Chapter 1), I was more interested in trying to identify what cultural forces might be causing young cohorts to think differently about gay marriage. I wanted to compare how two cohorts of Midwestern Americans talked about gay marriage and (using the parent-child relationship to control for the influence of socialization) to listen for evidence of just how the process of generational change might be working.

The heart of this book comes from these interviews. The voices of these Midwestern Americans come from a pivotal moment in time—a time of transition when a significant change was under way but the outcome was not yet clear. When I began my interviews, gay marriage was legal only in Massachusetts, but my informants also sensed that change was coming. The discourses I document in this book therefore provide a snapshot of the change as it was unfolding: of how people talk about a contentious issue that was once settled as nonsense, but had become unsettled and was on its way to being resettled as a new common sense.

As we will see, the gay marriage generation is not a cohort; to the extent that the label can be applied to a group of people, it is that fraction of the cohort who came of age after 1992 and imagined homosexuality in a way that was very different from their elders. In reality, though, the gay marriage generation is the decades-long process, involving people of all ages, by which our whole society collectively redefined what homosexuality is, and thus what the idea of gay marriage means. Fully understanding the gay marriage generation therefore means understanding the process by which new worldviews emerge in the first place.

Homosexuality and Marriage in the American Imagination

It took me many years of study to fully understand the voices of my Midwestern informants. The key to explaining how gay marriage was so quickly transformed from nonsense to common sense—and the process by which young people's generational encounter with history shapes their worldviews—is the *social imagination*. Not *your* imagination, like the unicorns and fairies of fantasy; *our* imagination—our "collective representations" of reality and how they influence our thought and behavior.[13] The social imagination of homosexuality in American society has changed twice during the past half century, such that young cohorts imagine gay marriage to mean something different than older cohorts; at the same time, older cohorts are being challenged by the youth and a rapidly changing culture to *re*imagine these same concepts.

This thesis builds on a cross-disciplinary body of research in anthropology, communication, philosophy, psychology, and sociology that shows that the imagination is a crucial component of our social mind. In purely psychological terms, we exercise our imagination whenever we create mental images of things that are not present in our current sensory envelope—the time and space in which our body experiences the world through perception (sight, sound, and so on). Sometimes, our imagination builds purely on our memory (I can imagine what my parents look like, even though I can't see them right now); at other times, it builds on our mental *schemas*—a type of cognitive structure in which a concept is defined by a collection of cultural associations we have with it.[14] To take a trivial example, if I ask you to think of eating a piece of fruit, you will probably imagine eating a prototypical one, like an apple or a banana, rather than a botanical fruit, like an eggplant or a zucchini. This is because our schema for "fruit" includes associations with "tastes sweet" and "good in a pie" and "eat it raw." Mental schemas are resources that our imagination uses to process information and act in the world.

Although all human minds operate by creating and using mental schemas, the exact pattern of associations—the content of a schema—varies by culture and social experience. We call them *cultural schemas* to signify this.[15] Fruit is one example of how schemas are affected by culture, but *stereotypes* of people are probably the most important type of cultural schema for sociologists.[16] Our stereotypes are based on our cultural experiences in a society (as shaped by media representations and socialization), and the network of mental associations we develop over time become lodged in our minds as a schema, which we then draw on either consciously or unconsciously when we encounter individuals we perceive as members of that group. Importantly, although the imagination can cause us to perpetuate a stereotype, we can also use our imagination to counter a stereotype—intentionally breaking the cultural schema and its effects.[17]

The above observations illustrate the importance of asking two questions: How do our schemas come to consist of one set of associations rather than another? And how can we break the pattern of associations and create a cultural schema with different content? I argue that the social imagination is the process that produces and modifies the content of our cultural schemas. Formally, we can define the *social imagination* as the process by which collectives jointly create or modify the cultural schemas that individuals encounter and internalize through social experience and that provide the cognitive foundation for future action. It is this collective, cultural process of imagination that creates the stereotypes and schemas that individuals inevitably encounter when they come of age, and it is by engaging in the process of social imagination that we challenge, modify, and replace them for new generations.

This book shows how our attitudes and discourses about gay marriage are premised upon how we imagine homosexuality and marriage, and that our cohort-related differences in support for gay marriage both reflect and affect the generational change in the social imagination. At the macro level, I trace the changing American imagination of homosexuality in politics and media representations; at the micro level, my interviews show how different cohorts express their various imaginations of homosexuality in communicative interaction. I argue that the rapid shift in public opinion about gay marriage is therefore due to a generational change in the social imagination of homosexuality in American culture that unfolded at the end of the twentieth century and the beginning of the twenty-first.

Plan of the Book

The seven chapters of this book expand upon this argument in greater detail using three kinds of evidence and analysis. Chapter 1 is primarily theoretical in nature; readers exclusively interested in the issue of gay marriage may safely skip this chapter, but it is essential reading for those who want to know what generations are really made of. In it, I explain generational theory in detail, describe five interrelated problems that the theory poses to students of generational change, and explain the theory of social imagination to which I have just alluded.

Chapter 2 is historical in nature, drawing primarily upon secondhand accounts of the rise and evolution of the LGBTQ movement and their representations in mass media since 1945. The history shows how the social imagination of homosexuality evolved over time and thus distinguishes different periods in American history; it further suggests why cohorts who reached adulthood in each period would develop different cultural schemas of homosexuality based on how it was constructed in the public sphere. Chapter 3 presents the quantitative analysis of public opinion data, which show the existence of cohort and period effects in attitudes, along with the ways in which people's opinions about gay marriage are shaped by gender, education, politics, religion, and their views about homosexuality.

Chapters 4 to 7 present my analyses of the interviews I conducted with two cohorts of Midwestern Americans. Chapter 4 describes the discourses of the culture wars, along with the ways in which ordinary Americans who were caught in the cross fire talked about the issue. It shows how people were influenced by both cohort and ideology in interactive, dialogic ways, thereby producing an array of discourses about gay marriage that was more varied than the culture war rhetoric usually suggests. Chapter 5 shows how people express their imagination of homosexuality through metaphors and analogies and thus accounts for the influence of cohort on discourse described in Chapter 4. Chapter 6 uncovers the existence of a paradoxical consensus about the practical, everyday meanings that marriage has for people—paradoxical because it exists beneath the surface-level disagreement about definitions of marriage and implicitly legitimates the battle for gay marriage, even for opponents. Finally, Chapter 7 examines the reasons why many older Americans are just as supportive of gay marriage as their younger counterparts and why many younger Americans are just as opposed to it as their elders. In the conclusion, I consider the practical implications of this study for the future of gay marriage and draw out the bigger lessons we learn regarding generational change.

Terminology and Standpoint

Before we begin though, I want to briefly address the terminology I use in this book and my standpoint. For the sake of readability, I have tried to excise as much academic jargon from this book as possible, at the risk of sacrificing precision. Although I have used "same-sex marriage" in my research and academic publications, here I use the popular term *gay marriage* because it rolls off the tongue more easily. Similarly, in my academic publications, I have used the phrases *social imagination* and *social generation* and insisted upon particular meanings; in this book, I frequently drop the word *social* from the front. Thus, in most cases, *imagination, generation,* and *generational change* should be read to emphasize their social, collective nature.

Different readers may find this book's focus and representation of homosexuality, lesbians, and gays objectionable for a variety of reasons. In the historical chapter, I try to represent cultural understandings accurately in the context of their times, which means laying bare the contested stigmas, prejudices, and values. In my interviews, I intentionally shifted my language when discussing homosexuality to meet the cultural norms and conversational styles of the people I was talking to. Academics and activists are right to emphasize the importance of labeling and word choice because of how language can frame issues and exclude people, but I made the choice as an interviewer to strive to be more conversational and to avoid making informants feel defensive about their own language. I believe this had the effect of encouraging them to open up to me in ways they might not have otherwise and thereby helped me to understand their worldview more fully.

Beyond my standpoint as a researcher, I made it a point to never inquire about my informants' sexual orientations or reveal my own (a few informants asked me about my sexual orientation during their interview). I do not know to what extent interviewees assumed anything about my own sexual orientation. I have often been mistaken for gay, but most Americans tend to assume people are straight unless given evidence to the contrary. I had gotten married the summer before I began my interviews, so some informants noticed the wedding ring on my finger. Thus, my standpoint as a straight, married researcher associated with a prominent university put me in a position of power and privilege, which certainly affected the things people said to me. Readers should keep in mind that another researcher might have asked different questions about gay marriage and elicited different answers; though as a social scientist, my sincere hope is that the overall story of generational change would be the same.

1

Imagining Generations and Social Change

Like many academic studies, mine has a story behind it. In 2006, when I was a graduate student at the University of Wisconsin–Madison, voters in the state confronted a referendum on gay marriage in the midterm elections. The question before voters was whether or not to amend the state constitution to define marriage as between one man and one woman—and thus prevent the courts from overturning the existing statutory ban as unconstitutional (what happened in Massachusetts in 2003, making it the first state to legalize gay marriage).

I was a teaching assistant for a class called "Contemporary American Society," and the week before the election, I decided it was my civic duty to have my students talk about voting and the issues that would be on the ballot. Predictably, at a liberal campus like Madison's, the students in my discussion section who supported gay marriage dominated the discussion and were quite vocal about voting "no" on the referendum. As an educator, I felt my role was to try to create space for the other side, so I asked the students, "Why do you think people oppose gay marriage? What reasons do you think they would give to explain why they would vote to define marriage as between one man and one woman?"

Silence. Even in my normally contentious discussion section, my question was met with awkward glances. Tentatively, one student raised his hand and said the opponents were religious and thought that homosexuality was a sin. Then, another student said that they were bigoted and intolerant. That was it. My students were extremely fluent in the language of support for gay marriage, but they had trouble explaining why people opposed it.

I found myself explaining to them the profound sociological significance of de-gendering marriage. Although there is no one "traditional" marriage, and although procreation has not been viewed as essential to marriage for decades, it is true that the opposite-sex couple had been a taken-for-granted part of the institution of marriage in modern Western societies. I explained that the very idea of gay marriage had been un-thinkable to most Americans until very recently and that it would be reasonable for someone to be upset that the conventional wisdom was being challenged.

This kind of classroom one-sidedness happens all the time, so nor-mally it would not have made an impression—except for the fact that the editors of the conservative student newspaper at UW–Madison also took a pro–gay marriage stance on the referendum. The *Mendota Beacon* was an activist newspaper funded by the conservative Leadership Institute, and its motto, "Shining Light on What's Right," truthfully advertised the right-wing viewpoint that could be found in its pages.[1] Normally, the newspaper followed the Republican Party line on most issues, and when it didn't, it advocated more conservative principles. But with gay marriage, the editors bucked the party line and advocated that students vote "no" on the constitutional amendment.

Together, these events made me wonder: Could this be a genera-tional issue? Could young people be that much more supportive of gay marriage that even the conservative activists approved? And if so, why? When I began studying public opinion data on the issue, it certainly seemed to be a clear-cut case of generational change. Both tolerance for homosexuality and attitudes about gender equality had liberalized in this manner: not only were young egalitarians replacing older tradition-alists in the population, but there was evidence that older Americans were adapting to the changing times by changing their attitudes.[2]

But when I began reading the research on generations, I was disap-pointed. In both scientific studies and popular books, I noticed a serious disconnect between what the authors were saying and what the classical theorists of generational change had written. In the popular literature, all I saw were crude stereotypes about Generation X, Millennials, and other broadly defined cohorts. By contrast, the scientific research on generations I found seemed totally unrelated to the popular understand-ing. There was a vast literature on relations of kinship descent across the life course (e.g., among grandparents, parents, and children) and an equally large literature on cohorts (focused on quantitative measure-ments of their similarities and differences), but very little research on cohorts' cultural distinctions. It was as if social scientists found the pop culture stereotypes of generations to be so appalling that they wanted nothing to do with them.

In this chapter, I explain why this puzzling gap in the literature about generations exists and how we can bridge it. First, I trace the source of the divergent meanings of the generation concept back to its classical foundations. Although philosophers throughout history have understood the importance of generational change, I discuss the work of Karl Mannheim, whose theory of generational change has been the most influential.[3] Second, I outline five key problems that Mannheim's theory poses to researchers who want to document and explain generational change. Third, I discuss recent innovations in generational theory and explain the importance of the social imagination; I argue that the concept is well suited to generational theory because it links society-wide changes in history and culture with the psychological processes by which individuals form and articulate their worldviews.

This lays the foundation for the study of gay marriage that follows in subsequent chapters. Generational theory requires us to combine three types of social research: a thorough description of historical events, a precise quantitative analysis of how the population changes over time, and a cultural and cognitive explanation of how young people develop distinctive worldviews, based on their biographical encounter with history while coming of age. When the insights from each of these types of research are combined, we can understand exactly how and why generational change occurs.

Generational Theory

Most people have a decent, intuitive understanding of generational theory. Social scientists have formalized and extended this basic view in important ways, and their efforts have produced some valuable insights. They also have debunked some important myths and can help us avoid common traps in our conventional thinking. But our everyday version of generational theory is a good place to start.

In general, we think of generations as groups of people who share a common location in historical time and who develop distinctive world-views and patterns of behavior because of the experiences they had while coming of age. Typically, the experiences we have during adolescence and early adulthood create a set of stable, enduring values and orientations that serve as foundations for future thought and behavior. Because different age groups go through this developmental phase during different historical periods, each *cohort* will be different from the ones before and after it. Sometimes the differences are so dramatic that young people have trouble understanding older people, and vice versa: old people complain about "kids these days," while young people tell their elders to "get with the times."

We use this commonsense view to talk about generations in two contrasting ways. First, when we think about groups like the Sixties Generation or Digital Natives, we think of significant historical events or societal trends and how growing up during that time produced a unique group of people. The Sixties Generation came of age during the Civil Rights Movement, the Vietnam War, and Woodstock, and they fundamentally reshaped American politics and culture with their protests, music, and sexual mores. Similarly, today's Digital Natives can't be separated from their smartphones, are in constant contact with their peers, and share everything about their lives online. In this view, generations emerge in response to some notable change to society; only some people belong to those generations, while others do not.

In the other view, everyone belongs to a generation that has some kind of unique worldview, based on the year they were born. The idea that the Millennial Generation follows Generation X, which follows the Baby Boomers, and so on, illustrates this latter view. The temporal boundaries between the generations aren't always clear, but this succession of generations is thought to follow a fixed interval of time that can be indexed to the life course. The labels capture the idea that people who grow up during different periods in history develop different psychological and behavioral traits that define them as a group.

Although this latter view of generations has some major flaws, which I explain below, both views illustrate generational theory's basic presumption that the process of coming of age during a particular historical era creates distinctive worldviews and acts as a potent force of change. However, the fuzziness of the character traits that we associate with different generations points to a big problem: generational research often produces one-sided stereotypes of whole age groups. Not everyone who came of age during the 1960s was a liberal hippie. Not all Millennials are constantly checking their smartphones. Stereotypes drive sociologists crazy, and no self-respecting social scientist can accept this basic view of generations, despite its intuitive appeal.

Karl Mannheim, the most influential generational theorist in the social sciences, confronted this challenge in the 1920s, and his discussion of what he called "The Problem of Generations" is Exhibit A for why generational theory is, on one hand, so evocative and important while, on the other hand, so stereotype-prone and resistant to scientific study.[4] Mannheim's theory of generations is worth discussing in detail because it provides the framework for a more comprehensive and nuanced analysis of generational change.[5]

Mannheim's thinking on the subject was inspired by the Marxists' problem of class consciousness. Like most social scientists of his time, Mannheim was familiar with Karl Marx's theory of communist revolutions and the debates about why workers did not rise up to overthrow capitalism, as Marx predicted. Why did workers fail to develop the working-class consciousness that one might expect of those exploited, paid meager wages for dangerous work, and subjected to terrible living conditions? Mannheim reasoned that developing a working-class consciousness depended upon much more than simply being part of the working class. Workers *also* had to experience the deprivation that Marx predicted (not all workers did); *then* they had to be connected to a Communist Party organizer (not all workers were); and *then* they had to actualize this working-class consciousness by acting on their identity as workers and suppressing other status group identities (like occupation, religion, and ethnicity) that might inhibit mobilization. Only if all four of those conditions were met would the workers rise up against the capitalists.

Mannheim argued that the same logic held for generations. Simply being part of a cohort—being the same age as someone else—wasn't enough to make you part of a generation. You also had to share a common experience with others in that cohort, develop meaningful personal relationships with others who also shared those experiences, and then develop a common identity, worldview, or set of behaviors to bring your distinctive generation into being.

Mannheim therefore distinguished among four separate generation concepts, the interrelations of which define the *problem* of generations and serve as the foundation for subsequent generational research. The *generation location* is what we, today, call a cohort; it refers simply to a group of people defined by a shared location in historical time and space.[6] Members of a cohort have nothing in common, other than the fact that they were born during the same historical period into the same society. There is potential for a generation to emerge from a generation location, but something else is required. Put differently, being in the same cohort is a necessary but not sufficient condition to being part of a generation.

Mannheim defines the "generation as an actuality," or *actual generation*, as those members of a cohort who "participate in the characteristic social and intellectual currents of their society and period."[7] What Mannheim means is that to become a generation, members of a cohort must share a common and distinctive experience with history that is made possible by their unique position in historical time and in social space. Not only must you be in the same age group in the same society, but you also must occupy similar social positions in that society, such that you *experience* history in the same way.

An example may clarify this distinction. In a classic study, sociologist Glen Elder Jr. studied the effects that growing up during the Great Depression of the 1930s had on that cohort as they moved through the life course. Generational theory predicts that this would have a variety of long-lasting effects on the cohort's behaviors and worldviews: we might expect them to be more frugal and to value steady employment more than older and younger cohorts. But this was not true for the whole cohort. Elder found that only people who experienced deprivation firsthand were affected in lasting ways; those who lived through it but weren't adversely affected by it were no different from other cohorts. Thus, the *actual Depression Generation* comprised only a certain subgroup of the cohort—those who experienced the historical event directly.[8]

Before moving on, it is worth pausing to draw out one important implication that this example illustrates regarding the distinction between cohort and generation. In reality, only certain members of a cohort become a part of the actual generation, so our tendency to identify whole cohorts as generations should be presumed wrong until proven otherwise. What separates the actual generation from the cohort are the cultural and social psychological processes that emerge when people experience the unique conditions of history in a particular way. These "social generational" processes translate the experience of history while coming of age into the enduring worldviews and behaviors that we observe in some members of the cohort.[9]

The third generation concept described by Mannheim is what he called a *generation unit*. Just as the actual generation is only a subset of the generation location, so too is a generation unit a subset of the actual generation. Mannheim argued that each actual generation is composed of multiple generation units, which are concrete groups that "work up the material of their common experiences in different specific ways."[10] In other words, members of the actual generation experience the same social and historical forces of their era, but they react to them differently. So while some people in the Depression Generation might have joined the Democratic Party, others might have joined the Communist Party. To the extent that people in the actual generation form identifiable, concrete groups that display a shared reaction to their generational experiences, we can speak of generation units.

Many of the groups that come to mind when we think of generations are actually generation units. For example, when someone mentions the Sixties Generation, she is probably thinking of the hippies of the late 1960s who went to Woodstock and protested the Vietnam War or maybe the Civil Rights activists of the early 1960s. These are both generation units because they represent concrete, identifiable groups who reacted to the shared experience of a historical moment in a similar way. Because there are multiple generation units in the actual generation, we should be able to identify other generation units as well. What about the white Southerners who fought against the Civil Rights Movement? Or the young people who became soldiers and fought in the Vietnam War? The fact that we tend to think about some generation units and not others shows just how easy it is to stereotype whole cohorts in the name of generational theory.

It also points us toward the fourth generation concept that Mannheim describes: the *generation entelechy*. An entelechy is a philosophical concept that refers to something coming into being—the realization of a potential. In this sense, a generation entelechy refers to a particular generational style, identity, or behavior coming into being—the uniqueness of a generation becoming actualized as a real social force.

The generation units that we notice and remember created a generation entelechy, though not in isolation. In reality, the generation entelechy emerges out of the relations among generation units with one another and with contemporaries from other cohorts.

Mannheim's theory of generational change is therefore based on a three-way distinction among groups of people within cohorts, with the generation entelechy being the visible manifestation of the whole process. In essence, multiple generation units sit within the actual generation, while the actual generation is only one part of the generation location. What distinguishes the actual generation from the generation location is a shared experience with history, and what distinguishes among generation units are their divergent reactions to the shared experience.

Let's take one more example from sociological research to illustrate how these distinctions can make the difference between stereotype and reality. Research has shown that when people are asked to name important historical events that have happened during their lives, they are more likely to name things that occurred during adolescence and early adulthood— just as generational theory predicts. In 1989, sociologists Howard Schuman and Jacqueline Scott showed this to be true for a wide variety of issues, but generational memory of the Civil Rights Movement failed to fit the pattern.[11] The reason for this exception was a mystery until sociologist Larry Griffin reanalyzed the data, this time dividing people according to the region of the country in which they lived. He found that people in the South but not those who lived elsewhere were more likely to mention the Civil Rights Movement.[12]

Griffin's findings confirm a logical expectation and illustrate the importance of distinguishing between the generation location and the actual generation: because people in the South experienced the Civil Rights Movement more directly than people in the North, it stands to reason that they would be more influenced by it. Thus, in terms of collective memory, the actual Civil Rights Generation is composed of only one fraction of the cohort—those who grew up in the South; and within it are some generation units who supported integration and others who opposed it.

Even though Mannheim's theory of generations is consistent with our commonsense view of it, his distinctions among the four generation

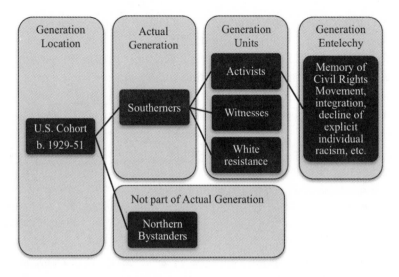

Figure 1.1: The Civil Rights Generation
Note: Based on Griffin, "'Generations and Collective Memory' Revisited."

concepts show just how easy it is to caricature a whole cohort inappropriately and how careful we must be when studying generations scientifically. Considering these examples from the Sixties Generation and the Depression Generation, it should be clear that distinguishing among these generation concepts can make the difference between accurately describing social change and perpetuating generational falsehoods.

Problems of Generational Analysis

Mannheim's theory of generations is both profound and alluring in the ways it promises to unlock the mystery of how society slowly changes as history evolves and young cohorts replace old ones in the population. However, the complexity of Mannheim's theory makes it difficult for researchers to fully validate the predictions of generational theory. Specifically, generational theory poses five interrelated problems for social scientists seeking to document and explain generational change.

First, the previous section illustrated the *problem of intra-cohort variation*—that there are several levels of difference among groups within the cohort. The *actual generation* is only a subset of a *cohort*, so one cannot study generations by defining them as cohorts. Moreover, the actual generation consists of multiple *generation units*, so not all members of an actual generation think and act alike. It should cause no great controversy to assert that not all people of the same age are alike; yet scholars and popular writers routinely equate the actual generation with the cohort or with the generation unit.

Starting first with academic research, it is common for scholars to define intra-cohort variation in terms of generation units (or what are sometimes called "political generations"), because it is clearly true that different groups in society would respond differently to events like the Vietnam War or 9/11.[13] However, scholars rarely make the distinction between cohort and generation in tandem with the distinction between generation and generation unit. Thus, most research never accounts for multiple levels of intra-cohort variation.

If there were an act of original sociological sin to which we could trace the consistent failure of social scientific research to distinguish between the cohort and the actual generation, it would be the publication of Norman Ryder's classic 1965 essay on the cohort concept, in which he largely transposes Mannheim's entire generational theory onto the "generation location."[14] Ryder's essay helped to establish the field of cohort analysis as an important sociological subject, but he did so by flattening the multilayered richness of Mannheim's theory.[15]

When American sociologists, inspired by the social turmoil of the 1960s, set out to measure exactly what was distinctive about the Sixties Generation, they used the cohort concept as their measure. The researchers usually found that anything distinctive about the cohort disappeared once they took educational attainment and political ideology into account. In other words, what made the Sixties Generation distinct was not the fact that they came of age during a unique historical period, but the fact that more liberals were going to college than ever before. Indeed, the uprising of the New Left during the late 1960s was largely centered on college campuses among political liberals. So when scholars set out to measure the unique attitudes of the Sixties Generation, they found that education and ideology, not age, explained the difference.[16]

These findings are entirely consistent with Mannheim's theory, taking into account the fact that only certain subgroups of a cohort would be part of an actual generation, and that there would be many distinct generation units within that; but because Ryder had successfully redefined the problem in terms of cohorts, scholars interpreted their findings as evidence *against* generational theory. Literature reviews from that period confronted the problem that researchers never could confirm their hypotheses about the existence of the Sixties Generation, despite what appeared at first to be clear evidence that it did.[17]

Social scientist David Kertzer's solution to this problem unintentionally reinforced the one-dimensional flattening of generational theory in terms of the cohort.[18] Noting the many different meanings of the word *generation*, Kertzer argued that the word should be restricted to its narrow, kinship-descent meaning and that it should not be used to describe differences between age groups. Thereafter, in American sociology at least, the field of cohort analysis flourished, as did research into (kinship-descent) generations; but generational theory was emptied of its research warrant. Several outstanding empirical studies inspired by Mannheim's theory were produced after Kertzer's 1983 article, but sustained attempts to analyze generational change declined after the theory's apparent failure to account for the Sixties Generation.[19]

Popular writers on generations committed a different sort of sin. Whereas academic researchers tried their hardest to measure actual generational distinctions in terms of cohorts, popular commentators tended to construct one-dimensional stereotypes of whole cohorts on the basis of a single generation unit, making little effort to acknowledge the variation among its members. Social scientists, in a way, needed to jettison the complexities of generational theory in order to produce rigorous, academic studies of cohorts; by contrast, popular writers found the cultural generalizations to be more appealing to general audiences. Their books may be compelling and provocative, but only because they traffic in half-truths.

Take, for example, several notable books describing the Millennial Generation. If you believe the cynical analyses of English professor Mark Bauerlein and psychologist Jean Twenge, authors of *The Dumbest Generation* and *Generation Me*, respectively, these young Americans are the most selfish, individualistic, narcissistic, and academically ill-prepared cohorts in recent history.[20] By contrast, if you believe Neil Howe and William Strauss, authors of *Millennials Rising*, or Morley

Winograd and Michael D. Hais, authors of *Millennial Momentum*, these same youth are the next great civic saviors of American society—more altruistic, politically engaged, and hardworking than previous cohorts.[21] The comically different caricatures that these authors have created testifies to the failure of their enterprise: because they overlook differences within the cohort, they merely select some stereotypical traits from particular subgroups to apply to the entire cohort.[22]

The problem of intra-cohort variation is, to some extent, both amplified and caused by the *problem of measurement*. For social scientists, the problem of measurement is both simple and fundamental because we must base our studies on what we can measure. We have tools to measure cohorts, generation units, and generation entelechies; but until recently, social scientists did not specify the procedures to measure Mannheim's "actual generation," even though that concept is the crux of the whole theory. Cohorts are easily measured using quantitative surveys: you simply ask people what year they were born. Generation units and generation entelechies are also easy to measure because those are the most visible manifestations of change.

But the actual generation—the subset of the cohort who shares an experiential encounter with history but does not react to it in a particular way—is harder to identify by conventional methods. The actual generation can be identified not by either similarities or differences alone, but by a particular pattern of similarities and differences, both between and within cohorts. The works by Elder and Griffin discussed above are examples of how it may be done, but a commitment to distinguish the actual generation from the cohort and from the generation unit is essential. Had the social scientists studying the Sixties Generation interpreted their quantitative studies of the cohort with this in mind, they might have reached different conclusions about generational theory.[23] In recent decades, social scientists have developed new methods for measuring the processes that distinguish the actual generation from the cohort, as I discuss below.

The problem of measurement is also linked to the *problem of perspective*. Any scholar who wants to conduct a study must adopt a particular methodological perspective or approach in order to carry it out. From the formulation of a research question to the choice of methods to the analytic procedures, one's orientation toward the object of interest is consequential. What makes this a problem is that rigorous analysis of generational change must combine three distinct perspectives simultaneously, and it is difficult to overcome because researchers tend to specialize in specific subject areas and methods, to the neglect of others. Thus, it would be quite difficult to test generational theory in its entirety in a single study.[24]

Adopting a *demographic perspective* to the problem of generations demands that the researcher concentrate on disaggregating age, cohort, and period effects in longitudinal, quantitative data. Such studies can differentiate the amount of the total change over time that is due to cohort replacement from the amount that is due to intra-cohort attitude change. Additionally, they can provide clues about how much demographic and attitudinal factors are correlated with the observed generational change. However, longitudinal studies from a demographic perspective alone are insufficient to fully explain how and why change happens.[25]

Adopting a *narrative, historical perspective* to the problem of generations demands that the scholar concentrate on qualitative, historical research to determine the boundaries of historical periods, the nature of critical events and turning points, and the substantive facts of the change. Such studies can produce a description of how individuals, institutions, and organizations that make up society changed from one era to the next. Coupled with the demographic perspective, a historical study can define meaningful boundaries of cohorts and suggest plausible causes and covariates of generational change.

Adopting a *cultural, interpretive perspective* to the problem of generations demands that the scholar concentrate on analyzing how people's worldviews are shaped by the historical events that they experience while coming of age. Such studies can produce an explanation of the cultural and social psychological mechanisms that cause changes in the larger social structure (documented by the historian) to result in the formation of unique attitudes, orientations, and behaviors among members of the actual generation. The first two perspectives alone are insufficient because the actual generation is distinguished from the cohort by cultural and social psychological processes that are often best studied from an interpretive perspective.

Fourth, the *problem of reification* is that even though generations are most easily defined as groups of people, the generation is really an active and ongoing process, not a static and unchanging group. In one respect, the problem is grammatical: "generation" is both a collective noun and an abstract noun. It refers both to a group of people and to the process of generating, and since it is often easier to grasp abstract concepts by personifying them, we tend to think of generations as people rather than as processes.

The issue is not merely grammatical, however; it has major empirical and theoretical implications. Empirically, it is one thing to measure a group of people, but another to measure a process; so how you conceive of the thing you are measuring both affects and is affected by your research method. Theoretically, the relation of a group to a process is essential to understand because different groups may exhibit varying levels of agency in the overall process of generational change. To what extent are young generations created by forces outside their control, and to what extent are they active creators of generational change? Some groups, like the Depression Generation, appear to be passive victims of circumstance; while other groups, like the Sixties Generation, appear to be the source of their own generational distinction.

This is not an "either-or" dilemma but a "both-and" conundrum. We have to understand the *generation-as-group* as both a cause and an effect of the *generation-as-process,* and we can gain some clarity on this issue only if we focus on the process, not the people. There is no consensus on the nature of the generational process, but much of the existing research treats the group as an outcome of the process. Strong evidence exists for both the impressionable years hypothesis and the persistence hypothesis—that late adolescence and early adulthood are the phases of the life course in which people develop foundational attitudes and orientations, which then remain relatively stable throughout the life course.[26] Scholars have also used constructs like socialization and generational imprinting to describe the process that creates new generational groups.[27]

More recent theories view young generations as agents of change, not just as products of forces that are beyond their control. Concepts like cohort norm formation and historical participation suggest that young generations are actively creating social change.[28] Similarly, scholars inspired to think of generations in more contemporary theoretical terms—in Bourdieuian terms of habitus, field, and doxa, or in terms that derive from a variety of discursive, performative, and queer theories—start from the implicit assumption that structure and agency are mutually intertwined, and therefore that young generations both shape and are shaped by the generational process.[29]

In short, it is easy to reify the generation, stamping a group of people with a label that is actually about a set of ongoing, active processes; but we do ourselves a disservice if we forget the process meaning of generation when we talk about people as generations. It is not wrong to use the term as a collective noun, but when we do, we must remember that it is perhaps nothing more than a convenient shorthand way of referring to those groups who have created and endured the things that both distinguish them from others and have the potential to transform society. Studying the generational process is therefore of utmost importance for those who want to understand what generations are and how they work.

The fifth and final problem facing people who want to understand generational change is the *problem of boundaries*, especially the *temporal* boundaries that define periods and cohorts and the *substantive* boundaries that define the scope of generational distinction. These boundaries are defined in relation to each other and to the historical events, trends, and structural changes that give young cohorts "fresh contact" with society.

In general, there are two broad approaches to the problem of boundaries: the *imprint paradigm* and the *pulse-rate paradigm*.[30] Mannheim's theory and other social scientific studies like this one are examples of the former, which takes a particularistic, inductive approach to identifying boundaries, while latter approach is universalistic and deductive. Unfortunately, the pulse-rate paradigm has tremendous popular appeal and has produced enduring popular beliefs about cycles of generations, despite it being little more than social astrology. Therefore, it is necessary to explain the problems with the pulse-rate paradigm before turning to the more scientific approach.

The pulse-rate paradigm assumes that generations are tied to the biological rhythm of the life cycle (birth, adolescence, adulthood, etc.), that a society's whole population can be divided into a series of non-overlapping cohorts of fifteen to twenty-five years in length, that these cohorts develop "peer personalities" that distinguish them from their elders and juniors, and that the history of societies is marked by repeating generational cycles.[31] This approach has a philosophical pedigree that has given it a gloss of authority and some cultural staying power. Most notably, the Spanish philosopher José Ortega y Gasset argued that generations, like our life stages, are fifteen years in length, and that Western Europe's cultural, political, and economic history can be explained according to the regular fifteen-year generational cycle beginning in 1626 (why, the year of René Descartes's thirtieth birthday of course!).[32]

Historian Hans Jaeger rightfully observes that "the grotesque ineptness of this thesis prohibits any closer scrutiny," yet the foremost popular commentators on generations in the United States, Neil Howe and the late William Strauss, use this very approach.[33] Together, they authored seven books on generations and founded a private consulting business to help organizations develop strategies for dealing with generational change. In their master treatise, *Generations: The History of America's Future, 1584 to 2069*, Strauss and Howe propose that life stages and generations are twenty-two years in length and that the generations constitute a four-part repeating cycle, with each adopting one of four peer personalities—Idealists, Reactives, Civics, and Adapters—depending upon the part of the cycle in which they come of age.[34]

It is this view of generations that gives rise to the very idea of Generation X, Millennials, and iGen (or Generation Z, or whatever label they get stuck with), which are almost purely social fictions.[35] By contrast, the Baby Boom cohort is actually a meaningful group that is defined demographically; because of its size, the Baby Boom cohort affects many aspects of society—from employment rates to government budgets.[36] The same cannot be said about the younger generations, which have been concocted as the pulse-rate successors to the Baby Boomers, but which primarily serve as Rorschach blots upon which different groups project their prejudices.

The pulse-rate view of generations has all the appeal and problems of astrology: it is a deceptive mix of existential complexity with elegant simplicity that invites us to focus on confirming evidence and overlook disconfirming evidence. We *want* to believe because of the power of suggestion—and it would be so cool if it were true! Unfortunately, society is so messy, complex, and shaped by the unpredictable actions of people with free will that social scientists have long given up the search for the sort of natural laws that appear in math, physics, and chemistry.

The imprint paradigm, exemplified by Mannheim, and the pulse-rate paradigm thus constitute fundamentally opposite views about how generations are formed: the imprint paradigm begins from observable social change and asks how generations emerging from the flow of chronological time could have caused the change, whereas the pulse-rate paradigm imposes a single, arbitrary chronological time scheme indiscriminately onto the social world and forces observable social change to conform to it. When reputable research organizations like the Pew Research Center fail to distinguish between the two and adopt the labels and methods for defining periods and cohorts from the pulse-rate paradigm, their well-intentioned generational research becomes deceptive *generational mythology*. The age differences between cohorts in whatever attitudes they are measuring may really be there, but simply adopting labels like "Generation X" and "Millennials" obscures the real cohort and period boundaries that define them. For example, the analysis in this book shows that the gay marriage generation comes from the cohort born after 1974—this includes people from both the Generation X and Millennial cohorts. All of the research that singles out Millennials for being more supportive than their elders not only misleads people about who the real generation is and what the real dynamics of change are, but also perpetuates the mythology that Millennials constitute a meaningful cohort at all.[37]

Social scientists must take the particularistic, inductive approach of the imprint paradigm to defining generational boundaries. The temporal boundaries of periods should be determined by examining the historical events, trends, and changes in society that distinguish qualitatively different conditions in which people live. Depending upon the topic of interest (gay marriage or something else), the temporal markers of periods will vary.

Determining the temporal boundaries of cohorts is even more challenging. They should be based on the period boundaries, but altered to center on the psychological process of coming of age during late adolescence/early adulthood. There is an inherent "fuzziness" of the temporal boundaries with respect to cohorts because different people mature at different ages; moreover, people's impressionable years probably depend upon the issue. For example, we tend to become sexually mature much earlier than we become politically aware. Thus, the temporal boundaries of cohorts should be based on period boundaries but modified to take into account the variable process of coming of age.

Following the imprint paradigm, the substantive scope of generational distinction will be narrow and particular, not broad and all-encompassing. What makes an actual generation with respect to gay marriage will be different from what makes an actual generation with respect to social media use. Members of the actual generation will be distinguished from the cohort as a whole by the generational processes that set them apart both from their elders and juniors and from other age mates. Thus, even if some people in the same cohort happen to both support gay marriage and use social media frequently, it makes more sense to view them as belonging to two separate generations.

In sum, the problem of boundaries with respect to generational theory requires the analyst to inductively determine the temporal boundaries of periods and cohorts, delimit the boundaries of generational distinction in terms of substantive scope, and identify the generational processes that distinguish the actual generation from the cohort. These tasks involve significant work, combining multiple research perspectives, and the results will not lend themselves to alluring soundbites about Millennials or other popular stereotypes. But this is exactly what must be done in order to rescue generational theory from the suffocation of pop culture clichés.

How do I handle these five problems in this book? This study combines research about generational change in opinions about gay marriage from all three perspectives. In Chapter 2, I adopt a historical perspective on the gay marriage generation to derive the temporal boundaries that define unique historical periods. I use that periodization to define the cohorts for the longitudinal, demographic analysis in Chapter 3, which examines how public opinion is affected by cohort replacement, intra-cohort attitude change, and related covariates. Last, in Chapters 4 to 7, I adopt a cultural, interpretive perspective to distinguish among different levels of intra-cohort variation and to determine how generational processes contributed to the rapid evolution in Americans' views of gay marriage. Altogether, this book shows how the gay marriage generation arose because of the interactions among activists, celebrities, political and religious leaders, and ordinary people, who together reconfigured Americans' social imagination of homosexuality in a way that made gay marriage seem normal, logical, and good.

Social Generation and the Social Imagination

The gay marriage generation is what scholars would call a *social generation*, which I define as the set of cultural and social psychological processes whereby a young cohort's encounter with society during the historical period in which they "come of age" shapes their worldviews. Social generational processes distinguish the actual generation from the cohort, so to the extent that we apply the "gay marriage generation" label to a group of people, it would be to that subset of the cohort who developed a unique worldview because of their encounter with history.

Where does the phrase *social generation* come from, and why do we need it? In 1984, one year after David Kertzer recommended that sociologists define generation narrowly in terms of kinship descent and drop the cohort-related meaning of the word from the scholarly lexicon, historian Anthony Esler published an unassuming article in the *Journal of Political and Military Sociology*, in which he argued that the reliance of social scientists on opinion surveys to measure generational change resulted in a shallow understanding of Mannheim's theory.[38] Referring to Mannheim's "actual generation" as the "social generation," Esler argued that social generations are distinguished from cohorts by a shared collective mentality and that social scientists should take a qualitative and interpretive approach to generational analysis, in contrast to the quantitative and positivistic approach of cohort analysis.[39]

In effect, Esler agreed with Kertzer that the research on generations coming out of the 1970s was flawed but disagreed with his solution. The British sociologist Jane Pilcher would later reconcile Kertzer's and Esler's competing recommendations, using the phrase *social generation* to distinguish cohort-related generational phenomena from kinship-related ones.[40] By preserving Kertzer's distinction between generation and cohort and defining the social generation as a distinct phenomenon, these scholars opened the door for a parallel research agenda to emerge: one that focused on the cultural and social psychological processes that shape the worldviews and behaviors of young cohorts.

As described above, there is no consensus on the exact nature of the generational process, and there may be many different generational processes that work in different ways, depending on the circumstance. For the case of the gay marriage generation, I will argue that the *social imagination* is the generational process that caused support for gay marriage to increase so quickly and in the manner documented by scholars. I do not believe that the social imagination is the only such process or that it will apply to every case of generational change, but it is the theoretical explanation that emerged from the analysis of my interviews (especially Chapter 5).

To best understand the social imagination, we should start with our everyday understanding of imagination, then move to its broader psychological meaning, and finally advance to the sociological level. Typically, we think of imagination as fantasy: Children have wonderful imaginations. Not only can they think of things that don't really exist, like unicorns, but they have a tremendous capacity to do so. In our everyday usage, imagination is the capacity to produce mental images of things that exist only in our minds.

However, imagination is not just about fantasy; it is what we use to comprehend reality. Whether one imagines something that exists or something that doesn't—a horse instead of a unicorn—the process is the same. In psychology, the imagination is the individual's capacity to produce mental images of any nonpresent phenomena—things outside the current realm of perception. When an individual uses her imagination, she activates her existing mental structures—schemas, prototypes, memories, and so on—to create a mental image that exists inside her mind.

For example, imagine stumbling upon a news story about the problems of piracy in the Indian Ocean. A typical American who reads the story might immediately, unconsciously activate her cultural schema for pirates—guys with beards, swords, and eye patches sailing around the Caribbean Sea three hundred years ago on wooden ships looking for treasure. This stereotype of a pirate, learned through some combination of popular culture and history books, might help you understand some aspects of the story—like the threat piracy poses to ships transporting cargo—but it might make it surprising to learn that piracy happens today, that it happens in places like the Strait of Malacca, and that pirates use modern technology like guns and motorboats. Reading the story would then prompt you to reimagine piracy as you strive to comprehend the new information.[41]

This exercise, however trivial, illustrates the dynamic interplay between the imagination and the cultural schemas that it utilizes. Whether we use our imagination consciously (in slow, deliberate cognition) or unconsciously (in fast, automatic cognition), the mind uses cultural schemas—a type of mental structure in which a concept is defined by a collection of cultural associations we have with it.[42] Schemas are essential resources for the imagination. The typical American's schema for "pirate" might include associations like "man," "sword," "eye patch," "wooden sailing ship," "illegal," "treasure," and many more—a collection of attributes that automatically come to mind during the process of imagination. For the most part, these cultural schemas confront us as taken-for-granted entities because we did not actively choose to make them; like it or not, these schemas affect how our mind processes information, how we behave, and how we communicate.

Although all human minds use schemas to make sense of the experiences we have in the world, the exact pattern of associations that make up our schemas vary by culture: our life experiences, social networks, and media representations all influence the nature and strength of associations that define our schemas. Thus even though all humans have schemas, and even though we are all forced to live with our schemas to some extent (we did not choose to make them, although we can work to change them), we cannot simply ignore the process by which they emerged. The distinctively cultural nature of our schemas requires us to question why a given association exists. Put simply, if Captain Hook is our prototypical pirate, then it should be obvious why we can't simply assume that a schema is natural. Cultural schemas are not given; they are made.

So how do cultural schemas get made? I argue that they are made (and continually remade) through the process of *social imagination*. I add the word *social* to emphasize the fact that the imagination is not just individual and cognitive, but also collective and cultural (just like our schemas). The process of imagination might happen inside individuals' heads, but it cannot be a coincidence that the mental images that individuals produce when they imagine are so broadly similar to others in the same group. The imagination, therefore, is not a purely cognitive endeavor carried out by isolated individuals; it is fundamentally social.

Your imagination is powerfully shaped by the broad cultural context of your life in society.

Formally, we can define the *social imagination* as the process by which collectives jointly create and modify the cultural schemas that individuals encounter and internalize through social experience and that provide the cognitive foundation for future action.[43] Philosophically, the theory of social imagination (and, not coincidentally, modern schema theory) is grounded in Kant's *Critique of Pure Reason*, in which he posits the "transcendental power of imagination" as the essential, synthetic capacity that combines individual intuition and understanding, thus rendering human knowledge and experience possible.[44] Durkheim's theory of collective representations effectively transposed Kant's theory to the social level, while Castoriadis was the first to argue that the social imaginary is the essential ontological root of all sociohistorical phenomena.[45]

The theory of social imagination synthesizes current research in cognition and culture to model the dynamic interaction between mind and society.[46] In essence, society—via the social imagination—furnishes individuals with the cultural schemas that serve as the basis for the mind's operation and for future action in the world. Individuals use their cultural schemas, prototypes, and concepts when they process new information and when they say or do things. Then, the results of what the individual says and does feed back into the collective, social process of imagination—by reinforcing, modifying, or undermining the dominant cultural schemas.

In psychology, the significance of the imagination has been illustrated with respect to stereotypes. Research shows that stereotypes furnish some of the raw materials of the imagination, and when people are asked to imagine different kinds of people, attitudes are either attenuated or reinforced, depending upon the consistency of the mental image with existing stereotypes.[47] For example, when psychologist Irene Blair and her colleagues asked research participants to imagine a strong woman, they found that gender stereotypic attitudes were reduced, compared to those asked to imagine something that was not counterstereotypical.

In other social sciences, scholars have conceptualized the imagination at the collective, cultural level as an ongoing, contested process of meaning making in which social actors create, use, modify, and challenge the meanings of collective representations. In the earliest and most famous usage, anthropologist Benedict Anderson provocatively defines nations as "imagined communities" and shows how people's feelings of nation-hood and nationalism are nourished by cultural objects like maps and newspapers.[48] Fellow anthropologist Arjun Appadurai develops the con-cept further, describing the imagination as a social capacity that builds on a group's vast background of taken-for-granted understandings and that acts as a resource for social behavior.[49] Philosopher Charles Tay-lor argues that the social imaginary forms a link between structure and agency because it is both factual and normative, contains an implicit moral order, and functions as a cultural repertoire from which we draw in practice.[50]

This conception has proven useful in empirical research, too. Soci-ologist Luc Boltanski argues that the capacity of imagination is essen-tial for developing empathy for distant, suffering others, and sociologist Andrew Perrin shows that the "democratic imagination" is a capacity that empowers ordinary citizens to formulate possible solutions to social problems.[51] Finally, communications scholar Shani Orgad demonstrates how media representations in a globalizing world enrich our imagina-tions by furnishing them with such raw materials as cultural scripts, stereotypes, and narratives.[52]

How is the social imagination different from other sociological con-cepts like collective representation, understanding, and framing? In essence, the process of social imagination differs in that it is keyed to a specific cognitive process—just like the notion of collective memory must be theorized in relation to the psychological process of remember-ing.[53] By contrast, Durkheim's theory of collective representation has no particular cognitive referent; understandings are best conceived as the *result* of the process of imagination; and framing works psychologically through processes that are more slow and deliberate than the schematic processing of the imagination.[54] To be sure, collective representations, understandings, and framing do influence the imagination, but the concept of social imagination is valuable because it indexes one mecha-nism of social, cultural, and communicative influence to its cognitive counterpart.

Because this book is about gay marriage, let's translate this into rel-evant terms. Take, for example, the phrase *that's so gay*. Research shows that phrases like this draw on two schematic associations: gay is bad or deviant, and gay is insufficiently masculine.[55] People who use such phrases may not consciously believe such things to be true and may even be supportive of gay rights, but their continued use of this language per-petuates the implicit schema of homosexuality as deviant and deficient. By contrast, when we become aware of such implicit associations and consciously refrain from saying such things, our actions have the effect (however small) of undermining the imagination of homosexuality as a negative thing.

This book examines how the social imagination of homosexuality and gay marriage has changed over time at the collective level and how in-dividuals give voice to it when they talk about these subjects in interac-tion with others. Chapter 2 illustrates the process of social imagination at the collective, cultural level by analyzing how popular discourse and media representations about homosexuality in the public sphere change over time. Chapter 5 measures the process of imagination at the indi-vidual level by analyzing the metaphors, analogies, and figurative tropes that people articulate in discourse. These forms of speech all indirectly, obliquely give voice to the cultural schemas that usually remain unex-pressed. By analyzing the social imagination at both levels, we will see how changes in the social imagination of homosexuality are related to the generational change in attitudes about gay marriage in the United States.

Conclusion

The overarching aim of this book is to fulfill the promise of genera-tional theory, as laid out by Karl Mannheim: to account for how cohort replacement, combined with the manifold mysterious ways that an individual's biography interacts with history, works to slowly, inexora-bly change society over time. This goal has eluded both scholars and popular commentators because of the five problems that confront gen-erational analysts; but advances in social scientific theory and methods finally allow us to measure generational change from three perspec-tives and triangulate the results to form a coherent account. Moreover, this book offers the theory of social imagination as an important tool for interpretive social scientists who strive to understand what people say and do—to fully understand the intersection of culture and cogni-tion and the dynamic interaction of individual and society.

Practically speaking, this book uses the case of gay marriage to develop a deeper understanding of the process of generational change. The heart of the book (Chapters 4–7) follows a qualitative, interpretive approach to Mannheim's problem of generations in an effort to uncover the generational processes that caused support for gay marriage in the United States to increase so quickly. This approach focuses on the cultural and social psychological processes that have caused young cohorts to be more supportive than older cohorts, and also that have caused members of older cohorts to rethink their prior views. With respect to gay marriage, I aim to solve a puzzle that has so far eluded analysts and commentators: how one of the most prominent battles in the culture wars moved so quickly from being a lopsided rout on the part of gay marriage opponents to a resounding victory for supporters.

By taking an interpretive approach, this book makes an epistemological commitment to develop a multidimensional account of how people make sense of the world in the ways they do. However, interpretive social scientists are not free to interpret a person's actions in any way they choose; our interpretations must be faithful to the broader social context in which people live. In this case, interpretive analysis must be triangulated with the other two perspectives required by generational theory: a historical analysis of the events that would cause young cohorts to imagine the world differently than their elders, and a demographic analysis of how public opinion changed from some combination of age, cohort, and period effects. In the next two chapters, I lay out precisely the historical and demographic parameters for the interpretive analysis of generational change in attitudes about gay marriage.

All three approaches, taken together, show how the gay marriage generation was both a product and a cause of social change. The gay marriage generation emerged because of the changing social imagination of homosexuality, and its effects on both the court of law and the court of public opinion brought about the ultimate legalization of gay marriage in the United States.

2

Contesting Homosexuality's Imagination, 1945–2015

Not that there's anything wrong with that.
—*Seinfeld*, "The Outing" (Season 4, Episode 17)

If I had to choose one utterance that epitomizes the status of gay rights in the 1990s—poised as it was on the brink of a revolution—I would choose this one. Simultaneously forward- and backward-looking (in historical terms at least), "not that there's anything wrong with that" was a stroke of rhetorical genius. The phrase was used not once but six times—and by four different characters—on the February 11, 1993, episode of the NBC sitcom *Seinfeld*.[1] Repetition is powerful as a source of both humor and learning: the sitcom made the problem of homophobia accessible through humor, and the learning came through Jerry's character, who packaged the catchphrase with a ready-made repertoire of retorts—a script for viewers to use in their own lives to acknowledge but delegitimate homophobia:

"I mean, that's fine if that's who you are. . . ."
"I have many gay friends. . . ."
"People's personal sexual preferences are nobody's business but their own!"

The repetition and humor, augmented with supporting tropes, turned a simple catchphrase into a moral lesson: even though we might dislike or even feel repulsed by homosexuality, we should not judge others. The episode was seen by twenty-eight million viewers originally—over 10 percent of the US population—and by tens of millions more during reruns.[2] "Not that there's anything wrong with that" became part of the essential inner monologue for social liberals who wanted to be more tolerant of lesbians and gays, but who had to get over society's disapproval of homosexuality. Those seven words helped shift the discourse about homosexuality in the United States from one of unambiguous moral condemnation and disgust to one of tolerance and acceptance.[3]

The *Seinfeld* episode is emblematic of representations of homosexuality in mass media during the early 1990s. As communication scholar Ron Becker observes in his analysis of lesbians and gays in prime-time television during the decade, it is a classic mistaken-identity narrative (in this case, Jerry and George are labeled as gay) that allowed viewers to work out their anxiety about homosexuality by watching fictional characters do so.[4] The laughter was a nervous, self-conscious kind. But more to the point, "not that there's anything wrong with that" was powerful because it resonated with the prevailing cultural Zeitgeist even as it pushed beyond it.[5] It appeared at a historical moment in which a shift in the social imagination of homosexuality had begun, but had not fully coalesced: the dominant cultural schema of *homosexuality as behavior* was being challenged by a new cultural schema of *homosexuality as identity*.

This chapter examines the historical trends in media representations of homosexuality and the evolving political battleground over gay rights in order to document the changing social imagination of homosexuality in the United States. In the lifetimes of contemporary Americans, what it means to be "homosexual" in society has changed significantly—not just in the sense that it is easier to be openly gay today than it was in 1945, but also in the sense that the very meanings of the terms have changed. People growing up in the United States at different points in time encountered very different constellations of meaning surrounding homosexuality, and the understandings of it that they developed while coming of age shaped the beliefs, attitudes, and values that they articulated in the political arena.

This chapter is organized chronologically to show how the social imagination of homosexuality changed between 1945 and 2015. In each historical period, the narrative weaves together two domains in which the symbolic contests over the social imagination are particularly important: politics and media. The ongoing political battles between the lesbian and gay (later, the LGBTQ) movement and the conservative countermovement were extremely important in shaping the social imagination of homosexuality because each side strategically framed the debate for ordinary Americans in distinct ways. Not only were these political battles covered in the news media, but entertainment media also shaped the social imagination with their fictional portrayals of lesbians and gays.

By tracing the evolution of these two realms of culture, this chapter shows how the social imagination of homosexuality in American society shifted over time. The changes happened slowly and unevenly, and there are few dramatic moments that constitute distinct markers of change. But if you adopt a long-term perspective and know where to look, the change is unmistakable. Looking at representations in the mass media, and especially the actions of media gatekeepers and other privileged communicators in the public sphere, we can identify turning points in which contrasts between older and newer ways of imagining homosexuality are brought into stark relief.[6] Change never happened overnight, but change did come. We are living with the evidence all around us today.

The Social Imagination in the Public Sphere

In the previous chapter, I defined the *social imagination* as the process by which collectives jointly create and modify the cultural schemas that individuals encounter and internalize through social experience and that provide the cognitive foundation for future action. Although it is really a continuous process, it is easiest to think of the social imagination as a static entity: *the social imaginary*. If one could take a snapshot of the social imagination at a single point in time, the resulting picture would show the social imaginary—the collection of culturally dominant meanings that exist in a given society at that time. As an individual, each of us usually confronts the social imaginary as a force that shapes and constrains the things we can say and do. I cannot change the meanings associated with particular words at will; I must adapt my own speech and behavior to the social imaginary.

However, that stability is only illusory. The social imaginary is constantly contested, multiple, and changing; and even though we typically have to accept the dominant social imaginary as it exists in order to have our speech and actions be comprehensible to others, change is possible. As a society, we invent new words and forget old ones; we try to influence people's attitudes and values, and we resist changing our own; society comes to accept things that it used to reject, and vice versa. Thus, the process of social imagination is ongoing: every communicative and behavioral action both builds upon and contributes to the evolving social imagination somehow.

Although in principle every action, no matter how small, contributes to the social imagination, the size of the impact varies. Every time people come out to their family and friends as gay, and every time they confirm or undermine a stereotype, they affect the social imagination—if only for those who know them. But because we are interested in public opinion about gay marriage, we have to think about changes in the social imagination that affect the whole society. In other words, it is one thing if my neighbor comes out as gay; it is another thing if a famous celebrity does so; and it is still another if one million people do so as part of a coordinated social movement.

In this chapter, therefore, we will analyze changes in the social imagination of homosexuality in the *public sphere*, not in everyday life. It is not that ordinary people are unimportant; it is that if we want to see evidence of how the social imagination changes over time, we must look where we are most likely to detect it. We will examine how representations of homosexuality in the mass media changed over time because, by definition, the mass media transmit cultural meanings across boundaries of time and space to an audience of theoretically limitless size.

Within the public sphere, we will focus on four categories of people who are privileged communicators within it. Three of them—*recognized political actors* (elected representatives, parties, interest groups, and social movements), *celebrities*, and *experts from epistemic communities*—are privileged because their claims to power, status, and authority grant them standing to speak in the mass media.[7] The fourth type—*journalists and producers in the culture industries*—are privileged both because of their gatekeeper roles and because they create the discursive terrain of the public sphere itself.

The *public sphere* is a concept first advanced by philosopher Jürgen Habermas to explain the significance of communication and media in democratic societies. Habermas initially defined the public sphere, akin to the "marketplace of ideas," as "the sphere of private people come together as a public"—a place in which ordinary people could come together to talk about matters of common concern. Habermas held that this public sphere initially emerged in seventeenth-century Europe, as people began assembling in salons, coffeehouses, and other public places to discuss literature, news, and economic issues. After the democratic revolutions in the United States and France, the ideal of free speech in the public sphere was codified in law, and in practice the news media became "the public sphere's preeminent institution" in large-scale democracies.[8]

Habermas was critical of the ways in which the rise of the mass media in the twentieth century effectively transformed the public sphere from a realm of deliberation and debate into a realm of publicity and consumption—in which citizens were reduced to consuming audiences, not full participants, in public communication. Moreover, Habermas saw that access to the means of message production was stratified by wealth and power in the mass-mediated public sphere, which meant that both wealthy capitalists who controlled the mass media and political figures who controlled the government had disproportionate influence. Critics will recognize the threat to democracy represented by this stratification of influence over political discourse; nevertheless, this did not change the essential function of the mass-mediated public sphere as the venue in which people could hear information and opinions about matters of common concern.

The idea of the public sphere is important for our discussion of the social imagination for two reasons. First, the reality (if not the ideal) of the public sphere directs our attention to those organizations and individuals who will be most influential: journalists, mass media organizations, celebrities, epistemic communities, political parties, and organized social movements shape the public conversation more than ordinary people. Thus, if we want to document how the social imagination of homosexuality has changed in American society over time, we would be most likely to find the evidence there. Second, what we call public opinion emerges out of the public sphere, so the causes and effects of change in public opinion should also be evident there.

The results of the following analysis show that the dominant social imaginary changed twice in the lifetimes of contemporary Americans, and that each change followed a similar pattern. At each of the turning points, a precipitating event (Stonewall in the first instance, *Bowers v. Hardwick* in the second) caused the lesbian and gay movement to adopt new tactics and discourses—innovations that were especially influential in campaigns targeting particular epistemic communities (mental health professionals in the first instance, journalists and media producers in the second). Changes in the practices and discourses of those epistemic communities were then transmitted to the public via mass media, and both public opinion and the dominant cultural schema for homosexuality changed afterward. Although this is not the only way in which the social imagination can change, this model twice proved effective for the burgeoning LGBTQ movement.

Homophile Period (1945–1968): Homosexuality as Mental Illness

Neither Sigmund Freud nor Alfred Kinsey—arguably the two most influential writers on homosexuality in the early twentieth century—viewed it as a mental illness; nor did they think negative moral judgments about homosexual behavior were appropriate. However, their writings nonetheless cemented its status as both undesirable and a treatable medical condition in the broader social imagination. Freud's psychoanalysis of homosexuality gave authority over its diagnosis and treatment to psychiatrists—represented by the American Psychiatric Association—while Kinsey's behavioral studies created a sensation among readers by showing that homosexual behavior was more widespread than previously imagined.[9] While Kinsey's *Sexual Behavior in the Human Male* (1948) provided support for the homophile view that homosexuality is normal and natural, it also stoked Americans' fears that homosexuality posed a threat to heteronormative society.

Homosexuality first became a national political issue in the United States after World War II. Approximately nine thousand soldiers were discharged from the US military during the war because of allegations of homosexuality, and the general public first became aware of gays in the military in a June 9, 1947, article in *Newsweek*, titled "Homosexuals in Uniform."[10] The fundamental cultural assumptions that Americans shared—that homosexuality is bad but changeable—are evident in the text:

> To screen out this undesirable soldier-material, psychiatrists in induction-station interviews tried to detect them (1) by their effeminate looks or

behavior and (2) by repeating certain words from the homosexual vocabulary and watching for signs of recognition. . . . Once this abnormality was detected, the man was usually evacuated by the unit doctors to a general hospital where he received psychiatric treatment while a military board decided whether or not he was reclaimable.[11]

This language of deviance and illness both reflected and perpetuated the imagination of homosexuality as a mental illness that was dominant in American culture during this period.

The repression of lesbians and gays continued throughout the 1950s. Lesbians and gays were drawn into the anticommunist hysteria of 1950 to 1953, during which time thousands of federal government employees were fired because of allegations of homosexuality. In 1952, the American Psychiatric Association published the first edition of its *Diagnostic and Statistical Manual of Mental Disorders* (*DSM*), in which it classified homosexuality as a type of "sexual deviation" that can be diagnosed and treated as a "sociopathic personality disturbance."[12] Also during this decade, police departments in urban areas intensified their use of raids, entrapments, and other tactics designed to arrest and prosecute lesbians and gays.[13]

Despite the climate of fear and persecution, lesbian and gay networks and identities slowly strengthened during the postwar years. The two most well-known homophile movement organizations—the Mattachine Society and the Daughters of Bilitis—were founded in 1951 and 1955, respectively. Initially, the organizations served primarily as safe spaces for lesbians and gays to meet and discuss their shared experiences, and they were structured to be protective of members' identities. Far from attracting public attention or subverting social norms, these early homophile organizations were primarily accommodationist in nature: the groups sought to educate society about homosexuality, not through mass mobilization but by developing relationships with experts in science, law, and education.[14]

In popular culture, lesbians and gays were almost entirely invisible to the American public during the forties and fifties. Even the mocking representations that were legacies of Vaudeville—the "sissy" character, cross-dressing, and "swish routines"—were censored. In Hollywood, the 1930 Motion Picture Production Code was established to keep offensive content out of movies; beginning in 1934, the Production Code Admin-istration reviewed movie scripts and final products to ensure that films were in compliance with the code.[15] This system infamously caused Hol-lywood writers and directors to eliminate or mask representations of lesbian and gay sexualities in films through the end of the 1950s, before it finally unraveled.[16]

In radio and television, not only were stations subject to the Federal Communications Commission's mandate that networks serve "the pub-lic interest," but networks also maintained their own internal censorship departments. For example, NBC's Continuity Acceptance Department reviewed scripts for programming and advertisements and filtered out most depictions of lesbians and gays.[17] In 1952, the National Association of Radio and Television Broadcasters approved a self-regulatory code designed to keep offensive content off the air—a code to which all the networks and 80 percent of broadcast stations subscribed.[18]

The homophile movement's very perseverance through the 1950s may have been its greatest accomplishment. None of the homophile magazines and newsletters had large circulations, and by the dawn of the 1960s the Mattachine Society and Daughters of Bilitis counted fewer than 350 members nationwide between them.[19] Nevertheless, the estab-lishment and survival of an organized movement provided the foun-dation for the political uprisings that would follow in the tumultuous sixties.

The sixties, as the conventional wisdom goes, changed everything. But the decade did not change the social imagination of homosexuality. Most Americans would continue to imagine homosexuality as a mental illness or deviant lifestyle throughout the decade, despite the gradual emergence of a movement that began to contest its oppression openly. As late as 1970, fully 62 percent of Americans said that, for most lesbians and gays, homosexuality is a "sickness that can be cured." The stigma of homosexuality remained so strong that 81 percent of Americans agreed that "I won't associate with these people if I can help it."[20]

If anything, what changed in the 1960s was the nature of the social and symbolic annihilation of lesbians and gays: their trivialization and absence in 1950s mass media were replaced by their emphatic condem-nation in news, television, and film.[21] In October 1961, the prohibition against depicting homosexuality in Hollywood film was eliminated from the Motion Picture Production Code and replaced with a statement: "Restraint and care shall be exercised in presentations dealing with sex aberrations."[22] Hypothetically, this would allow writers and directors to create positive representations of lesbians and gays, but that would have been unpopular. Instead, lesbian and gay characters were clearly denoted by signs of pathology: they were mentally tortured, socially outcast, and suffered frequent on-screen deaths. Hollywood's message to mass audiences in the 1960s thus reinforced Americans' negative views about homosexuality.

The national news media changed their reporting on homosexuality in the 1960s as well, framing it as a full-blown social problem. Several high-profile exposés of lesbian and gay life were printed in newspapers and magazines in the early 1960s, and television news followed suit later in the decade. On December 17, 1963, the *New York Times* published a front-page story titled "Growth of Overt Homosexuality in City Provokes Wide Concern." The social problem framing is evident in both the title and the lead sentence: "The problem of homosexuality in New York became the focus yesterday of increased attention by the State Liquor Authority and the Police Department." The article is peppered with warnings that "sexual inverts have colonized three areas of the city" and that some "homosexual bars" are operated by "the organized crime syndicate," providing safe havens for "the dregs of the invert world." The status of homosexuality as a mental illness is not disputed in the article; the homophile movement is merely reported as favoring the view that "homosexuality is an incurable, congenital disorder," rather than a curable, developmental one.[23]

Seven months later, *Life* magazine produced an in-depth exposé of the "sad and often sordid world" of "practicing homosexuals." The warnings for the American public are explicitly stated in the opening paragraphs: "This social disorder, which society tries to suppress, has forced itself into the public eye because it does present a problem—and parents are especially concerned. The myth and misconception with which homosexuality has so long been clothed must be cleared away, not to condone it but to cope with it." The understanding that homosexuality is an unwanted "affliction" dominates the essay. A lengthy story on the attribution of homosexuality presents a range of opinions from medical and psychiatric experts, but it devotes only one paragraph to the research of

Evelyn Hooker, which showed that there was no difference between gay and straight men in psychological tests.[24]

On television, the first national exposé of homosexuality appeared on *CBS Reports* on March 7, 1967. In "The Homosexuals," reporter Mike Wallace discusses homosexuality from the personal, social, legal, religious, and medical points of view. The show begins with a three-minute interview with Warren Atkins, a twenty-eight-year-old articulate Mattachine Society activist who describes "sexual orientation" as an important part of one's identity, no different from eye color or skin color. In doing so, CBS allowed the homophile movement to contest the mainstream imagination of homosexuality. Nevertheless, that interview was immediately followed by an interview with an anonymous gay man who confirmed the dominant view: "I know that inside, now, I'm sick. I'm not sick just sexually, I'm sick in a lot of ways: immature, childlike. And the sex part of it is a symptom, like a stomachache is a symptom of who-knows-what." Overall, the program devotes over 20 percent—about nine of forty-three minutes—of its content to explaining the psychiatric view that homosexuality is a mental illness.[25]

Thus, mass media representations of the 1960s elevated the political and social significance of homosexuality: what was once a private, isolated behavior became a public epidemic and a cultural malaise. The media encouraged audiences to see homosexuals everywhere: they might be your neighbors, your grocery store clerks, and your children's teachers. Despite the advances made by lesbian and gay activists during the 1960s, the social imagination of homosexuality remained unambiguously negative.[26]

Turning Point 1 (1969–1973): Demedicalization

The year 1969 is justifiably remembered for the June 27–28 Stonewall Rebellion—when patrons of a gay bar in New York City, the Stonewall Inn, fought back against a routine police raid. But Stonewall was neither the first such uprising nor qualitatively different from others; what makes Stonewall significant is what happened afterward.[27] By 1969, the lesbian and gay movement had become emboldened by the tumultuous sixties, had grown in number and organization, and had become national news. Thus, both mainstream and alternative news sources covered the Stonewall uprising more than others, and activists responded by deploying new tactics of protest publicly.

For the social imagination, 1969 is also noteworthy for the release of the final report from the National Institute of Mental Health Task Force on Homosexuality. One could hardly expect the NIMH to steadfastly deny that homosexuality has anything to do with their expertise, so the final report does not exactly read like a revolutionary statement. However, the recommendations of the task force codified a significant divide within the epistemic community over the status of homosexuality, and it marked the beginning of its demedicalization.

In general, the report makes clear that it is straight society who must change—not lesbians and gays. It recommends that virtually everyone become better educated about homosexuality, naming specifically those professional groups—from law enforcement personnel and lawyers to teachers and ministers—whose emotional reactions to homosexuality "interfere with an objective understanding of the problem."[28] Moreover, the task force argued that government policy should change:

> Most professionals working in this area—on the basis of their collective research and clinical experience and the present overall knowledge of the subject—are strongly convinced that the extreme opprobrium that our society has attached to homosexual behavior, by way of criminal statutes and restrictive employment practices, has done more social harm than good and goes beyond what is necessary for the maintenance of public order and human decency.[29]

Thus, the task force argued that private homosexual contact between consenting adults should be decriminalized and employment policies revised in order to reduce the anxieties that lesbians and gays experience.

The publication of the NIMH report codified the disagreement among psychiatrists and mental health professionals about whether or not homosexuality was a mental illness that could be cured. Proponents of the illness model, such as Irving Bieber and Charles Socarides, continued to make the case that homosexuality was a medical issue. In a 1970 article published in the *Journal of the American Medical Association*, Socarides pleads with his fellow physicians to swim against the tide of popular culture:

Together with the mainstream heterosexual revolt has come the announcement that a homosexual revolution is also in progress and that homosexuality should be granted total acceptance as a valid form of sexual functioning, different from but equal to heterosexuality. Such acceptance of homosexuality, as being a simple variation of normality, is naïve, not to say grounded in ignorance. . . . That we, as physicians, could be persuaded to overlook such tendencies among our young people is a harmful fantasy.[30]

By contrast, dissenters like Evelyn Hooker and Thomas Szasz maintained that millions of people engaged in homosexual behavior without exhibiting any signs of mental illness and that efforts to treat homosexuality as such were a form of social control.

It was this divide in the epistemic community into which lesbian and gay activists drove a tactical wedge, creating an opening for changing the whole society's imagination of homosexuality. How did they do it? After Stonewall, lesbians and gays turned away from established homophile associations and began founding hundreds of new organizations, which transformed the issue of homosexuality's repression into a multifaceted and contentious movement for sexual liberation.[31] These groups pioneered new tactics of protest—especially "coming out," public marches, and "zapping"—and deployed them in a triumphant four-year campaign to demedicalize homosexuality.[32]

Activists especially targeted the American Psychiatric Association and demanded the removal of homosexuality from the *DSM*. In 1970, gay liberationists in San Francisco organized a protest of the APA's annual convention, causing such a disruption that some panels discussing research on homosexuality and aversion therapy could not be finished. The incident prompted the APA Program Committee to convene a panel at the 1971 convention for lesbians and gays to present their views formally, but that accommodation failed to avert further disruption.[33]

At the 1972 convention in Dallas, lesbian and gay activists were again invited to present, but this time the result was more conciliatory. Attendees learned for the first time that lesbians and gays were their peers: a masked gay psychiatrist, Dr. H. Anonymous, spoke at the panel for himself and the other two-hundred-plus gay psychiatrists he knew were in attendance and who had to conceal their true identities. In the exhibition hall activists Frank Kameny and Barbara Gittings presented a poster called "Gay, Proud, and Healthy: The Homosexual Community Speaks," which invited conference attendees to help make psychiatry an "ally." Overall, the message to conference attendees was that the APA had a choice to make: would it continue to stigmatize lesbians and gays with diagnoses of mental illness, or would it repudiate its past?[34]

The opportunity to make that choice soon emerged. At the May 1973 convention, over a thousand psychiatrists gathered to hear a debate organized by Robert Spitzer, a member of the APA's Committee on Nomenclature, regarding the removal of homosexuality from the *DSM*. Also at the convention a New York GAA activist, Ronald Gold, brought Spitzer with him to a social function of the "Gay-PA"—the clandestine group of gay psychiatrists who met every year at APA conventions. Years later, Gold recalled an incident at that gathering in which a man broke down in tears in his arms—an event that spurred Spitzer to action:

> He was a psychiatrist, an army psychiatrist, based in Hawaii, who was so moved by my speech, he told me, that he decided that he had to go to a gay bar for the first time in his life. . . . It was a very moving event. I mean, this man was awash in tears. I believe that that was what decided Spitzer right then and there. "Let's go." Because it was right after that that he said, "Let's go write the resolution." And so we went back to Spitzer's hotel room and wrote the resolution.[35]

By the middle of December, Spitzer had successfully steered a resolution through the Committee on Nomenclature and the Board of Trustees that declassified homosexuality as a mental illness and replaced it with "Sexual Orientation Disturbance"—which allowed someone who was "disturbed by, in conflict with, or wish to change their sexual orientation" to seek treatment.[36]

The impact of the APA's decision was immediate. As Barbara Gittings recalled, "When the vote came in, we had a wonderful headline in one of the Philadelphia papers, 'Twenty Million Homosexuals Gain Instant Cure. . . .' It was a front-page story. I was thrilled. We were cured overnight by the stroke of the pen."[37] The *New York Times* also ran a front-page story, emphasizing the historic proportions of the declaration in the lead paragraph: "The American Psychiatric Association, altering a position it has held for nearly a century, decided today that homosexuality is not a mental disorder."[38] For decades, lesbians, gays, and heterosexuals alike had been convinced that they were sick; now, those psychiatrists—whose claims to expertise over the true nature of homosexuality had been hegemonic—declared that they had been wrong.

This authoritative shift in the social imagination of homosexuality did not, however, end the discrimination against lesbians and gays. Although expert authorities no longer claimed homosexuality to be a mental illness, ordinary Americans would nonetheless continue to imagine it as abnormal, criminal, immoral, and repulsive. In Gittings's words:

> Now that people don't have the sickness label, they're coming out with more reasons for being against us: "I don't like you." "I don't like the way you live." "I think you're immoral." "I think you're rotten." All of that is more honest than this "you're sick" nonsense.[39]

Throughout the 1970s and 1980s, this was exactly the cultural climate faced by lesbians and gays. They were no longer stigmatized by the sickness label, but the American public remained as intolerant of homosexuality as ever.

Resistance Period (1974–1986): Homosexuality as Deviant Lifestyle

Today, it is strange to think of homosexuality as a crime, but by 1974 only eight states had repealed their sodomy laws. In most parts of the United States, people could be arrested and prosecuted if they were caught engaging in homosexual sex—even privately in their own home. Despite demedicalization and gay liberation, most Americans would continue to imagine homosexuality as a deviant or criminal behavior through the late 1980s. In its 1986 ruling in *Bowers v. Hardwick*, the US Supreme Court lent its institutional weight and authority to this understanding of homosexuality by upholding sodomy laws as constitutional.[40]

If the fifties and sixties represent the story of the lesbian and gay movement's emergence, then the seventies and eighties mark the story of conservative opposition. Although efforts by lesbians and gays to gain equal rights and political power strengthened during these decades, their gains were surpassed by the countermobilization of religious and conservative groups who were alarmed by the revolution occurring in their midst. In the early 1970s, the lesbian and gay movement was coalescing at the same time as second-wave feminism, and the perceived threat of these two movements to orthodox worldviews should not be understated. It was compounded by the landmark 1973 Supreme Court decision *Roe v. Wade*, which guaranteed all women access to abortion, and the campaign to add the Equal Rights Amendment to the US Constitution.[41]

This unholy trinity—gender equality, gay liberation, and abortion rights—induced religious conservatives to build a resistance movement, the result of which was that by the end of the 1980s, the public's acceptance of lesbians and gays was no greater than it had been in 1973. Between 1973 and 1987, the percentage of Americans who said that "sexual relations between two adults of the same sex" is "always wrong" actually increased from 70 to 75 percent.[42] In effect, this period of resistance bolstered the social imagination of homosexuality as a deviant, immoral behavior for most Americans.

The year that conservative opponents gained the upper hand against the lesbian and gay movement was 1977. That year, the "homosexual agenda" became thoroughly integrated into the national New Right movement, via Miami, Florida. A mere six months after the Dade County Commission voted to add sexual preference to its nondiscrimination law, the voters overturned it by a vote of 69 to 31 percent, thanks to a campaign spearheaded by celebrity Anita Bryant. According to communication scholar Fred Fejes's authoritative history of this episode, Bryant's campaign, called Save Our Children, used local churches and synagogues as the initial sites for organizing before going public. Their discourse was firmly rooted in religious opposition to homosexuality, but it also included secular appeals, such as allegations that gays were targeting children for conversion to homosexuality. Bryant's campaign attracted national media attention and inspired conservative activists in Wichita, Kansas, Saint Paul, Minnesota, and Eugene, Oregon, to launch similar campaigns in the next twelve months.[43]

This episode was tactically and discursively important. Tactically, it provided New Right activists with a tool—the ballot initiative—that they would use to successfully combat the lesbian and gay movement over the next several decades. Discursively, it introduced a coherent counterframe into the public sphere, three aspects of which seem especially potent: it defined homosexuality as a moral issue, rather than a matter of civil rights; it stoked fears that heterosexuals—especially children—could be influenced to adopt the homosexual lifestyle; and it portrayed gay rights as "special treatment" that was not available to others.[44]

The discourse resonated with individuals at the time because, regardless of demedicalization, Americans still imagined homosexuality as a learned behavior, not as an inherent, unchanging identity. In fact, the oppositional discourse of New Right activists magnified and crystallized one of the main frames that the media used to talk about homosexuality after demedicalization: the lifestyle frame. Fejes traces the origins of this frame to marketing researchers of the mid-1960s who used the term to categorize consumer groups by their activities, interests, and opinions, not just demographics.[45] Lesbian and gay activists had adopted the term as an alternative to the sickness label during the demedicalization campaign, and by the mid-1970s, lesbian and gay media had embraced it. According to Fejes: "In 1974 the *Advocate*, the major national gay magazine, in revamping itself with an eye toward making itself more mainstream both in advertising and politics, adopted as its cover slogan, 'touching your lifestyle,' thus giving its imprimatur to the term."[46]

Although characterizing homosexuality as a "lifestyle" was certainly preferable to "illness," the adoption of the term by many in the lesbian and gay movement was problematic, to say the least. Even if there were such a thing as a gay lifestyle, the ways that lesbians and gays might have imagined it—as happy, healthy, normal, and functional—were opposite to how most Americans imagined it—as sad, unhealthy, deviant, and dysfunctional. In the 1970s, the opposition's judgment resonated with the public, and the imagination of homosexuality as deviant lifestyle became dominant.

The onset of the HIV/AIDS epidemic both reinforced this understanding and intensified the stigma: there could be no greater symbol to reinforce the public view that homosexuality is unhealthy than a lethal "gay cancer" with no cure. The impact of HIV/AIDS on the gay community and the movement cannot be understated and has been written about extensively; but many in the general public felt their condemnation of homosexuality was validated by HIV/AIDS.[47] Religious conservatives interpreted HIV/AIDS as divine punishment for sin; ordinary Americans blamed people with AIDS (PWAs) for their condition because they thought of homosexuality as a freely chosen behavior; and fears that HIV/AIDS could be spread by insignificant contact—for example, merely touching objects that a PWA had touched—exacerbated homosexuality's stigma.

The case of popular movie star Rock Hudson illustrates the cultural dynamics surrounding HIV/AIDS. According to communication scholar Larry Gross, the mass media paid little attention to HIV/AIDS until it became clear that heterosexual Americans might be threatened by it; the June 25, 1985, revelation that Hudson had AIDS was the turning point.[48] The absence of early media attention was in part due to the public's presumed lack of concern about gay men, but also to journalists' own prejudices and fears that they would be suspected of being gay themselves if they covered HIV/AIDS: "It was only after Rock Hudson had raised the status of AIDS to that of a front-page story that reporters could safely be associated with the topic."[49]

A celebrity icon since the 1950s, Hudson was the epitome of what art historian Richard Meyer calls "relaxed masculinity": he was physically imposing (six-four, two hundred pounds) but cultivated a nonthreatening image that appealed to both men and women.[50] The revelation that he had AIDS provided every American with a face that they could associate with the disease, but also outed Hudson as gay, and in doing so overturned Americans' assumptions about homosexuality. Meyer observes that the social commentary on Hudson's outing at the time carried a "tone of betrayal" because of how the on-screen heterosexual romances his audiences admired were really those of a gay man.[51] There is bitter irony in the fact that a man who would die from AIDS three months later was accused of deceiving the American public because of the closeted life he was forced to lead.

Summing up the significance of HIV/AIDS on the American imagination, Gross observes a paradox:

> By the late 1980s, the AIDS epidemic had accomplished something that the lesbian and gay movement had not been able to achieve—the end of gay invisibility in the mass media. Even so, nearly all the attention to gay men was in the context of AIDS-related stories, and because this coverage

seems to have exhausted the media's limited interest in gay people, lesbians became even less visible. AIDS also reinvigorated the two major mass media "roles" for gay people: victim and villain. The public image of gay men was becoming inescapably linked with the specter of plague.[52]

In short, HIV/AIDS—via Rock Hudson and the threat it posed to straight society—brought homosexuality into the center of the American collective consciousness, but the mental image that it produced was one of a deadly malady unleashed upon society by the deviant lifestyle chosen by an irresponsible minority.

The status of homosexuality as a deviant behavior was institutionally affirmed by the 1986 Supreme Court ruling *Bowers v. Hardwick*, which upheld the constitutionality of sodomy laws. Although Georgia's sodomy law applied equally to both heterosexual and homosexual acts, the Court transformed the case into a question of homosexual sodomy specifically. In a five to four decision, the majority ruled that the right to privacy, which covered matters of marriage and reproductive behavior, did not extend to homosexual behavior and that state legislatures were free to criminalize homosexual behavior on the basis of moral disapproval. The Court viewed homosexuality as being antithetical to the institutions of marriage and family and that the state was therefore justified in declaring it illegal.

The journalists Dudley Clendinen and Adam Nagourney note that the ruling was handed down on June 30, the day after many cities' annual gay pride celebrations, and that the unambiguously anti-gay ruling sparked both despair and anger from lesbians and gays around the country.[53] The despair is easy to understand: taken together, the opposition of the New Right, the emergence of HIV/AIDS, and the affirmation of societal intolerance for homosexuality constituted a dramatic setback, if not reversal, of the progress made by the lesbian and gay movement. The anger has been best explained by sociologist Deborah Gould, who argues that the court ruling was so sudden and severe that it forced the diffuse frustration that had long been simmering among lesbians and gays to bubble over:

> *Hardwick* laid bare dominant society's hatred for lesbians and gay men, and made clear the hopelessness of a strategy for gay rights based on being

"good" lesbians and gays. In doing so, *Hardwick* reconfigured lesbians' and gay men's feelings about state and society, and simultaneously rearranged their self-feelings, paradoxically, perhaps, easing gay shame and fear of further social rejection. At the point of complete social annihilation, there was no *further* to be feared.[54]

In essence, *Bowers v. Hardwick* radicalized lesbians and gays because they had nothing left to lose.

Thus, the emotions that *Bowers v. Hardwick* elicited proved to be the beginning of yet another turning point; enraged and motivated activists began planting the seeds for a new phase of contention. Within hours of the ruling, three thousand people blocked traffic in Greenwich Village; two days later, six hundred people were arrested for civil disobedience at the US Supreme Court; and another five thousand activists attempted to disrupt the Independence Day celebration in Lower Manhattan.[55] But most importantly, activists began channeling their anger into organization building: by building radical direct action movement organizations, like the Silence = Death Project, and making plans for a second March on Washington.

Turning Point 2 (1987–1992): Legitimation

The year 1987 was pivotal for two reasons: the Second National March on Washington for Lesbian and Gay Rights and the founding of the AIDS Coalition to Unleash Power (ACT UP). The events surrounding the March on Washington expressed the whole range of emotions—from outrage and sadness to pride and love—felt by the lesbian and gay community. On Tuesday, between 650 and 850 protestors were arrested for nonviolent civil disobedience at the US Supreme Court. On Saturday, a wedding demonstration (more on this below) was held to celebrate love and demand equal rights for same-sex couples. On Sunday, the seventy-thousand-square-foot AIDS Memorial Quilt was tearfully unveiled on the National Mall to pay tribute to those who had died. At the end, over two hundred thousand people—including allies like Jesse Jackson, César Chávez, and Whoopi Goldberg—marched to combat HIV/AIDS and end discrimination against lesbians and gays. The march's most significant and enduring victory is that it is commemorated every October 11 as National Coming Out Day, and thus represents the fulfillment of one of the main slogans and promises of the march: "For Love and for Life, We're Not Going Back."

The founding of ACT UP in 1987 was also important because the organization had a disproportionately large influence in forcing the government, scientific and medical authorities, and the American public to take the HIV/AIDS crisis more seriously. Originally founded in New York, ACT UP was a network of over 110 national and international groups united by shared goals and similar tactics of direct action protest. Before the movement's decline in the 1990s, ACT UP groups around the United States committed scores of creative, spectacular, and disruptive actions that both drew attention to the AIDS epidemic and forced authorities like the FDA and CDC to prioritize treatment and education.[56]

Taken together, the radicalism of ACT UP and the more reformist tone of the 1987 March on Washington changed the national discussion of homosexuality. It became increasingly difficult for the news media to portray lesbians and gays as one-dimensional stereotypes; HIV/AIDS had become such a multifaceted issue that the news media began to humanize them more fully. At the same time, the practice of coming out—institutionalized in National Coming Out Day—began to appear in mass media and therefore gave American audiences an opportunity to witness lesbians and gays at their most vulnerable moment—of confessing to a stigmatized, secret aspect of their identity.[57]

Nowhere was this humanizing effect on clearer display than on the *Oprah Winfrey Show*, October 11, 1988—one year after the March on Washington. The producers decided to devote an entire episode to the first annual National Coming Out Day. It included activists, experts, and other notable figures as panelists to talk about the coming out experience; the studio audience was even composed of movement sympathizers. Audiences at home witnessed Winfrey moderating an open, frank discussion about the necessity and the emotional difficulties of coming out to their loved ones. One guest, Greg Brock, the assistant managing editor at the *San Francisco Examiner*, used his appearance on the show as an opportunity to come out to his parents privately the night before the taping. His mother spoke on the show via telephone about her feelings, and Brock recalled her concluding, "But the bottom line is that he's my flesh and blood and my only son and I love him."[58]

The significance of such a mass-mediated coming out is twofold. First, straight audiences at home were suddenly able to imagine how they might react if they were in Greg's mother's shoes; she both role-modeled how the bonds of family and friendship conquer stigma and provided audience members with a script to follow in case someone they knew ever came out to them. Second, lesbian and gay audiences who had not yet come out were given Greg's role and script, and thus furnished with the materials necessary to imagine their own coming out. This, then, was the primary impact of the March on Washington and National Coming Out Day: the more people came out and the more people witnessed it, the more fully lesbians and gays became integrated into Americans' everyday lives.

Just as importantly, the effects of these changes were felt inside the newsrooms—the places where media gatekeepers were daily concocting the authoritative account of the day's events for Americans at home. Prior to 1987, few employees in a typical newsroom had come out as gay, and few knew enough about lesbian and gay issues to cover them adequately. In 1982, the *Columbia Journalism Review* reported that "nearly 200 interviews at news organizations in ten cities indicate that, with rare exceptions, gay reporters and editors believe they must stay in the closet to keep their jobs, and that their fear of being perceived as gay inhibits them from making suggestions about covering stories about gays."[59] The article cites a half dozen stories that were flawed as a result: for example, the *New York Times'* coverage of a mass shooting that killed two and wounded six at a gay bar in Greenwich Village failed to include any statement from the city's gay community.[60]

Communications scholars Fred Fejes and Kevin Petrich argue that the AIDS epidemic and AIDS activism "force[d] the media to regard the gay and lesbian community more seriously and in a different light" because of the ways in which the requirements of news reporting led journalists into new territory:

> Reporters and their readers were exposed to a view of gay and lesbian life very different from the 1970s hedonistic stereotypes of gay life. Accounts of the fundraising, the patient care efforts, the political lobbying efforts for more AIDS funding, and AIDS education campaigns began to characterize the gay community far more than the "exotica" of gay and lesbian

life. . . . Moreover, the political activism of groups such as ACT UP served to further educate media reporters how homophobia was woven into the government's and media's response to the AIDS crisis.[61]

Thus, a combination of the AIDS crisis and movement activism forced journalists to confront the multidimensional lives of lesbians and gays and correct the stereotypic representations that had previously dominated the news.

Occasionally, this process unfolded dramatically on the newsroom floor itself. On December 21, 1990, a deputy national editor at the *New York Times*, Jeff Schmalz, stood up from his desk in the middle of the newsroom, had a seizure, and fell to the ground as coworkers watched helplessly. At the hospital, he tested HIV-positive, and the episode contributed to a dramatic shift at the *New York Times*—both in its organizational culture and in its outward depictions of lesbians and gays. Between 1990 and 1991, the number of stories about the gay community in the *New York Times* increased 65 percent, causing observers to marvel at the "Lavender Enlightenment" at the newspaper. In reality, the improvement in coverage had its origins in 1986, when longtime executive editor Abe Rosenthal was replaced by Max Frankel, who began to allow journalists to use the word *gay* in their stories. Nevertheless, as more and more journalists came out of the closet, experiences like those of Schmalz made HIV/AIDS and homophobia personal for many straight journalists. They weren't abstract issues anymore; they were affecting people they cared about.[62]

The *New York Times* was not the only news organization that changed its tone. In 1990, the American Society of Newspaper Editors released the results of a survey of two hundred lesbian and gay journalists about their experiences in the newsroom and their perceptions of the quality of reporting on lesbian and gay issues, indicating significant room for improvement on both fronts. Accompanying the survey results was a series of short essays giving practical tips on improving reporting, notes on preferred terminology, and recommendations on issues that should receive more coverage. The release of this report is significant because it brought the issue of media representations and workplace climate to the attention of newspaper editors across the country and set clear professional expectations that newspapers should improve their reporting and treatment of lesbians and gays.[63] Additionally, the leader of the survey, Leroy Aarons, personally came out at the ASNE meeting in which the survey results were reported, went on to establish the National Lesbian and Gay Journalists Association, and worked with the Radio and Television News Directors Foundation to create a similar survey and report for broadcasters.[64]

Thus, as the 1990s dawned, the tenor of news discourse about homosexuality had undergone a significant shift since *Bowers v. Hardwick*. It was around this time—1988 or 1990—that public opinion surveys began to detect an increase in tolerance for homosexuality, which would continue as a long, steady trend over the next twenty-five years. To be sure, the vast majority of Americans still disapproved of homosexuality, and representations in popular culture were still tepid and trivializing, at best. Entertainment media depictions still relied heavily on stereotypes and never portrayed same-sex intimacy; fictional characters were rarely central to any plot or developed in much depth; and mass media producers still felt the need to conform to the tastes of the mass audience.

Now, however, media producers were beginning to face pressure from groups like the Gay and Lesbian Alliance Against Defamation. GLAAD was formed in 1985 in order to counter the negative representations in the New York City press and quickly became an effective national media watchdog. For example, a 1988 episode of the NBC series *Midnight Caller*, the 1991 Hollywood film *Silence of the Lambs*, and the 1992 film *Basic Instinct* all depicted lesbian, gay, or bisexual characters as depraved killers and were fiercely protested. The pressure from GLAAD and others pushed the entertainment industry to change their tone and begin planning more positive representations for 1993 and beyond.[65]

The emergence of GLAAD as a media advocate and the shift in the organizational cultures and practices of mainstream newsrooms meant that the terms in which the social imagination of homosexuality was created and distributed would be changed forever. Journalists and Hollywood storytellers, more than anyone, have the power to construct our imagination of the world. Journalists, through the news, aspire to tell us what is *true* in the world; writers and entertainers in the culture industries, through their stories, teach us how to *feel* in the world. Because of this, the production of more positive representations of lesbians and gays was a significant development in the evolving social imagination of homosexuality: beginning around 1990, the news and entertainment media would increasingly portray homosexuality as part of one's identity—who one is, not what one does.

In 1991, this shift toward representing homosexuality as identity crystallized around new scientific research that homosexuality was, at least in part, biological. A neurologist, Simon LeVay, published an article in *Science* that documented a difference in the anterior hypothalamus (one part of the brain that regulates sexual behavior) between straight men on one hand and both straight women and gay men on the other hand—a finding that purported to show a biological basis for homosexual attraction among men.[66] The study received over two minutes of coverage on both the CBS and NBC evening news on August 29, was part of a twenty-nine-minute show regarding the causes of homosexuality on *Nightline* on August 30, was front-page news in the August 30 *New York Times*, *Washington Post*, and *Los Angeles Times*, and was covered in both *Time* and *Newsweek* the following week.

Although LeVay and other scientists urged caution in interpreting the findings, many journalists immediately framed the study as being much bigger than it was by raising the question that audiences most urgently wanted answered. Curt Suplee of the *Washington Post* led his story with it: "Are homosexuals born gay and heterosexuals born straight?"[67] The headline in the *Los Angeles Times* read, "San Diego researcher's findings offer first evidence of a biological cause for homosexuality."[68] After reflecting on the uproar caused by the study's release, *Newsweek*'s Sharon Begley intoned, "Despite the questions, the study fit the emerging theory that sexual orientation is determined more by nature than nurture."[69] In short, although journalists did not say so explicitly, the coverage clearly implied that homosexuality is probably an innate part of your identity, not something freely chosen. By 1993, when the first scientific evidence that homosexuality may be genetic was released, the news narrative that homosexuality might be due more to nature than nurture had been firmly established.[70]

The final crucial development in the legitimation of lesbian and gay identities is the movement's full inclusion in the 1992 presidential campaign of Bill Clinton. Although gay rights had been part of the Democratic Party platform since 1980, never before had the movement been so fully embraced by a candidate in the country's most important election.

Clinton not only actively sought the support of the gay community but also included them as part of his message of unity in his acceptance speech at the Democratic National Convention:

> We must say to every American: Look beyond the stereotypes that blind us. We need each other—all of us—we need each other. We don't have a person to waste, and yet for too long politicians have told the most of us that are doing all right that what's really wrong with America is the rest of us—them. Them, the minorities. Them, the liberals. Them, the poor. Them, the homeless. Them, the people with disabilities. Them, the gays. We've gotten to where we've nearly themed ourselves to death. Them, and them, and them. But this is America. There is no them. There is only us.[71]

The fact that Clinton actually won the election while outwardly support-ing gay rights meant that lesbians and gays had real national political standing and that they would be a political force to be reckoned with in the decades to come.

Gay Rights Period (1993–2015): Homosexuality as Identity

By the end of President Clinton's first hundred days in office in 1993, a new gay identity discourse was ascendant in American culture, and "not that there's anything wrong with that" signaled its contrast with the pre-vailing attitudes. The discourse was not yet dominant over the immoral lifestyle discourse, but its propagation by the Democratic Party and mainstream media provided the LGBTQ movement with strong insti-tutional counterweights to the immoral lifestyle discourse put forth by the Republican Party and New Right. Progress in winning equal rights would be painfully slow, but the rise of the identity discourse in news and popular culture was so fast, and so dramatically different from the cultural climate of the 1980s, that *Entertainment Weekly* dubbed the decade the "Gay 90s" when it was only half finished.[72]

In politics, April 25, 1993, was the date of the Third March on Wash-ington for Lesbian, Gay, and Bi Equal Rights and Liberation, which at-tracted almost one million participants. As sociologist Amin Ghaziani notes, the inclusion of "Equal Rights" in the title of the march indi-cates the consolidation of a discourse of equal rights that emerged in response to state-level political battles with conservative opponents in Oregon, Colorado, and elsewhere.[73] Also at this time, President Clinton attempted to fulfill his campaign pledge to allow gays to serve in the military. In the face of widespread opposition, he was forced to issue a compromise decree in December 1993, known popularly as "Don't Ask, Don't Tell," which effectively left the existing ban in place but instructed members of the military to neither inquire about nor reveal one's sexual orientation.

Although political success would remain frustratingly elusive in the 1990s, popular culture evolved steadily between 1993 and 2000, especially in television and film. Looking only at prime-time network television series, the number of openly gay characters increased from five in the 1992–1993 season to thirty-three in the 1996–1997 season, and the number of gay-themed episodes in those series increased from eleven in 1992–1993 to thirty-two in 1997–1998. The reason for the increase, according to Ron Becker, is a shift in the marketing strategies of the broadcast networks. Competition with cable channels had eroded the networks' traditional advertising advantage, so they began to target the narrow demographic groups that advertisers most coveted in their programming decisions. Led by the Fox's "edgy" programming that appealed to young, educated, liberal, urban, and affluent audiences (*The Simpsons, In Living Color, Beverly Hills, 90210*, etc.), broadcast networks began to incorporate gay content into their episodes in order to attract these desirable viewers. As Becker puts it, "By 1993 homosexuality was actually becoming chic in certain circles," and the controversy surrounding it gave programming that edgy appeal that advertisers wanted.[74]

By the 1995–1996 season, all the broadcast networks had increased the amount of lesbian and gay content on television, but none of the characters were protagonists and the representations were sanitized so as to avoid controversy. That changed with the April 30, 1997, coming out of Ellen DeGeneres as both the actress and the character on *Ellen*. The month-long controversy that preceded the actual airing of the episode merely increased its profile. As Becker notes, only one of ABC's 225 affiliates refused to air the episode, and a threatened boycott of advertisers by conservative groups appeared to have little effect; by contrast, GLAAD held coming out parties to coincide with the airdate, and the episode's forty-two million viewers got yet another opportunity to develop an emotional identification with a lesbian who was struggling to overcome stigma and admit who she is to the world.[75]

Even though *Ellen* was canceled the following year, in the fall of 1998 NBC introduced the series *Will & Grace*, which ran 189 episodes over eight seasons and featured two leading gay male characters.[76] Many have criticized the show for its avoidance of same-sex intimacy and for the heteronormative pairing of an openly gay man with a straight woman as the show's title characters; but it is probably because of those features, rather than despite them, that *Will & Grace* helped shift public opinion. Back then, majorities of Americans still disapproved of homosexuality, even as they became increasingly supportive of gay rights; and there is some evidence to suggest that regular viewers of the show became more tolerant of homosexuality by virtue of their identification with the gay characters.[77]

The representations of lesbians and gays in Hollywood films followed a different trajectory, though the ultimate outcome was largely the same. Whereas the "culture of homosexual pollution" determined how homosexuality was depicted in the 1980s, lesbian and gay characters in the 1990s increasingly took on the form of the "normal gay."[78] The film that most clearly marks the rise of the "normal gay" is *Philadelphia* (1993), the story of a successful lawyer who is fired after the partners at his law firm learn that he has HIV. Tom Hanks won an Academy Award for his portrayal of the suffering gay lawyer, Andrew Beckett, but the film is also noteworthy for Denzel Washington's homophobic character, Joe Miller, whose anti-gay prejudice ultimately does not prevent him from helping Beckett win justice. The film invites straight audiences to identify with both characters: they sympathize with Beckett because his character suffers while exhibiting no stereotypically gay character traits, and they sympathize with Miller because audiences at the time shared his moral disapproval of homosexuality. By watching Washington's character work through his homophobia, audiences learned how they could stand up against discrimination while at the same time acknowledging their discomfort with homosexuality.

Through the rest of the decade, lesbian and gay characters appeared in an increasing variety of roles and contexts that collectively attest to the diffusion of the "normal gay" throughout society. In *The Bird Cage* (1996), Robin Williams plays a gay drag club owner with a straight son and who humorously adopts a straight persona when meeting the daughter-in-law's conservative parents. In *As Good as It Gets* (1997), Greg Kinnear earned an Oscar nomination for playing the gay neighbor and witness to an antisocial Jack Nicholson's romantic pursuit of Helen Hunt. Also in 1997, cult classic film director Kevin Smith's *Chasing Amy* depicts Ben Affleck's pursuit of Joey Lauren Adams, whose sexual orientation is far from clear.

Thus, in Hollywood's gay nineties, lesbian and gay characters appear as parents, neighbors, friends, potential romantic partners, professionals, business owners—all defined by attributes other than sexual orientation. Sexual orientation in the 1990s thus became only one part of a person that stood alongside all others. To be sure, sociologist Steven Seidman's conclusion that these films "at best promote a fairly narrow type of social tolerance, not equality" is accurate: films of the 1990s rarely featured lesbian or gay leads or depicted homosexuality as equal to heterosexuality.[79] However, Hollywood at least relegated homophobia to the negative half of the semiotic ledger.

Critic Suzanna Danuta Walters observes that homosexuality's "new visibility" in the 1990s was deeply embedded in paradox: for just as American popular culture seemed to embrace lesbians and gays more than ever, acceptance in real life lagged far behind.[80] According to the 1996 General Social Survey, there was still a 30-point gap between the percentage of Americans who said that homosexuality was "always wrong" versus "not wrong at all" (56 to 26 percent). In politics, this period has been characterized as one in which the state refused to see lesbians and gays in law and policy: both "Don't Ask, Don't Tell" and the 1996 Defense of Marriage Act (DOMA) illustrate how policy makers tried to render same-sex sexuality invisible.[81] And in everyday life, lesbians and gays faced persistent homophobia and anti-gay violence, as the gruesome 1998 murder of Matthew Shepard illustrates. Thus, just as it became easy and cool to consume gay culture, Americans remained resistant to real equality.

Americans' acceptance of lesbians and gays in politics and real life would lag behind mass media representations for most of the 2000s as well, but as the new millennium dawned, the social imagination of homosexuality as deviant behavior was no longer dominant. The religious and conservative opposition to homosexuality remained quite strong—and appeared to strengthen after George W. Bush, an evangelical conservative, assumed the office of president after the 2000 election. However, the news media, culture industries, and the Democratic Party provided a secular, youthful alternative. Throughout the 2000s, moral disapproval of homosexuality steadily declined, support for gay rights steadily increased, media representations continued to push the boundaries of acceptability, and the social imagination of homosexuality as identity became increasingly powerful. Tolerance and equality for lesbians and gays never progressed quickly or dramatically, but the tastemakers in the media continued to tell an ever-widening story about normal gay identities, while the demographic metabolism of society slowly and inexorably churned out a new generation who saw the world in a new light.

The Battle for Gay Marriage

Looking back on the history, it seems to be no coincidence that the first significant push for gay marriage by the LGBTQ movement occurred in 1987 at the Second National March on Washington as part of a momentous turning point. True, the first legal requests for same-sex marriage licenses appeared in the 1970s; but back then, when homosexuality was broadly understood to be either a mental illness or a deviant behavior, such a proposition was nonsense.[82] Gay marriage would make sense only in the context of a full-throated demand for the recognition of lesbian and gay identities.

Gay marriage was a significant component of the 1987 March on Washington in two respects. First, although the word *marriage* did not appear, the first of the seven major demands made in the activists' platform was "The Legal Recognition of Lesbian and Gay Relationships." The platform further alluded to gay marriage—albeit in a variety of euphemistic phrases—by demanding access to the rights and benefits given to heterosexual couples:

> Lesbian and gay male domestic partners are entitled to the same rights as married heterosexual couples. . . . Changes must be made in the courts and the legislatures to provide homosexual couples the same privileges and benefits as heterosexuals who commit themselves to similar relationships.[83]

Although the platform did not demand gay marriage per se, the call for rights, benefits, and legal status equivalent to marriage was effectively the same.

Second, as mentioned above, organizers held a mass wedding ceremony on Saturday, October 10. Ghaziani reports that the decision to hold a wedding was highly contentious, garnering opposition from several constituencies within the movement.[84] Nevertheless, about two thousand same-sex couples, along with their supporters, gathered in front of the IRS building in Washington to enact their vision of marriage equality.[85] One participant in the event recalled:

> The wedding ceremony was conducted by a woman. She said, "Now, for those of you who aren't getting married, move to the outside and join hands." The people who were going to marry moved in. All of us who had joined hands were told to raise our hands and hold them in the air while she said some kind of prayer. The emotion and the sincerity were very unexpected. Tears were streaming down everybody's faces. It was like this circle of love. I think people might have expected more of a show, and it turned into something very real.[86]

Gay marriages would become very real indeed. In a tension that would characterize the battle over gay marriage from beginning to end, this public, political demonstration that, legally, was about rights and benefits provided by government to married couples was also an intensely emotional, personal affair that invoked transcendent values of love, acceptance, and recognition.

During the 1990s, gay marriage became a nationwide issue. Activists at the 1993 March on Washington demanded its legalization explicitly in their platform, and a mere ten days later, the Hawaii Supreme Court issued the first (albeit temporary) legal victory for gay marriage proponents. In *Baehr v. Lewin*, the court ruled that the government must demonstrate that "compelling state interests" are served by denying someone a marriage license on the basis of sex. The ensuing legal battle lasted for much of the remainder of the decade, and it prompted both federal and state-level legislation to define marriage as between one man and one woman only. In 1996, President Clinton signed DOMA, which both defined marriage thusly and explicitly allowed states to refuse to recognize same-sex marriages that were granted in other states. Two years later, voters in Hawaii and Alaska amended their state constitutions to define marriage as an opposite-sex union, thereby preempting any court ruling that would permit gay marriage there.

In 2004, Massachusetts became the first state to grant marriage licenses to same-sex couples after the Supreme Judicial Court ruled, in *Goodridge v. Department of Public Health* (2003), that it was a violation of the state constitution to deny the rights and benefits that come from marriage to someone on the basis of the sex of the individual's partner. Legislators were given six months to correct the problem, but the court rejected a proposal for same-sex civil unions (similar to what Vermont legislators created in 2000) because it would relegate same-sex couples to "second-class status." On May 17, the first marriage licenses to same-sex couples were issued, and over 8,100 couples received them during the next two years.[87]

Although this was a significant milestone, the most dramatic effect of gay marriage's legalization in Massachusetts was the nationwide moral panic that ensued: opponents sounded the alarm that liberal courts would redefine marriage to include same-sex couples if they did not take drastic measures.[88] President Bush endorsed a proposed amendment to the US Constitution banning gay marriage and rode a tidal wave of anti–gay marriage ballot initiatives to his 2004 reelection. Prior to 2003 only four states had banned gay marriage in their state constitutions, but in 2004 citizens in thirteen voted to do so. Between 2005 and 2008, thirteen more states passed such constitutional amendments. In all but two of these twenty-six referenda, gay marriage opponents won with more than 56 percent of the vote.[89] It is perhaps shocking to recall that the day after President Obama's election in 2008, gay marriage was legal only in Massachusetts and Connecticut, and no state that had proposed banning gay marriage via constitutional amendment had ever failed to do so. At the time, only 39 or 40 percent of Americans supported gay marriage, according to Gallup and the Pew Research Center.

Something happened in 2009, however. That year Iowa became the third state to legalize gay marriage via the courts, while New Hampshire and Vermont (along with Washington, DC) became the first American states to legalize gay marriage through legislative action. New York followed suit in 2011. For reasons that are still unclear, public support for gay marriage rose 10 points during President Obama's first term, crossing the 50 percent threshold sometime in 2011 or 2012. Shortly afterward Obama came out in support of gay marriage, and the 2012 election marks the first time that gay marriage was legalized through popular vote. Voters in Maine, Maryland, and Washington all legalized gay marriage in their states, while Minnesota voters defeated a proposed constitutional amendment to ban it. Only in North Carolina did voters approve another constitutional ban on gay marriage.

The pace of change quickened further in 2013. In June the US Supreme Court (*United States v. Windsor*) simultaneously legalized gay marriage in California and struck down as unconstitutional Section 3 of DOMA (passed only seventeen years earlier). The writing was now on the wall. Over the course of the next eighteen months, courts legalized gay marriage in twenty states, and public opinion polls continued to show rapid increases in support across all demographic groups.[90] Only the Sixth Circuit Court of Appeals upheld the preexisting state bans against gay marriage as constitutional, which prompted the US Supreme Court to finally settle the dispute. Two years after the US Supreme Court struck down DOMA, a majority of justices ruled that a federal constitutional right to marriage exists for all couples regardless of sex. Although the ruling did not end the battle over gay marriage permanently, it did legalize it in all fifty states and brought an important chapter in the battle for lesbian and gay equality to a close.[91]

Cohorts Coming of Age

Readers will be forgiven for their disappointment that this chapter says so little about what happened after 2000.[92] We have grown accustomed to thinking about politics within short-term time horizons, and the methods of social scientists are much more amenable to documenting the direct causes of social change. It is much easier to show that some social change was spurred by an immediate cause—a protest, a lawsuit, a change in political regime—than a distant influence, the effects of which are usually indirect and contingent on subsequent events.

Yet, it is the thesis of this book that the rise of gay marriage in the United States owes more (or at least more than we usually think) to these long-term, indirect effects than to short-term, direct effects. The social imagination that dominates each period lays out the cultural terrain on which all battles are fought by political actors, and the two turning points constituted major shifts in the landscape. Thus, the LGBTQ movement actions that brought about those turning points had long-term effects on the culture war that were far greater than the short-term outcomes of any one battle.

Moreover, the processes of generational change that shape the formative experiences and worldviews of young cohorts work slowly and cumulatively, not quickly and dramatically. It may take decades before the unique attitudes and dispositions of young generations become sufficiently widespread in the population to make a difference in the outcomes of elections. And because the effects of generational change are indexed (at least partially) to the demographic metabolism of cohort replacement in a society, this type of change tends to be incremental and gradual.

This is not to say that nothing important happened in the 2000s to cause the legalization of gay marriage; nor would I argue that the outcome was inevitable. The LGBTQ movement's actions after 2000—on the streets, at the ballot box, and in the courtrooms—all worked to make gay marriage a reality. San Francisco mayor Gavin Newsom's bold decision to begin issuing marriage licenses to same-sex couples in 2004 helped catalyze the movement, as did the decision of every same-sex couple who got married, knowing that their papers might ultimately be meaningless.[93] The alliance of the so-called dream team of lawyers to challenge the constitutionality of California's Proposition 8 was also a bold step and fiercely debated within the LGBTQ movement, because it was by no means clear that their case would succeed.[94]

Moreover, media representations of lesbians and gays continued to evolve after 2000 in ways that supported the marriage equality movement. The 2005 release of the Academy Award–winning film *Brokeback Mountain* broke new barriers for its loving depictions of homosexual male intimacy, and it gave audiences insight into the heartbreak felt by generations of lesbians and gay men for being unable to marry the person they love. In 2009, *Milk* won two Academy Awards, while *Modern Family* and *Glee* debuted on network television, bringing same-sex families and LGBTQ issues to the forefront of popular entertainment. Later, the 2012 release of the Grammy Award–winning song, "Same Love," by hip-hop artists Macklemore and Ryan Lewis, no doubt fueled the pro–gay marriage electoral victories in Washington state and elsewhere.

But these are stories for another book. In this chapter, I have documented the long-term evolution of the social imagination of homosexuality because people who grew up in different time periods came of age imagining homosexuality to mean fundamentally different things. The oldest living Americans, born before 1951 and reaching adulthood before 1969 or so, came of age in a society that characterized homosexuality as a mental illness; we can call them the *Illness Cohort*. Organizations like the American Psychiatric Association and World Health Organization listed homosexuality as a mental disorder in their official diagnostic manuals, and lesbians and gays were regularly institutionalized in psychiatric facilities. In the mass media, lesbians and gays were symbolically annihilated: their representation as either comic, effeminate buffoons or tragic, mentally disturbed victims was scarcely better than blanket censorship. The homophile movement was largely covert, and lesbian and gay activists rarely challenged their stigma publicly. Accordingly, cohorts coming of age in this period grew up imagining homosexuality as something to be eliminated, not just for the sake of society, but for the health and well-being of the afflicted.

Between 1969 and 1973, lesbian and gay activists challenged the cultural schema of homosexuality as mental illness and substituted a more positive image of gay identity and gay lifestyle as an alternative, but they only partially succeeded in changing the social imagination. They demedicalized homosexuality because they were able to influence the judgments of an important epistemic community—the psychiatrists and mental health professionals who claimed the expertise to label or de-label mental illnesses—but most Americans were not yet willing or able to imagine homosexuality in the positive terms set out by the activists.

Instead, between 1974 and 1986, religious and conservative activists successfully neutralized the lesbian and gay movement's victories and framed homosexuality negatively; meanwhile, the scourge of HIV/AIDS and *Bowers v. Hardwick* affirmed the American public's understanding of homosexuality as deviant behavior. Americans born between 1956 and 1968 (and reaching adulthood between 1974 and 1986) therefore came of age imagining homosexuality as a deviant lifestyle (we can call them the *Lifestyle Cohort*) and lesbians and gays as deviant or immoral individuals whose behavioral choices could lead to social condemnation, serious disease, or criminal prosecution.

This began to change between 1987 and 1992 when lesbian and gay activists adopted increasingly radical tactics to call attention to the HIV/AIDS epidemic and began to pressure the media to produce less offensive representations. During this six-year turning point, the social imagination of homosexuality was fiercely contested, with both old and new understandings of homosexuality competing for symbolic dominance. Like the first turning point, the activists again successfully influenced an epistemic community—journalists and media producers in the culture industries—to change the ways they communicated with the public about lesbians and gays.

By 1993, the LGBTQ movement had succeeded in bringing the Democratic Party, mainstream news organizations, and culture industries over to its side. Although it was far from clear at the time, the battle lines in the ongoing contest over homosexuality's imagination were now set for the next two decades. One side imagined homosexuality as identity, while the other side—institutionalized in the Republican Party and religious organizations—continued to imagine homosexuality as behavior. Each side attempted to frame the entire debate over gay rights in favorable terms: their discourses both presupposed and furthered their own cultural schema of homosexuality in a symbolic struggle for the minds of straight Americans. With each passing year after 1993, the imagination of homosexuality as an identity would increasingly prevail over the imagination of homosexuality as behavior. Thus, only Americans born after 1974 (and reaching adulthood after 1992) came of age in a society that imagined homosexuality as an identity; we can call them the *Identity Cohort*.

As the years progressed and the demographic metabolism kept churning away, the Identity Cohort grew while the Illness Cohort shrank. Popular culture continued to cater to the young, desirable market niches; public tolerance of homosexuality and support for gay rights gradually increased; and the view that homosexuality is a deviant, immoral lifestyle became increasingly confined to conservative religious communities. With every passing year, the youngest cohorts were growing up in a culture that was progressively removed from the historical conditions that older Americans knew so well, and gay marriage proponents found increasingly favorable conditions for fighting court battles and winning elections. The culture war, declared by Pat Buchanan in 1992, became a war of attrition. It took twenty years for gay marriage activists to begin winning battles consistently, but the fight over gay marriage effectively ended a mere three years after the turn of the tide.

What has this chapter taught us about why and how the social imagination changes? In the culture at large, the social imagination of homosexuality changed as an indirect response to the activism of the LGBTQ movement, mediated by shifts in the discourse and practices of epistemic communities. Each of the two turning points began with changes in the tactics and strategy of lesbian and gay activists, who succeeded in extracting changes from important epistemic communities in how they defined and represented homosexuality to the general public. Because these epistemic communities laid claim to the expertise to define homosexuality and the media power to broadcast it to a mass audience, public opinion began to shift afterward.

In the next chapter, we turn to the quantitative data to see exactly how public opinion about homosexuality and gay marriage evolved over time. We expect to see not only shifts in public opinion that correspond to the historical events described in this chapter but also cohorts who came of age during different periods expressing different levels of support for gay marriage. As we shall see, the data are mostly (though not entirely) consistent with the story I have just told, but they do not provide clear answers for why and how different cohorts developed different attitudes about gay marriage. We learn much about the dynamics of generational change from these data, but we will also be called to look beyond them in order to fully explain the rise of gay marriage.

3

The Evolution of Public Opinion about Gay Marriage

Demography is destiny, as the saying goes.

According to government figures, every year about four million people are born in the United States (a figure that has been roughly the same since 1989) while about two and a half million people die—about 73 percent of whom are over age sixty-five.[1] For most of the 2000s, support for gay marriage among the youngest cohort was about 30 percentage points higher than among the oldest cohort. So every year, if six out of ten senior citizens who oppose gay marriage die, they are replaced in the electorate by young people, only three out of ten of whom oppose gay marriage.[2] If you do the math, counting both births and deaths, the number of gay marriage supporters relative to opponents would increase by almost two million per year—19.6 million over a decade. And this is only because of population turnover; it doesn't count the untold numbers of Americans who change their minds about the issue.[3]

The inexorable process of population turnover—or *cohort replacement*—is evidence of what sociologist Norman Ryder famously described as the "demographic metabolism" of society.[4] It is a powerful engine of social change. Through cohort replacement, like our own body's metabolism, society continually gets new supplies of energy even while it burns through the older supplies. The rate of change in the social body due to the demographic metabolism may not be dramatic—after all, it's much easier to lose weight by getting surgery than by burning stored-up calories—but it is constant and unyielding.

Cohort replacement is not the same as *generational change*, however. Cohort replacement is inevitable, but generational change is not. If the newborn cohorts who replace the dying cohorts in society share the same attitudes, beliefs, and values, public opinion will not change. If newborn cohorts adopt the same behaviors and lifestyles as their elders, we will get *social reproduction* instead of social change; society will simply reproduce itself over time. So, in order for generational change to occur, cohort replacement must be combined with some other force that causes young cohorts to develop distinctive worldviews or behaviors.

The changing social imagination of homosexuality is one such force. Americans reaching adulthood during different historical periods developed different cultural schemas of homosexuality while coming of age; these changes in the social imagination, combined with cohort replacement, produce generational change. As members of the Illness Cohort die off, they are replaced in the population by members of the Identity Cohort, and their differing understandings of homosexuality are a source of social and political instability.

When we talk about generational change, we usually focus on young people. It's easy to notice the distinctiveness of young cohorts because they often act and communicate differently from what elders are used to. But this view is incomplete. We have to look at young cohorts in relation to older cohorts—not just because old cohorts were the ones who created the society into which young people are unwittingly brought, but also because the attitudes of older cohorts may be more or less similar to those of the young cohorts they are replacing.

Moreover, old people are not as set in their ways as popular stereotypes suggest. It may be hard to teach an old dog new tricks, but old humans actually learn a great deal—and from the young, no less. Attitude change in old age is much more common than previously thought, and in some ways senior citizens are more open to change than middle-aged adults.[5] While it is true that the worldviews we develop during our formative years are of enduring significance, it is emphatically not true that people do not change as they age. Thus, the kinds of historical forces that cause young cohorts to develop distinctive worldviews are sometimes strong enough to cause older cohorts to alter the worldview they adopted during an earlier era.

These observations complicate the conventional narrative of generational change. Cohorts are distinctive in part because their formative worldviews are relatively enduring, but the social forces that cause unique cohorts to emerge are precisely the kinds of forces that can undo an older cohort's distinctive markings. Sometimes older adults change their attitudes because of history, other times because of the young, still other times because of their movement from one phase in the life course to another (when people marry, have children, and retire, they change along with their roles). So attitude change among older cohorts can come from a variety of sources, and its relation to generational change is not always obvious.

The complete story of generational change must therefore address young and old, attitude stability and attitude change. It must account for how cohort replacement, life course transitions, and sociohistorical changes interact. When we try to make sense of how time, aging, demography, and the various forces of change influence one another, we quickly realize that any given outcome could be due to any combination of causes. Often the changes mutually determine one another, making it difficult, if not impossible, to distinguish what's what. When it comes to generational change, once you determine whether or not change is happening, it is a puzzle all its own simply to figure out why.

In this chapter, I document and explain the changes in public opinion about gay marriage from a quantitative point of view. We already know that public opinion is changing, and we have good reason to attribute at least part of it to generational change; but we need to subject the evidence to more rigorous tests. Thus, I begin this chapter by discussing what is required to determine that generational change is occurring from a quantitative point of view. Then, I present analyses of public opinion data from the General Social Survey and the Pew Research Center—two of the best data sources we have on gay marriage. The analyses show that generational change is indeed occurring, though in ways and for reasons that are not obvious. The change in public opinion is clearly affected by both cohort replacement and intra-cohort attitude change, but how exactly it is related to the changing social imagination cannot be explained quantitatively.

Age, Cohort, and Period Effects

Social scientists who study public opinion typically have approached the complicated relationships among history, aging, and demography by trying to quantitatively distinguish among age effects, cohort effects, and period effects. All three effects represent some relationship between time, age, and attitude change, and social scientists have spent decades refining the statistical techniques for determining how much of a given change in public opinion is due to each kind of effect. Unfortunately, a person's age, her birth year, and the current year can all be mathematically derived from one another, so it has proven difficult to determine the extent to which changes in attitudes, like we see with gay marriage, are due to aging, to cohort replacement, or to the influence of unique historical periods—or to any combination of the three. In fact, it is not clear whether the age-cohort-period problem can ever be solved in a purely quantitative fashion.

The good news is that it doesn't have to be. Make no mistake, it is vital to distinguish among age, cohort, and period effects because it is so easy to draw the wrong conclusion about society by mistaking one source of change for another. But even the best statistical analyses must be accompanied by clear historical or theoretical explanations for them. So after explaining each type of effect below, I make the case that we have to incorporate the insights from other chapters in order to truly understand how public opinion about gay marriage changed.

An *age effect* occurs when people's attitudes change as they get older. Typically, age effects happen either because people enter a new stage of the life course that causes their status and roles to shift, or because the simple accumulation of experience has caused them to change. For example, we will see some evidence of age effects in how people talk about marriage in Chapter 6 because people who have gone through that life-stage transition have a different perspective on it than those who haven't. By contrast, the old adage that people become more *politically* conservative as they age has little evidence to support it because there is no life-stage transition that regularly induces a change in political ideology.[6]

Cohort effects occur when one age group develops different attitudes than another age group during the period in which they come of age (the impressionable years hypothesis) *and* when those attitudes stay the same over time (the persistence hypothesis). The logic of a cohort effect implies both that there really is something special about one's "formative years" and that the worldview that is formed remains relatively stable, even as one ages.[7] In their formal definitions, a cohort effect appears to be the opposite of an age effect, but both age and cohort effects can happen simultaneously. For example, Americans' changing attitudes about premarital sex contain both age and cohort effects: younger cohorts developed more tolerant attitudes than older cohorts, but we tend to become more disapproving of premarital sex as we age.[8]

Finally, *period effects* occur when society enters a new historical era or experiences some event that causes the attitudes of people from all age groups to change. Scholars have found it easiest to identify period and cohort effects by focusing on "cultural traumas"—dramatic social and historical events that are clearly marked in time, like World War II—but in principle they can be caused by more gradual changes too.[9] Period effects that cause older cohorts to change their attitudes can look like age effects, and period effects that affect young people while coming of age can look like cohort effects; however, analytically, period effects are distinct from the other two.

Existing research suggests that public opinion about gay marriage is following the same pattern of change as public opinion about homosexuality more generally: attitudes are changing because of cohort and period effects, but not age effects.[10] If young cohorts are more supportive of gay marriage than their elders, and if they show no signs of becoming more opposed as they grow older, we can predict that cohort replacement is responsible for some portion of the increase in support for gay marriage—to the tune of two million Americans per year. However, support for gay marriage increased even more rapidly than cohort replacement alone would account for. The intra-cohort attitude change that is evidenced by declining levels of opposition across all age groups is indicative of period effects that compound the cohort effects.

From a quantitative perspective, it is important to distinguish the proportion of the change in public opinion that is due to cohort replacement and the proportion due to period effects. Logically, the larger the proportion that is attributable to period effects, the smaller the proportion that is attributable to cohort effects; and since cohort effects are the basic signature of generational change, evidence of period effects would seem to lessen the impact of generational change as the true cause of the change in public opinion.

However, to draw such a conclusion on the basis of quantitative reasoning alone would be a mistake. Generational theory does not map perfectly onto the age-cohort-period problem, and generational change is not a zero-sum accounting game. Although generational change is most clearly identified by cohort effects, the combination of cohort and period effects can be interpreted as an unusually powerful case of it—so powerful that it both molds the worldviews of impressionable youth and alters the worldviews of older cohorts who are more set in their ways. Combined, the same historical changes that cause older cohorts to increase their support for gay marriage could also cause young cohorts to develop more tolerant attitudes in the first place.

Moreover, cohort and period effects can mutually reinforce each other as they are happening, meaning that they are compounding, not competing, forces. Put simply, every time an older person changes her mind about gay marriage because of the influence of the younger generation, we see evidence of a cohort effect contributing to a period effect. Additionally, cohort replacement might increase the power of a period effect if it causes older Americans to conclude that the legalization of gay marriage is inevitable. Perhaps older cohorts perceived that the different attitudes of young cohorts were so steadily shifting the balance of power that they ought to rethink their positions—to get on the "right side" of history. These observations confirm that generational change is, above all, a historical process that causes both quantitative and qualitative changes in society, and we can no more explain generational change by disaggregating age, cohort, and period effects than we can explain the outcome of a war by counting soldiers on the battlefield.

Nevertheless, in this chapter I present analyses of the best public opinion data we have about gay marriage in order to show how public opinion changed between 1988 and 2014. I use multiple methods to estimate how much change can be attributed to age, cohort, and period effects, and I analyze how the cohort and period effects that we observe are related to individuals' demographic characteristics and to their views on homosexuality. From this, we gain valuable insights into how public opinion changed, and we will take a crucial step in our overall explanation of how and why generational change contributed to the rise of gay marriage.

The Data

As discussed in Chapter 2, the ways in which privileged communicators in the public sphere represent homosexuality are important because they have the potential to shape public opinion. As the discourses about homosexuality and gay marriage in the public sphere change, so too would we expect to see changes in public opinion. Thus, American public opinion about gay rights during the Homophile Period (1945–1968) should be qualitatively and quantitatively distinct from public opinion during the Resistance Period (1974–1986) and the Gay Rights Period (1993–2015).

Unfortunately, since the idea of gay marriage was nonsense in the American imagination for most of this time, researchers never asked Americans how they felt about it until 1988. Our knowledge about how public opinion about gay marriage has changed comes from two primary sources: the General Social Survey (GSS), conducted biennially by the National Opinion Research Center at the University of Chicago, and polling firms like the Pew Research Center. Each source offers distinct benefits for the analysis of public opinion.

The GSS is highly regarded because the in-person interviews provide high-quality data and because the high response rate (consistently over 70 percent) reduces nonresponse bias.[11] The GSS was the first to ask a nationally representative sample of Americans how they felt about gay marriage. In 1988, shortly after the platform of the Second National March on Washington for Lesbian and Gay Rights included a demand for the "legal recognition of lesbian and gay relationships," the GSS asked how much people agreed or disagreed that "homosexual couples should have the right to marry one another." The fact that this question was asked as early as 1988 provides us with an estimate of how people felt about gay marriage prior to the Gay Rights Period. However, the GSS did not ask the question again until 2006, so we don't know how public opinion changed during the 1990s and early 2000s.

In this chapter, I analyze GSS data for the purposes of disaggregating age, cohort, and period effects, and for analyzing authoritatively how cohort and period are related to the demographic and attitudinal characteristics of individuals. Scholars who first analyzed these data identified both cohort and period effects as causes of the change in public opinion.[12] However, because the GSS asked about gay marriage only once prior to 2006, early analyses generally compared Americans' 1988 opinions with those from after 2006. This is unfortunate because Americans born after 1970 were too young to be included in the 1988 survey, making a before-and-after comparison impossible for young cohorts. Now, sufficient data after 2006 exist to provide a more detailed view of how attitudes changed among young cohorts.

Polling firms like the Pew Research Center began asking Americans about gay marriage in 1996, the year that the Defense of Marriage Act (DOMA) was signed into law, and they have regularly asked Americans about the issue since then. They have also asked a variety of questions at different times about aspects of people's worldviews that pertain to gay marriage—so these data allow us to investigate how people's opinions about gay marriage are related to their definitions of homosexuality, their feelings about lesbians and gays, and their personal contact with them. Thus, data from the polling centers can provide valuable insights into how public opinion evolved in relation to other aspects of people's worldviews and life experiences. Because these polls have low response rates, the amount of bias in the statistical estimates we get from them is probably greater than for the GSS; however, the Pew data can offer a more detailed glimpse into people's worldviews about homosexuality.[13]

In this chapter, I report on both the scholarly literature and my own analyses of these two sources of data. From the GSS, I use data from six years (1988, 2006, 2008, 2010, 2012, and 2014) to examine the overall trend in public opinion, how it varies by period and cohort, and the extent to which attitudes about gay marriage are related to demographic variables (like gender and education) and to moral judgments about homosexuality. Then, from the Pew Research Center I use data from two years (2003 and 2013) to examine how the changes in public opinion are related to other aspects of people's worldviews regarding homosexuality. Both datasets provide unique glimpses into the collective mind-set of the American population at the crucial moment right before the US Supreme Court legalized gay marriage in all fifty states and how it had evolved over the course of the previous decades.

The General Social Survey 1988–2014: Cohort and Period Effects

One indication of how opinions about gay marriage are related to cohort and period comes from Figure 3.1. It displays the level of Americans' opposition by birth year, as measured in each of the six available years of GSS data. Even as five-year moving averages, there is a good deal of random fluctuation in each line; but the general downward slope of all lines shows that older Americans are more opposed to gay marriage

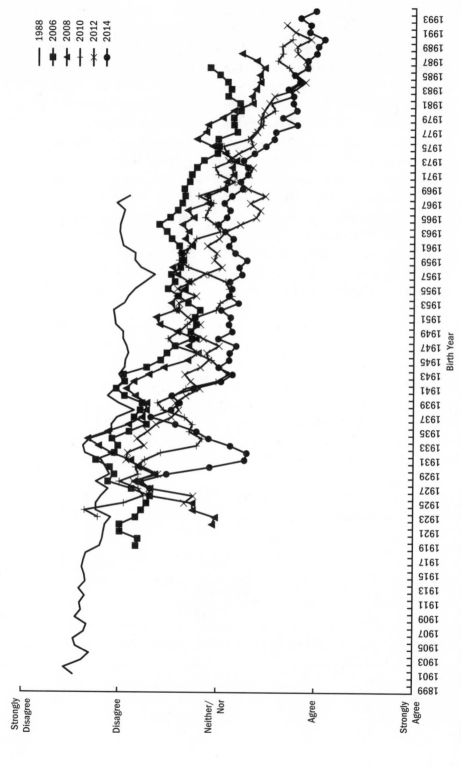

Figure 3.1: Five-Year Moving Average Opposition to Gay Marriage by Birth Year and Year

than younger Americans during every survey year. We can also visually see evidence of the period effect—the overall decline in opposition over time across all ages—in that lines from recent years are generally below those of prior years. This pattern is suggestive of cohort and period effects and resembles the pattern documented elsewhere with respect to increasing tolerance for homosexuality and support for gender equality.[14]

It is unclear from Figure 3.1 whether opposition to gay marriage is related linearly to age or whether there are distinct age cohorts that are qualitatively different from one another. In 1988, the relation between age and opposition is statistically insignificant; everyone of all ages was equally opposed to gay marriage.[15] However, by 2006, a strong and statistically significant relationship between age and opposition had emerged. Members of the Identity Cohort (born 1975 and after) are clearly more supportive of gay marriage than their elders, but there is no obvious "gap" in opinion between different age groups.[16]

The full magnitude of the shift in aggregate public opinion can be appreciated, however, only by remembering that cohort replacement was constantly reshaping the composition of the population represented by these lines. As the years passed, older individuals (displayed in the left-hand side of the figure) were continually dying and being replaced by young adults entering the population (displayed on the right-hand side of the figure). So not only were adults of all ages softening their opposition, but gay marriage opponents were continually being replaced in the population by supporters through population turnover.[17]

Figure 3.2 displays the change in public opinion in another way, this time grouping people of different ages by cohort. These cohort groups are derived from the periodization in Chapter 2 by subtracting eighteen years from those dates in order to determine the birth years of individuals who reached adulthood during each major period and turning point.[18] As expected, the Illness Cohort shows the highest opposition to gay marriage, while the Identity Cohort shows the lowest opposition to gay marriage. The fact that the slope of those lines is downward shows the period effect; the fact that the lines remain parallel shows that the distinctive imprinting due to their formative experiences as cohorts never disappeared. Thus, both the distinctive worldviews of the cohorts and the change in attitudes among people of all age groups simultaneously contributed to the aggregate change in public opinion.

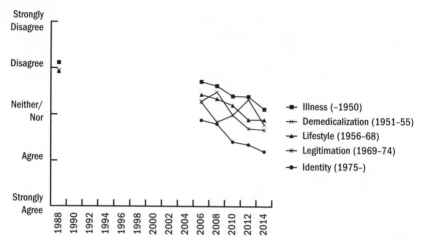

Figure 3.2: Opposition to Gay Marriage by Year and Cohort

Between the oldest and youngest cohorts, it is unclear exactly how similar or different people born between 1951 and 1974 are to one another and to the other cohorts. Because the turning points are much shorter and the cohorts who came of age during them are much smaller, the statistical estimates fluctuate more widely from year to year. To simplify the analyses, I combined these two smaller groups with the Lifestyle Cohort. This expanded Lifestyle Cohort represents all individuals who came of age between 1969 and 1993: between the time when the Stonewall Rebellion signaled the start of the public battle over gay rights and the time when Bill Clinton's election to the presidency solidified the partisan and cultural schism that would define the subsequent battle over gay marriage.

Figure 3.3 shows just how big the shift in public opinion was between 1988 and 2014, once cohort replacement and the period effects are combined. The percentage of Americans who "strongly disagree" that homosexuals should have the right to marry declined from 47 percent in 1988 to 20 percent in 2014. By contrast, the percentage of Americans who "strongly agree" increased from only 3 percent in 1988 to 31 percent in 2014. Put differently, whereas only one in eight Americans agreed (strongly) in the right to gay marriage in 1988, fewer than three in eight Americans disagreed (strongly) in 2014.

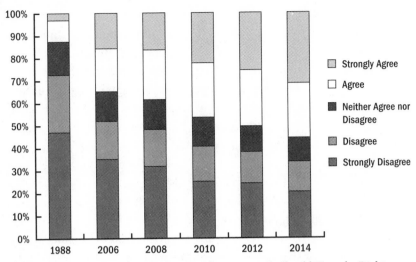

Figure 3.3: Percentage of Americans Saying "Homosexuals Should Have the Right to Marry"

How much of this overall change in public opinion is due to age, cohort, and period effects? One simple procedure that we can use to estimate this divides the total change in public opinion into two sources: change that comes from cohorts entering and leaving the population, and change that comes from the population that remains from year to year.[19] In these dichotomous terms, about one-third of the total change between 1988 and 2014 is attributable to cohort replacement, while two-thirds is attributable to intra-cohort attitude change. Although this technique is not able to differentiate how much of the intra-cohort attitude change is due to age effects and how much is due to period effects, the lack of evidence of age effects in attitudes about homosexuality leads me to interpret that attitude change as a period effect.[20]

This estimate likely understates the importance of cohort replacement because the procedure cannot determine the reasons for intra-cohort attitude change. Every time someone from a young cohort with a distinctive worldview influences someone from an older cohort to change her opinion—by introducing gay friends or by persuading her that marriage would be good for lesbian and gay families—would be counted as intra-cohort attitude change, even though the process of generational change is the process that gave rise to the young cohorts' distinctive attitudes in the first place. Therefore, if we want to know more about the cohort and period effects and how they are related to people's demographic characteristics and worldviews, we have to use other procedures.

Existing research has already taught us a great deal about this. Most notably, sociologist Dawn Michelle Baunach examined the similarities and differences between attitudes in 1988 and 2010, focusing on the ways in which demographic factors were related to people's views on gay marriage. In 1988, support for gay marriage was only weakly associated with demographics. It was (like it is now) higher among women, Democrats, people with higher levels of education, and people who attend religious services less frequently; but age, race, city size, and marital status were statistically unrelated to opinions about gay marriage. By 2010, public opinion was more strongly patterned: whereas demographic variables accounted for only 13 percent of the total variation in attitudes about gay marriage in 1988, by 2010 they accounted for 34 percent.[21]

The simplest interpretation of this fact is that opposition to gay marriage was so widespread in 1988 that the reasons people supported it had little to do with demographics. But after gay marriage became a contentious political issue, public opinion became more divided. For example, in 1988 age was statistically uncorrelated with support for gay marriage; but the size of the effect of age on attitudes (controlling for other variables) increased tenfold by 2010. Similarly, the impact of political and religious beliefs increased dramatically between 1988 and 2010: partisan political identity was almost five times more strongly associated with attitudes about gay marriage in later years, and the effect of frequency of religious service attendance more than doubled.[22] Evangelical Protestants were statistically no more likely than mainline Protestants to oppose gay marriage in 1988, but by 2010 the effect of being an evangelical Protestant on opposition had increased eightfold.[23]

From her analysis, Baunach concludes that the changing attitudes were due not to any overall shift in population demographics, but rather to some unspecified "cultural shift."[24] Unfortunately, there is no consensus on the nature of that shift. Scholars have offered several plausible explanations, all of which are probably part of it.[25] But the GSS data do not provide any definitive answers; at best, we can search for clues.

The most obvious place to start our search for an explanation for the trend is with people's attitudes about homosexuality in general. The sociologist Brian Powell and his colleagues showed that people's opinions about gay marriage are strongly correlated with their moral judgments of homosexuality. In their analysis of GSS data from 2006 to 2012, they showed that fully 90 percent of people who "strongly disagree" that lesbians and gays should have the right to marry describe homosexuality as "always wrong." Conversely, 83 percent of respondents who "strongly agree" that lesbians and gays should have the right to marry believe that homosexuality is "not wrong at all." These findings are an emphatic confirmation of the view that the controversy about gay marriage was mostly about our moral judgment of homosexuality.[26]

In order to determine how all of these factors—people's moral judgments about homosexuality, their demographic characteristics, and cohort and period—interact to shape public opinion about gay marriage, I conducted three kinds of statistical analyses that predict individuals' opinions on the basis of observed variables. Although the results differ somewhat depending upon the procedure, together they tell a fairly coherent story. In essence, people's moral judgments about homosexuality are the strongest predictor of their opinions about gay marriage, but both cohort and period have strong, statistically significant effects on both their moral judgments and their opinions about gay marriage, controlling for politics, religion, and other demographic characteristics.

Figure 3.4 provides a visual representation of this basic story. It is a path diagram that treats people's opposition to gay marriage as the dependent variable and their moral judgments about homosexuality as an intervening variable; thus, period, cohort, and other demographic characteristics are assumed to have both direct and indirect effects on public opinion. Each arrow represents a statistically significant influence of a left-hand variable on a right-hand variable; the number next to the arrow is an estimate of the relative strength of influence, all else equal. The larger the number, the larger the influence; the sign (positive or negative) indicates the nature of the association (opposition to gay marriage is coded with a higher value than support, and the judgment that homosexuality is "always wrong" is coded with the highest value, compared with other judgments).

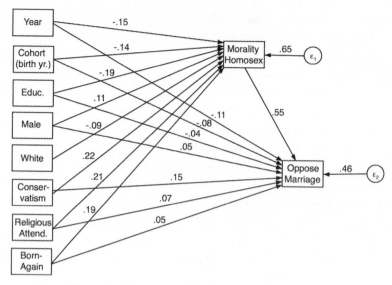

Figure 3.4: Opposition to Gay Marriage Mediated by Moral Judgment of Homosexuality

As you can see, judging homosexuality to be morally wrong is the single largest predictor of opposing gay marriage (ignoring the unexplained error terms on the right-hand side of the figure). Political conservatism and the two separate measures of religiosity (attendance at religious services and born-again Christian identity) are the next largest set of influences on public opinion, counting both direct effects and the indirect effects they have via moral judgments of homosexuality.[27] Neither of these results should be surprising: debates about gay rights have long centered on moral judgments of homosexuality, and as Chapter 2 described, the alignment of political and religious ideologies after 1992—with secular-liberals on one side and orthodox-conservatives on the other—set the stage for the battle over gay marriage.

After these ideological factors, both cohort (measured by birth year) and period (measured by survey year) have the next largest total effect size. This shows that the cohort and period effects in public opinion cannot be explained by changing moral judgments about homosexuality or by other factors, like education. It is certainly true that younger cohorts, people with higher levels of education, and people who were surveyed in later years were more likely to say that there is nothing morally wrong about homosexuality; but these groups were also less opposed to gay marriage, independently of how they judged homosexuality.

Using ordinal logistic regression to analyze the data produces similar results, even when we measure cohort in terms of the cohort categories discussed in Chapter 2 instead of birth year.[28] Moral judgments and political/religious ideologies are the strongest predictors of public opinion, but both cohort and period have statistically significant influences as well. With respect to period effects, the analyses show that levels of opposition to gay marriage fall with every passing survey year, compared to the 1988 baseline. Similarly, when compared with the Illness Cohort, members of the Lifestyle Cohort and especially the Identity Cohort are more likely to report lower opposition to gay marriage, all else equal.

A final, more exhaustive test of how age, cohort, and period effects contribute to the change in public opinion comes from a hierarchical age-period-cohort (HAPC) analysis.[29] This method solves the problem of the linear relationship between age, birth year, and survey year by conceptualizing individuals of a given age as nested within cohorts, which are then nested within years; thus, the effect of age on people's opinions about gay marriage depends on the cohort and year. Using this method, we learn that age has a linear, positive effect on opposition to gay marriage even within cohorts and periods; however, because the effects of age and cohort are both in the same direction, the age and cohort effects here may be two separate measurements of the same correlation.[30]

The HAPC analysis does suggest one tantalizing alternative, however: it may be that the Identity Cohort is the exclusive demographic home of the gay marriage generation. One measure of cohort that I used for this analysis simply compares people in the Identity Cohort (born 1975 or after) with all others, and it is this measure of cohort that generates the most parsimonious models. In other words, of all the possible ways that age, cohort, and period could explain the shift in public opinion, the simplest is that it is a function of year and whether or not one is part of the Identity Cohort.[31] This analysis suggests that the Identity Cohort has truly unique views of gay marriage, compared to their elders. The fact that the data from 1988 are so different from the post-2006 data certainly bolsters this conclusion: something momentous happened after

1988 that caused Americans coming of age after 1992 to develop markedly different attitudes.

In sum, we can draw three lessons from the GSS data. First, cohort matters. Members of the Identity Cohort, who came of age after 1992, are much more supportive of gay marriage than those who came before them, and even members of the Lifestyle Cohort are more supportive of gay marriage than their elders (though the exact cohort boundaries do not seem to matter much). Second, the change in public opinion is due to a combination of period effects and cohort replacement. The large size of the period effects show that Americans of all kinds were becoming more supportive of gay marriage as time passed. Whereas almost no one supported gay marriage in 1988, support was more common by 2006 and spread further with every passing year. Even though it appears that this intra-cohort attitude change accounts for the majority of the shift in public opinion, it may be that much of this attitude change was caused by the influence of the Identity Cohort over their elders. Third, Americans' judgment of the morality of homosexuality is the strongest single predictor of their opinions about gay marriage, but ideology, cohort, period, and demographic variables also significantly affect public opinion.

In general, the GSS data support the story of generational change laid out in theoretical and historical terms in previous chapters: Americans became increasingly supportive of gay marriage in the twenty-first century because of a combination of cohort replacement and intra-cohort attitude change. Not only did younger, more supportive Americans replace older, more opposed Americans in the population, but also processes of social influence during the Gay Rights Period caused Americans of all kinds to soften their opposition.

However, the story may not be so simple. Analyses of the GSS data still leave much of the variation in public opinion unexplained. Most notably, the GSS's sole measurement of people's feelings about homosexuality—their moral judgments—may not be sufficient. Might people's attitudes toward lesbians and gays, their beliefs about what causes homosexuality, and their level of personal contact with lesbians and gays also play a role in shaping opinions about gay marriage? It is to this question that we now turn.

Pew Research Center 2003–2013: Broader Views of Homosexuality

The Pew Research Center, like other polling firms, conducts dozens of surveys every year about a wide range of topics. This prevents the organization from gaining high response rates like the GSS, but it allows them to measure public opinion about issues like gay marriage more frequently and to ask a larger number of questions about it. In October 2003, Pew asked twenty-four questions that pertained to homosexuality and gay marriage, and a May 2013 survey featured nineteen questions on the subject.[32] Nine questions appeared on both surveys, so we can compare how different aspects of people's worldviews about homosexuality changed in the years leading up to gay marriage's legalization.

The timing is noteworthy: the 2003 poll of 1,515 adults was conducted just one month before the Massachusetts Supreme Court declared the state's ban on gay marriage to be unconstitutional, thereby opening the door to gay marriage for the first time in the United States. The 2013 poll of 1,504 adults was conducted less than two months before the US Supreme Court ruled that the federal definition of marriage specified in DOMA was unconstitutional. Analyzing these two datasets therefore allows us to get a glimpse inside the public mind at two critical junctures: at the last possible moment when gay marriage was illegal in all fifty states and at the moment just before the US Supreme Court opened the floodgates to gay marriage nationwide.

Let's begin with our variable of interest: opinions about gay marriage. In 2003, only 32 percent of respondents to Pew's survey said they favored gay marriage, while 59 percent opposed it; ten years later, opposition had fallen by 17 points, and 51 percent of respondents said they supported it. Support increased across every demographic and ideological group. For example, support for gay marriage rose 18 percentage points among the oldest Americans (members of the Illness Cohort, born 1950 or earlier); among those who identified as born-again or evangelical Christians, support increased 11 points; among those who identified their political beliefs as "very conservative," support increased 12 points. The fact that increases are evident among all groups is the signature of a period effect: clearly, some significant change was under way.

If we consider multiple aspects of Americans' worldviews regarding homosexuality—whether measured in terms of moral judgments, affective attitudes, or cognitive beliefs—Figure 3.5 illustrates just how much their thinking shifted over the decade. In terms of moral judgments, the percentage of Americans who said that homosexuality is not a sin increased 12 percentage points. Americans' self-reported attitudes about lesbians and gays changed, too: the percentage of Americans who said they have favorable opinions about them increased 18 points. Although only one in five Americans reported feeling uncomfortable around lesbians and gays in 2003, that number fell even further by 2013.

Combined, this represents a large shift in Americans' moral and affective attitudes: the majority opinion in 2003—an unfavorable view of lesbians and gays combined with the belief that homosexuality is a sin—was a minority view in 2013. Can this shift help explain the

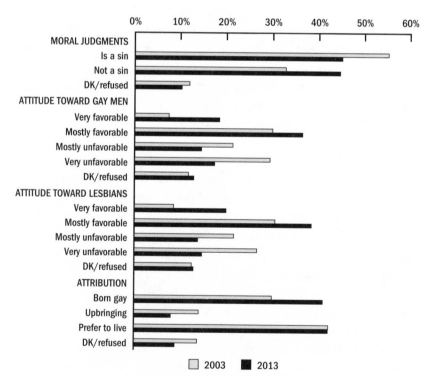

Figure 3.5: Americans' Views of Homosexuality, 2003–2013

transformation in public opinion? When I replicated the ordinal regression analysis of GSS data using the Pew data, I got the same results: cohort, period, demographics, and moral judgments about homosexuality were all associated with public opinion in the same way. Even though the two surveys phrased the question of moral judgments differently, I found that the associations of demographic variables with opinions about gay marriage are mediated by differences in their moral judgments of homosexuality.[33]

What is most interesting about this finding is that moral judgment about homosexuality is not an either-or issue. Even though overwhelming majorities of respondents to both surveys selected the extreme answer choices (always wrong vs. not wrong at all, and sin vs. not), the "middle" and noncommittal answers are meaningful as well. This is most surprising for the Pew data: almost 12 percent of respondents either refused to say whether or not homosexual behavior is a sin or said they did not know, and the odds that those individuals expressed higher levels of opposition to gay marriage were over four times higher compared to those who said homosexuality was not a sin.

A related issue is people's attitudes about lesbians and gays. Although many people's attitudes are rooted in their judgment of whether or not homosexual behavior is immoral, it is not hard to imagine why someone's judgment of a behavior might be different from how she feels about the person. Indeed, people's attitudes about lesbians and gays have a significant effect on their opinions about gay marriage, controlling for both their moral judgment of homosexuality and all relevant demographic variables. In fact, including this attitude measure in the analysis eliminates the statistical association of gender and education with gay marriage. Thus, the greater support for gay marriage among women and people with higher levels of education is at least partly due to their more favorable attitudes toward lesbians and gays.[34]

These results suggest that both moral judgments and attitudes affect people's opinions about gay marriage, so the substantial shift in both factors between 2003 and 2013 could account for a large portion of the overall change in public opinion. In 2003, when asked whether "more acceptance of gays and lesbians would be a good thing or a bad thing for the country," only 22 percent said it would be good. By contrast, in 2013, 60 percent of Americans agreed more with the statement "homosexuality should be accepted by society" versus "homosexuality should be discouraged by society."[35] The legalization of gay marriage could certainly be a consequence of this sharp increase in support for lesbians and gays.

What role does personal contact with lesbians and gays play in this shift? My results suggest that personal contact is associated with opinions about gay marriage not directly but only indirectly through moral judgments and affective attitudes. In fact, once these factors are taken into account, people who report knowing someone who is lesbian or gay are statistically more likely to *oppose* gay marriage than to support it. The Pew surveys are not directly comparable in this regard because the 2003 question "Do you have a friend, colleague, or family member who is gay?" was replaced with a set of three questions in the 2013 survey, the most comparable one being, "Do you personally know anyone who is gay or lesbian, or not?" In 2003, 60 percent of Americans said they had a friend, colleague, or family member who is gay, and 87 percent of Americans in 2013 said that they knew someone who is gay or lesbian.[36] Of those 87 percent who said yes in 2013, 56 percent of them said that one of their "close family members" or "closest friends" is lesbian or gay—so in all, about half of Americans reported being "close" to someone who is lesbian or gay in the year that the definition of marriage in DOMA was overturned.

Last, it appears that Americans' cognitive beliefs about the nature of homosexuality changed as well, and that the changing attribution of homosexuality may be associated with the increase in support for gay marriage. When asked what Americans think causes a person to be lesbian or gay—whether homosexuality is caused by nature, nurture, or a lifestyle choice—the percentage saying that they are born that way increased from 30 percent to 41 percent.[37] The view that lesbians and gays are born that way—perhaps due to genetic factors beyond their control—is significant because it suggests that they could not change their sexual orientation, even if they wanted to. Indeed, in the 2003 survey, 79 percent of people who said that homosexuality is something people are born with also agreed that lesbians and gays cannot change their sexual orientation.[38] Unsurprisingly, those who said that people are born gay were significantly more likely to support gay marriage, controlling for all other variables.

Conclusion

All told, these analyses provide important insights about the nature of the generational change that we would be unable to get from other sources. Three conclusions in particular stand out. First, public opinion about gay marriage is most strongly and immediately shaped by people's views of homosexuality, which includes more than just their moral judgment of it. Certainly, that judgment matters, but so do people's attitudes about lesbians and gays *as people* and their cognitive beliefs about what causes a person to be gay in the first place. For many people, these three aspects of their worldview are commonsensically and logically related, but it is also not difficult to understand why people's cognitive beliefs, affective attitudes, and moral judgments could operate independently of one another. Thus, any analysis of the evolving public opinion about gay marriage should place it in the larger context of homosexuality and gay rights. When we turn to the analysis of how people talk about gay marriage in the next chapter, a focus on how people talk about homosexuality is clearly warranted.

Second, we learned that people's worldviews about homosexuality can account for some of the association between demographic variables and opinions about gay marriage, but political and religious ideologies are especially important influences on both their moral judgments about homosexuality and their opinions about gay marriage. In the statistical models, the predictive power of all demographic variables vis-à-vis gay marriage is mediated by their views about homosexuality; including measures of people's attitudes about lesbians and gays accounted for the influence of both gender and education on public opinion. Similarly, personal contact with lesbians and gays affects public opinion only insofar as it improves people's moral and affective attitudes toward them. Thus, if women, people with higher levels of education, and people who know lesbians and gays personally are more supportive of gay marriage, it must be largely because their attitudes regarding homosexuality are different.

By contrast, the fact that political and religious ideologies have such strong independent effects on opinions about gay marriage, even after taking into account the influence of people's views about homosexuality, means that we should further explore how these ideologies are related both to gay marriage and to people's views on homosexuality. The ways in which politics and religion fit into the battle over gay marriage seem obvious in some respects, but it is not obvious how people's beliefs in all three domains—politics, religion, and homosexuality—interact.

Third, these analyses show that both cohort and period effects contributed to the increase in support for gay marriage, though in ways that are somewhat different from what the historical narrative in the previous chapter suggests. With respect to period effects, Chapter 3 shows that the Gay Rights Period from 1993 to 2015 was characterized by an accelerating pace of change, not a constant one. Cohort replacement alone—with no intra-cohort attitude change—during a given period is enough to produce generational change in public opinion; but these quantitative data show that intra-cohort attitude change was a significant force of accelerating change within the period. With every passing survey year between 2003 and 2014, more and more people began to support gay marriage for reasons that are not explained by cohort replacement or any of the demographic or attitudinal variables discussed here. The trend became especially pronounced after 2008: people of all political and religious persuasions and people of every color, shape, and size began changing their minds about gay marriage for reasons that remain a mystery. These statistical findings are not incompatible with the story told in Chapter 2, but clearly that historical narrative is not the whole story.

For cohort effects, the analyses leave two unanswered questions regarding the view that cohort replacement caused public opinion to shift. First, although we see clear evidence of cohort replacement, it is unclear whether the relationship between age and gay marriage is linear or categorical. Is it just the Identity Cohort that is different, or do the other cohort categories matter in ways beyond mere age? A related problem is the lack of difference that precise cohort boundaries make for these analyses: whether I identified five cohorts or three and whether I assumed that people "come of age" at age sixteen or eighteen made little difference. Although the historical narrative from the previous chapter implies that there *should* be significant categorical differences of opinion between cohorts and small differences within cohorts, the data do not confirm that age is related to public opinion in this way.

The second unanswered question with respect to cohort effects in public opinion is simply this: how much does cohort replacement per se matter in relation to period and in relation to the other variables? On one hand, cohort replacement appears to account for only half as much change as the intra-cohort attitude changes in public opinion between 1988 and 2014. On the other hand, it would be wrong to discount the power of the cohort effects on this account. Cohort is correlated with educational attainment, attitudes about lesbians and gays, and beliefs about whether or not homosexuality is immoral, and even so it retains a statistically significant, direct effect on opinions about gay marriage. Moreover, none of the statistical techniques used in this chapter capture the fact that members of the Identity Cohort were active agents of change during this period, persuading their elders to rethink their prior opposition to gay marriage. So if anything, these analyses probably lead us to underestimate the power of generational change if we follow the existing convention of equating it with cohort replacement.

The next chapter shows how people of different cohorts, with varying political and religious ideologies, talk about gay marriage. Located at a single point in time during the Gay Rights Period (2008–2009), Chapter 4 is the start of a multi-chapter exploration of how cohorts, ideologies, and worldviews all intersect to produce distinctive ways of thinking and talking about gay marriage. Combined with the history described in the previous chapter and the quantitative analyses discussed in this chapter, the qualitative interviews discussed in the next four chapters provide the final pieces of the puzzle and help explain how and why the generational change in public opinion occurred as it did.

4

Young and Old in the Cross Fire of the Culture Wars

One hour and twenty-two minutes into my interview with Tom, a forty-seven-year-old Catholic and moderate Republican, I asked him point-blank: "Do you personally have an opinion about whether or not same-sex marriage should be legalized?" After an agonizing nine-second pause, he responded:

> It really doesn't matter to me. I mean, it's a, again, it's a piece of paper that maybe to them means a lot. But to me, it doesn't really change my life or my outlook on life. You know, does it give them a tax break or something cause they can claim as dependents? I don't know. And if that's all it is, it's small potatoes. . . . If it means so much to them, and it means very little to me, why are we getting all bent out of shape about it?

During the interview, Tom never offered a clear opinion about gay marriage. It seemed that he was not opposed to it, but neither did he advocate for it. He seemed not to care one way or the other. Could that be possible? That night, and throughout my research, I struggled to understand what people like Tom were really saying; their patterns of talk did not fit clearly into one of the most polarizing fights in America's culture wars.

Tom, in particular, was a puzzle to me, given his age, gender, religion, and politics—four factors that statistically predict opposition to gay marriage. Tom grew up at a time when homosexuality was culturally understood to be a deviant lifestyle. His religion defines homosexuality as a sin and marriage as a procreative, spiritual relationship blessed by God. He said he was planning on voting for the Republican candidates John McCain and Sarah Palin in the presidential election that loomed a mere four weeks away. The public opinion data, not to mention common sense, suggest that he would be a strong opponent of gay marriage. But he wasn't. Or at least he didn't say so, despite my repeated efforts to draw it out. My field notes from the interview that night captured my perplexities: "Is he censoring himself? Does he think I'm trying to trick him or lead him on?"

Driving back to Wisconsin on I-355, the sprawling eight-lane freeway running through Chicago's vast territory of exurbs, I struggled to wrap my head around it all. This built environment seemed the perfect symbol of rapid social change. The quaint neighborhood near the high-voltage power lines that I saw out Tom's front window looked very different from how I imagined his boyhood home—five miles from there in a town that used to be nestled among the corn fields. As I drove through the sprawl, I listened to vice presidential candidates Sarah Palin and Joe Biden debate on the radio for the 2008 election. Both candidates endorsed civil unions for lesbians and gays, but not marriage. This just added to my perplexities. If this is a culture war, then why are Tom, Palin, and Biden sitting on the sidelines?

In the previous chapter, I showed that both cohort and period effects were causing public opinion about gay marriage to shift in the manner predicted by generational theory, but that people's worldviews regarding homosexuality and their political and religious ideologies were substantial influences on public opinion, too. I had gone out into "the field"—in this case, the fields of northern Illinois—during the fall of 2008 to interview college students and their parents, hoping that listening to people talk would help me explain what was driving the shift in public opinion. I knew that the college students I was talking to—members of the Identity Cohort who were all primarily from Chicago, Rockford, and the numerous suburbs and small towns surrounding them—would be more supportive of gay marriage than their parents. I also knew that the culture war imagery typically associated with the issue was overblown—that I would be talking to a more diverse group than just fervent opponents and rabid supporters. But I did not expect to be so puzzled at the variety of discourses I was hearing from both young and old.

This chapter is the product of my efforts to map the discourses I heard. It took dozens more interviews and months of analysis to unravel the complexities of the language that I heard. My initial reaction to discourses like Tom's—to psychoanalyze my informants and to wonder what I was doing wrong—turned out to be unnecessary. I ultimately realized that people like Tom were everywhere and that they spoke about the issue in remarkably similar ways. Tom was not being coy or wishy-washy; he was producing a discourse that I call *libertarian pragmatism*. As we shall see below, what he had to say about gay marriage is a kind of discourse that we find all over the country about all sorts of issues, from marijuana legalization to motorcycle helmet laws.

But more to the point, people like Tom were caught in the cross fire of the culture wars, and his discourse bears the marks of battle. The patterns of talk I found in my interviews show that there is nothing inevitable about the culture wars; it emerged in the discourses of two groups of people: those whose religious and political ideologies were compatible with their cohort-related attitudes about homosexuality. Young liberals and older conservatives articulated these discourses in dialogue with each other, and even though my informants were talking to me, their rhetoric was armed for semantic combat with the nonpresent opposition.

Although the culture wars discourses of support and opposition are most prevalent, fully one-third of my informants did not talk in such polarized terms. Between the two polar discourses were a variety of middle-ground discourses produced by people whose political and religious ideologies were not easily reconciled with their attitudes about homosexuality. Younger conservatives and older liberals shared affinities with both sides, and their patterns of talk showed signs of tension: their ideological peers were pulling them to one side, while their age mates were pulling them to the other. Both of these groups had different ways of expressing their conflicted views.

In this chapter, I describe the culture war discourses of *unambiguous support* and *unambiguous opposition*, along with two middle-ground discourses—*libertarian pragmatism* and *immoral inclusivity*—which are produced by the interactive influences of people's ideology and their cohort-related attitudes about homosexuality. The influence of political and religious ideology on the discourse will be easy to spot, so I focus my analysis here on how cohort affects how people talk. By comparing matched pairs of parents and children who agree with each other ideologically, I show that cohort influences the discourse through their attitudes about homosexuality. This chapter, therefore, begins the process of unpacking exactly how the processes of generational change affect people's attitudes and discourses. Overall, we see that cohort exerts a strong influence over the configuration of discourses about gay marriage in the population and that its influence varies by how it interacts with ideology; moreover, because cohort replacement is continually strengthening one side and weakening the other, we begin to see why the culture war—as loud and intractable as the fighting seems—ended so quietly and so suddenly.

The Dialogic Culture War: Why We Fight

Like mom always said, it takes two to fight. Arguments, battles, wars— they always have at least two sides. And sometimes people fight even when there's no real disagreement: many soldiers fighting wars would rather not be. This obvious point has a serious implication: the truth about the culture war is that it is *dialogic*, not monologic. The culture war isn't waged inside an individual's head, measured in terms of beliefs or attitudes; it emerges in interaction—in communication and discourse—between two or more parties. People's statements are not just expressions of inner belief; they also express collective identities, construct symbolic boundaries, and enter into a discursive field already thickly saturated with meaning. It is in that field—not in our heads— that evidence of the culture war abounds.[1]

Sociologist James Davison Hunter first noted the emergence of the culture wars in his 1991 book, *Culture Wars: The Struggle to Define America*, and Republican presidential primary candidate Patrick Buchanan made it famous during his speech at the 1992 Republican National Convention.[2] But when social scientists analyzed public opinion surveys to determine whether Americans' attitudes were becoming more polarized, they found little evidence of it. With the notable exception of political party identification, people's attitudes were not becoming more extreme, and people were not clustering themselves into two irreconcilable camps.[3] Moreover, although commentators frequently contrast secular liberal Democrats with religious conservative Republicans, there is tremendous diversity within each side, and the religious orthodox are actually more progressive than secular liberals about some issues.[4]

Despite the intuitive appeal of culture war imagery, there is a simple sociological explanation for why it turns out to be wrong, at least at the individual level: every individual holds a unique combination of status group identities, and the patterns of social alliance that we maintain are too complex to make a fundamental division of people into two irreconcilable ideological camps easy. For example, I am a professor, a parent, a neighbor, a Wisconsinite, a cyclist. In different situations, I identify more with one group than another, and given the large number of identities that we all hold, there is no one with whom we will always agree about everything.[5] Moreover, everyone has a unique biography, and our varied experiences make us capable of formulating an almost infinite variety of opinions about things.

That said, given the theoretically infinite variety of things that people *could* think and say, it is remarkable how many regularities exist in what people *do* think and say. Despite the potential for limitless individuality and creative expression, we actually think and talk in patterned ways. And here is where we must replace the monological focus on inner belief with the dialogical view of interacting communicators: the culture war may not exist in terms of individual attitudes and beliefs but still arise from social interaction. Just like soldiers don't like the wars they fight, so too do we find ourselves drawn into arguments we would rather not have. We can create a culture war to fight, even if we agree on more than we think.

Culture is what converts ideas into discourse, and *discourse* is what results when the infinite variety of verbal expressions become regularized and patterned.[6] Culture gives us shared ways of making sense of the world, a common language with common symbols to help us package the infinite variety of life experiences into communicable, repeating patterns. Culture is the glue that keeps society together. From the smallest family to the largest collectivity, every social group has some shared framework for mutual understanding and sense making. Those shared cultural frameworks make their marks in discourse, so analyzing discourses can provide insight into culture. Because culture helps to turn an infinite variety of unique life experiences into a much smaller number of regular, repeating, shared discourses, we cannot evaluate the culture wars on the basis of public opinion data. That's why it's called a *culture* war, not a belief war: it takes place between interacting groups, not inside individual minds.

This is, in fact, what Hunter talks about in his book. His argument has been widely mistranslated into studies of individual attitudes and beliefs, but it is really about how our cultural institutions—language, media, and politics—give voice to two major types of moral worldviews:

the orthodox and the progressive. Notably, it is not *people* who are orthodox or progressive; Hunter describes them as "formal properties of a
belief system or world view," but they are more like *interpretive tendencies.* The orthodox is "the commitment on the part of adherents to an
external, definable, and transcendent authority," whereas the progressive
is "the tendency to resymbolize historic faiths according to the prevailing assumptions of contemporary life."[7]

The culture wars occur when cultural institutions, like churches, mass
media, and the political system, "intensif[y] and aggravate" the differences
between the orthodox and progressive ways of thinking.[8] According to
Hunter, the lines of political conflict and alliance were redrawn in the
second half of the twentieth century, bringing together religious ortho-
doxies with social conservatism and economic libertarianism on one side,
religious progressivism with social liberalism and economic collectivism
on the other side.[9] The news media amplify this division by reducing
complex issues with many shades of gray to simplistic, black-and-white
conflicts because of the convention of demonstrating objectivity by getting
quotes from both (as if there were only two) sides of an issue.

The story told in Chapter 2 shows how these dynamics played out for
gay rights. By the late 1970s, the New Right coalition had united political
and religious conservatives around opposition to abortion, gay rights,
and gender equality; by the early 1990s, the Democratic Party and popular media had united as the voice of social liberals supporting these three
sets of rights. Activists and leaders on both sides became the primary
spokespeople in mass media and escalated the conflict, and Americans
watching at home from the sidelines were drawn in, even though many
probably would have preferred to ignore it. Gay marriage didn't have
to be a culture war, but it got created through the interactive process—
between religion and politics, through media and social networks.[10]

In sum, there is nothing inevitable about the culture wars, and they
might not exist on their own—monologically—because of the infinite
variety of status sets and life experiences that define our identities and
beliefs. But because people always speak in dialogue with each other
and with the shared collective identities and cultural contexts in mind,
we can highlight and magnify differences, converting the innumerable,
unique perspectives we have into a handful of regular discourses. This
chapter shows how people can perpetuate a culture war through dialogic

argumentation, but that a substantial, diverse middle ground exists as a testament to the fact that culture wars are neither ubiquitous nor unwinnable. In a way, this middle ground is the best place to look for clues as to how the war is really playing out.

The Discursive Field and the Interaction of Cohort and Ideology

The two most common kinds of discourse that people construct about gay marriage are *unambiguous opposition* and *unambiguous support*; together, about two-thirds of my informants articulated one of these discourses. On one hand, this large majority articulating polarized discourses might make gay marriage feel like a battle in the culture wars. On the other hand, the fact that one-third of my informants articulated a *middle-ground* discourse of some sort should prompt questions about what sort of culture war we are fighting if the proportion of people in the middle is roughly the same as the proportion fighting it out on either side.

Despite this middle ground, it is nonetheless true that the polarized discourses of support and opposition carry added weight because

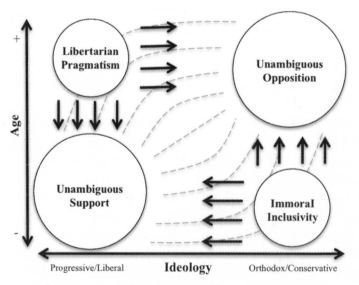

Figure 4.1: Dialogic Tensions in the Discursive Field

they anchor the field as a whole. Not only are these two discourses in dialogue with each other, but even the middle-ground discourses are meaningful mainly in relation to the polarized ones. We can think about the discursive field as a battlefield, but the metaphor of a magnetic field is more apt: it is as though the supportive and oppositional discourses at the two poles exert forces on both the people and the discourses in between them.

When analyzing the field, we need to keep both the social and discursive levels of analysis in mind. At the discursive level, the various elements of discourse and their manner of combination exist in dialogue with one another. So in the descriptions of discourses below, we will see how words, statements, and questions not only express something the speaker is thinking, but also make some implicit or explicit reference to other utterances elsewhere in the field. At the social level, speakers are communicating their collective identities and life histories in relation to the collective identities of the interviewer and the broader imaginary audience—which makes demographic characteristics and social networks of the communicators important factors. Words communicate social identities, and they cannot be analyzed in isolation from the social context of the interview or the broader political, cultural context of the controversy surrounding gay marriage.

As Table 4.1 shows, members of different cohorts were not equally likely to construct supportive and oppositional discourses. Members

TABLE 4.1: Percentage of Students and Parents Articulating Discourses about Gay Marriage

	Students (%) ($n = 65$)	Parents (%) ($n = 32$)	Total (%) ($N = 97$)
Unambiguous support	54	38	48
Libertarian pragmatism	6	13	8
Other middle ground	20	16	19
Immoral inclusivity	11	0	7
Unambiguous opposition	9	34	18
Total	100	100	100

Note: Not all percentages sum to 100 due to rounding.

of the Identity Cohort were more likely to support gay marriage, while their parents—members of the Illness and Lifestyle Cohorts—were more likely to oppose it. And while both students and parents were equally likely to produce a middle-ground discourse of some kind, members of the Identity Cohort were more likely to produce a discourse that I call *immoral inclusivity*, whereas members of the older cohort—like Tom—were more likely to produce the discourse of *libertarian pragmatism*.[11]

In sociological terms, these four discourses can be understood as the product of how one's religious and political ideologies interact with cohort. But what exactly does this mean discursively? To understand why this table looks the way it does, we need to examine each discourse in detail. Table 4.2 describes the four major discourses discussed in this chapter by summarizing the key components that make them up. Only when we look at the recurring patterns in how different kinds of people talk about gay marriage do we see how cohort and ideology influence discourse about gay marriage.

TABLE 4.2: Characteristics of Gay Marriage Discourses

	Unambiguous Support	Unambiguous Opposition	Libertarian Pragmatism	Immoral Inclusivity
Opinion about gay marriage	Support	Oppose	Don't know or refuse to state	Varies
Attitudes about homosexuality	Tolerant or nonnegative	Explicitly negative	Implicitly or explicitly negative	Tolerant or nonnegative
Moral judgment of homosexuality	Not immoral	Wrong, immoral, sinful	Seems unnatural or wrong, but cannot judge	No more sinful than other sins
Claims about attribution	Born gay, not a choice	A choice, not born gay	Varies	Varies
Gender in marriage	Any two people who love each other	Man and woman only	No specific statement, but gender not an issue	Man and woman only
Roles of government and religion	Government guarantees equal rights to all, regardless of religion	Government should not undermine religious/moral standards of society	Support for equal rights; freedom to live as you want, as long as no harm caused to others	Government should treat all people equally, but marriage is not a purely legal matter

Polarized Discourses of Support and Opposition

People who articulated a discourse of *unambiguous support* tended to be politically liberal (or libertarian) and young: 54 percent of students constructed this discourse, while 38 percent of parents did so (eleven of these twelve parents were politically liberal or libertarian). By contrast, 34 percent of parents in my study constructed a discourse of *unambiguous opposition*, while only 9 percent of students did so. All opponents in my study identified as Christians, and all but one (a parent) justified their opposition by referencing orthodox religious beliefs that homosexuality is immoral.

Two broad characteristics define these discourses, which together frame the debate about gay marriage: their ideological embeddedness and their dialogic antagonism. To be clear, these are not the only discourses that are ideologically coherent, and all discourses are dialogic in some way. What makes these two discourses significant is that they are *antagonistic* to one another and draw prominent political and religious ideologies into what might otherwise be a stand-alone disagreement about gay rights. These discourses are the easiest to articulate because each presupposes the other, and they are the most commonly heard in mass media because of how journalistic norms privilege the voices of elites from major political and religious organizations.[12]

The ideological embeddedness of these discourses is easy to understand. Logically, opposition to gay marriage builds on religious opposition to homosexuality, and the conservative value of minimal government interference in civil society is an important part of the opposition because the moral standards of the communities must be defended against unwanted intrusions by secular government. Likewise, support for gay marriage builds on the liberal political value of equality under the law, regardless of one's beliefs; and in recent history, liberals have supported the intervention of a powerful federal government to extend constitutional rights to previously marginalized groups.

Nevertheless, it would be a mistake to assume that it could not have been otherwise since neither religious nor political ideologies align perfectly with either side. For instance, not all religious values are incompatible with gay marriage, nor is religion a necessary ingredient for opposing gay marriage. Similarly, as gay marriage is a contentious social issue, libertarians align with liberals in supporting it, while they tend to align with conservatives on economic issues; logically, a libertarian could adopt the minimal-government argument that the legalization of gay marriage should be left up to the states.

As for their dialogic antagonism, the first two columns of Table 4.2 illustrate that each of the key identifying features of supportive and oppositional discourses either explicitly or implicitly contradicts the other. Opponents say homosexuality is immoral, and supporters deny it. Supporters say you are born gay, and opponents deny it. Opponents say marriage is between a man and a woman only, while supporters say that it's for any two people who love each other. In short, when supporters and opponents talked about gay marriage, they were speaking against one another through me.

The ways Natalia talked about gay marriage were typical of the supporters. Natalia was a twenty-two-year-old student at Northern Illinois University (NIU) whom I interviewed in the student center cafeteria. A Hispanic Catholic who was raised in Chicago, she identifies as a liberal Democrat and had begun exploring other religious beliefs in college. Like other gay marriage supporters I interviewed, she voted for Obama in the 2008 election and said she was "thrilled" that he won. When I first brought up the subject of gay marriage, she immediately stated her support for it by refuting the opposition's claims about the definition of marriage:

> I think that marriage is between two people regardless of sex or religion or anything, so if two girls want to get married, completely fine by me. If two guys want to get married, completely fine by me. Like I'm, you know, totally for it. You know, I'm very liberal with that so if two people love each other and, you know, want to live life together, why not? You know, just because that's their sexual preference, it's not any of my business.

Natalia not only begins her statement of support by implicitly rejecting the opposition's argument, she adds at the end that a person's sexual preference is none of her business. Of course, what she really means is that it's none of their (the opponents') business.

My informants frequently used rhetorical questions in dialogically antagonistic ways to reject opposing arguments. Natalia asked one in her opening statement and several others during the interview. For example, when I asked her why she thought gays and lesbians wanted the right to marry, she asked almost as many rhetorical questions as she made argumentative claims:

> Well, because they think, you know, they should be viewed fairly, just like everybody else. I mean this is supposed to be democracy and you know, equal rights to everyone, so why not grant them what everybody else has? I mean, that's just, you know, discriminating against—I mean, if they want to share a life together, I mean, why can't they have what everybody else gets when they want to share a life together?

What is striking about this passage is that her first statement above was sufficient to answer my question; but she added to it two statements and two rhetorical questions that explicitly challenge the opposition's position on gay marriage. Like all supporters, Natalia expressed her support for equal rights for lesbians and gays, but in such a way that delegitimized the opposition as prodiscrimination and antidemocracy.

Not all supporters went to this length to rebut the opposition's arguments, and not all parts of my interview with Natalia were this antagonistic. At times, she made her contrast with gay marriage opponents clear—as when she described opponents as scared of change and "closed-minded," or when she denied that homosexuality is immoral, saying that "it's just a way of expressing yourself." At other times, though, she appeared not to be thinking about the opposition at all. For example, most supporters denied that legalizing gay marriage would affect children, as many opponents feared, and most supporters denied that homosexuality was a choice. But Natalia thoughtfully considered how children raised by lesbian or gay couples might get outcast or teased by their peers, and she discussed quite matter-of-factly how bisexuals and others do make choices in how they express their feelings of sexual attraction.

These observations are important because the context of the interview itself both encouraged and discouraged the sort of dialogic antagonism that characterized the supportive and oppositional discourses. On one hand, many of my questions were designed to be dialogic in that I asked informants to respond to claims made by the other side. On the other hand, the fact that my primary role as interviewer was to ask questions and listen, rather than debate, tended to suppress the antagonism. Taking these dynamics into account, along with the stylistic variation in speech patterns of all my informants generally, the discourses of unambiguous support and opposition united the informants who uttered them in a co-constitutive argument that transcended the specific answers of individual informants. Taken together, this was the discursive give-and-take of the culture wars.

On the side of the opposition, Dana's statements and rhetoric are typical. I interviewed the forty-eight-year-old Rockford resident at the nondenominational Christian church she had attended for the past twenty years. She described herself as a born-again believer, and although she identifies as politically independent, she tends to vote Republican because they better represent her conservative values. When I first asked her about gay marriage, she responded by saying something that might surprise most liberal supporters before treading onto more familiar terrain:

> I struggle with it because—homosexuality in general—because coming from the dance field, my dance partner was gay. I saw it from the inside. You can love the person, and I did love him very much, he was a good person, but it was a weakness in him, and it opened up doors to a lot of other areas in his life that I don't think would have been opened up to if he would've not been in that lifestyle. I do not believe it is something you are born with. I do not believe that God would say that something is detestable to him and then create it that way. That is not the way God works.

It would be of no surprise to anyone that Dana's opposition to gay marriage ultimately centers on her religious conviction that homosexuality is a sin, and her statement at the end is a clear rebuttal of supporters' arguments that people are born gay.

But Dana's views about homosexuality—like those of most opponents whom I talked to—are much more complicated than the typical gay marriage supporter imagined. Contrary to the conventional wisdom that opponents of gay rights don't know anyone personally who is gay, Dana reports that her former dance partner, with whom she was close, is gay and that she "struggles" with the issue of homosexuality. The fact that she ultimately denies that people could be born gay should not be mistaken for animosity toward lesbians and gays; it reflects her religious faith, her beliefs about the nature of homosexuality, and her views about the consequences of it. Indeed, therein lies her "struggle": how can she simultaneously "love the sinner and hate the sin"?

The religious teaching that homosexuality is a sin was a prominent theme in oppositional discourse. As a sin, homosexuality is defined not just in behavioral terms, but as an emotional-spiritual force with which human beings must contend. Dana explains her beliefs this way:

> I think [homosexuality] comes from the Enemy. . . . There are three differ-
> ent desires that man has: spiritual, Godly desires; his own selfish desires;
> and then the desires that are placed to him by the Enemy. You are given
> the choice of which one you are going to follow. You can follow the Lord,
> you can follow your own self, or you can follow the Enemy. Self doesn't
> always completely go against God, it's usually just fulfilling what you want.
> Anything against God comes from the Enemy. That's how I see it.

Although not every opponent defined homosexuality in exactly these terms, they all agreed that homosexual acts are sins against God. But because Dana and other opponents see themselves as fighting against larger spiritual forces, they also see themselves as fighting for, not against, lesbians and gays:

> If you see someone is going down a path that is going to ruin their life,
> are you loving them by allowing them to do it, or are you loving them by
> telling them it's wrong? . . . I'm not trying to point the finger and tell them
> they're terrible people; I'm trying to tell them what is best for your life
> because of what research has shown it does to a family, a couple, children.
> It's not healthy.

To "love the sinner and hate the sin" was central to most opponents' doctrine. Because they saw themselves in those terms, they felt like they were the ones who were being attacked by gay marriage advocates. Their view of marriage as a relationship between one man and one woman, once taken for granted as common sense, now appears to opponents to be under siege by a secular society. As a result, they imagined far-reaching negative consequences from gay marriage's eventual legalization:

> It would not surprise me in the next five to ten years that it will be legal. I see that's the path we are headed, and if that happens, there—we will become a nation that has followed, going to be falling under the wrath of God. And the consequences of children understanding at all—right and wrong is no longer going to be available to them because there's no foundation of truth.

Oppositional discourse about gay marriage is dialogically antagonistic to the supportive discourse in ways that reflect the parallel feelings of victimization and attack that exist on both sides. Supporters perceive lesbians and gays to be victims of discrimination, while opponents perceive Christians to be victims of an antireligious agenda. Supporters perceive themselves to be attacking historic injustices, while opponents perceive themselves to be working to prevent moral catastrophe. Both sides lay claim to the value of love and condemn the opposite side as perpetuating hate. The dialogic antagonism of the discourses reflects the real, dialogically antagonistic relationship between the two groups in society.

Clearly, each side imagines itself a hero to the other's villain. But how accurate is their imagination of the other side? Although both supporters and opponents were familiar with the rhetoric of the other side, the accuracy of their perceptions about who the other side was and how they felt varied tremendously. Beyond the obvious truth that people on each side were variously empathetic or hostile to the other side, I did notice that each side's perception of the other side was consistently distorted in certain ways.

As Dana's quotes above illustrate, supporters were generally correct in their belief that gay marriage opponents based their opposition primarily on religious beliefs. However, supporters were generally incorrect in diagnosing the true nature of those beliefs and the impact of personal contact with lesbians and gays. Supporters often dismissed opponents as closed-minded, bigoted, or hateful, and supporters frequently talked about having gay friends as evidence for their own tolerant, supportive attitudes. However, like Dana, many opponents had close, intimate relationships with gay friends or family members, so personal contact was not an indicator of any particular opinion or discourse about gay marriage. To the extent that opponents expressed negative attitudes toward lesbians and gays, it was not for lack of contact; it was because they felt they had to condemn the body in order to save the soul.

Conversely, opponents were generally correct in diagnosing why lesbians and gays sought the right to marry, but they seemingly failed to understand the moral claims that supporters were making. Since opponents valued marriage a great deal, most of them could easily explain that lesbians and gays were seeking societal recognition and validation of their relationship as much as any basket of legal rights and benefits. In this sense, opponents had no difficulty understanding why lesbians and gays would want what they had. However, they failed to appreciate that the language of supporters was filled with moral claims about right and wrong. Supporters spoke at length about love, fairness, equality, tolerance, security, happiness, and refraining from judgment—all of which are deep, moral values that transcend the issues of rights and recognition. Thus, although opponents perceived their own moral worldview as threatened, they failed to appreciate that supporters were sticking up for a moral worldview that upheld many of the same values.

These discursive and social dynamics—the fact that those on each side saw themselves as the heroes, the fact that each side failed to perceive the depth and complexity of the other side's worldviews, and the fact that each side either explicitly or implicitly advanced their argument by impugning the other's—are fuel for the culture wars. Each side's ability to marshal dominant religious and political ideologies to support their view only enhanced the power and the reach of these discourses. Moreover, they were widespread among my informants and easy to articulate because of how common they are in mainstream media. Thus bolstered by the support of major social institutions—churches, political parties, and the media—these dialogically antagonistic discourses dominated the gay marriage debate. However, these dynamics did not work for everyone, and it is to their nonpolarized discourses that we now turn.

Middle-Ground Discourses

Middle-ground discourses emerge because the people who articulate them share social or ideological affinities with both supporters and opponents. Because their worldviews are influenced by both sides, they give voice to both when they speak about gay marriage. Although there are many such middle-ground discourses, this chapter focuses on two that feature a conflict between individuals' political/religious beliefs and their cohort-related attitudes about homosexuality: *immoral inclusivity* and *libertarian pragmatism*. Socially, these discourses emerge because people who share their religious or political ideology take one position in the debate about gay marriage, while their age mates take the opposite position. Given their immersion in social networks of people who articulate each of the polarized discourses just described, their own discourses were indelibly stamped with the strains of conflict.

Immoral Inclusivity: We Are All Sinners

The only people in my study to articulate the discourse of *immoral inclusivity* were young evangelical Christians who tried to reconcile their religious beliefs with their tolerant attitudes toward lesbians and gays. They all grew up in religious communities that taught that homosexuality is a sin, but they also expressed nonnegative attitudes toward lesbians and gays and said they should be treated equally under the law. I call this discourse immoral inclusivity because these young Christians identify *with*, not against, lesbians and gays: they believe that heterosexuals and homosexuals are equally immoral beings—albeit for different reasons— and that it would therefore be wrong to treat lesbians and gays differently.

It was difficult for some of these students to explain their views on gay marriage, and they used the interview to "talk it out." For example, take Elizabeth—a nineteen-year-old who described herself as "very artistic" and a "good student." It was no surprise that she, as a self-identified evangelical Christian with conservative political views, told me that she is against gay marriage because of how the Bible defined marriage and homosexuality. However, our interview that afternoon at the campus library happened at a serendipitous moment because earlier that day she had sat through a student's speech about gay marriage in one of her classes. As soon as I brought up the issue, she talked about what she had learned and explained that she felt differently from her fellow Christians:

> I don't know a lot about the topic from the other [supportive] point of
> view, so it's interesting to hear the person's speech in support of it. I found

out things like, you know, they aren't given a lot of the rights that they should be. So, I see that to be kind of upsetting that—oh, one thing that I don't like is that to me, Christians are picking this out as, you know, a worse sin than others, or like as unacceptable. They're just bashing the issue but it's really not anything worse than telling a lie.

It's not surprising that she reports being upset that lesbians and gays are denied certain rights. What is surprising is that this emotion seems to jog her memory about the thing that really upsets her: that other Christians are "bashing the issue." Here, Elizabeth articulates the central claim of immoral inclusivity: that the sins of lesbians and gays are no worse than anyone else's and therefore not worthy of special attention. Elizabeth empathizes with both Christians and lesbians and gays, and she is bothered that one group is attacking the other.

Elizabeth was unable to explain how she could simultaneously be against gay marriage and upset that lesbians and gays are denied equal rights on that account. In the quote above, Elizabeth accepts the premise that lesbians and gays should be accorded rights they do not have; but when I asked her directly whether lesbians and gays deserve equal rights, she contradicted herself:

I don't, not as far as marriage. I just don't like the idea that a man and a man can get married and then raise children. . . . As far as rights for people, I don't like that they're discriminated against. I think that they should be viewed as people. I mean, don't discriminate against them just like you wouldn't discriminate [against] someone because of their race. But then I guess I'm kind of contradicting myself when I say that I don't think that they should have the right to get married. So, I don't know, it's kind of a confusing issue for me.

Elizabeth acknowledges the apparent contradiction in her views and admits that she is not really sure how she feels about the issue. She implies that marriage is not one of those human rights she thinks everyone deserves. She clearly classifies lesbians and gays as human beings, equal to herself, and thus deserving of the same rights she has; however, her religious upbringing leads her to define marriage as between one man and one woman and thus not available to lesbians and gays.

Although Elizabeth might give the impression that immoral inclusivity is merely the result of an unsettled mind, other young evangelicals had clearly come to terms with the tension in their worldviews and found a logically stable foundation for it. They spoke confidently about the inerrancy of the Bible and the sinfulness of homosexuality, while maintaining that lesbians and gays should be accorded equal rights under the law. Carl, a nineteen-year-old pre-dental student with shaggy blonde hair and black rectangular glasses, was one such student. His quiet, studious demeanor was consistent with his willingness to accept and explain the ideological inconsistencies in the world, as he saw them. For example, when I asked him about his political beliefs, he said that he got irritated that Republicans and Democrats are unfairly labeled by his fellow Christians:

> I get so irritated with—being brought up in a Christian community and high school and everything, they're all, "Democrats are just from the devil." But they don't understand that, if anything, Democrats show more of a Christian-like attitude than Republicans. And the only thing they're kind of latching onto is abortion which I don't agree with. . . . But Democrats are all about giving back taxes, giving back to welfare, or something. The Bible talks so much more about giving to others and money and wealth—more than gay marriage, abortion.

Carl is clearly well aware that the political alignment of orthodox Christians with Republicans is based on social conservatism, not fiscal conservatism, and this quote shows that he doesn't simply follow group allegiances. It therefore should not have surprised me that his views about gay marriage were similarly resistant to groupthink.

Carl patiently helped me understand how he could simultaneously support and oppose gay marriage the way he did. Carl argued that gay marriage should be recognized on legal grounds, even though he personally disagrees with it on religious grounds:

> I believe you should have gay marriage, because constitutionally, if you look at the Constitution, that's what it says. Why should someone be denied a right? . . . Scripturally, I do think it's wrong, but I think they should have a right to.

From a legal perspective, Carl said that gay marriage should be allowed; but from his personal and religious perspective, he thought legalizing it would "degradate [sic] the meaning of marriage" and would make people "more predisposed to becoming a lesbian or homosexual." Ultimately, Carl said he would vote against gay marriage if given the chance because of the religious conception of marriage that he finds meaningful.

Carl's supportive-yet-opposed stance on gay marriage was bolstered by his continual rejection of the binaries established by the polar discourses of support and opposition. For example, he said that homosexuality is both a genetic predisposition and a choice. Additionally, he rejected the argument made by opponents that the Bible requires you to oppose gay marriage, and he also rejected as nonsense the progressive interpretation of the Bible as supporting gay marriage. This rejection of the binaries is what provides the ideological foundation for immoral inclusivity. To him, the Bible clearly says that homosexuality is a sin, but it says much more about divorce and other sins:

I mean, it's pretty explicit in the Bible: Romans. . . . To me, I think it says that [homosexuality is] immoral. And then you have to go on the other end, too, not to be judgmental at all. I mean, their sin isn't any worse than anyone else's, so why would—that's why I think it's horrible when some people just go on this tirade about gay marriage and stuff. There's no room whatsoever for someone to act like that.

In this quote, Carl affirms that homosexuality is immoral, but he also criticizes those who judge lesbians and gays more severely than they would judge straight people like him. Thus, he dislikes the anti-gay rhetoric he hears from his fellow Christians as much as he fears the consequences of legalizing gay marriage.

In the end, immoral inclusivity did not lead to any specific opinion about gay marriage. Some were opposed, some mixed, some in favor. Faced with the tension between their orthodox religious beliefs and their inclusive attitudes toward lesbians and gays, young conservative Christians constructed the discourse out of necessity. Immoral inclusivity comes from one's immersion in two very different social worlds: one composed of family, friends, and congregations who furnish the religious teachings and oppositional discourse, and the other composed of one's age mates, who set the cultural norms of inclusivity and equality.

Libertarian Pragmatism: It's a Free Country

Like immoral inclusivity, *libertarian pragmatism* is a discourse that is driven by a tension between people's attitudes about homosexuality and their ideological beliefs. In this case, their negative attitudes about homosexuality come from the older periods that defined it as deviant, but they also share the politically liberal belief that minorities should not be discriminated against, even if you disapprove of them. These informants, in effect, suppress their negative feelings about homosexuality and argue that lesbians and gays should be treated equally because sexual orientation is a private matter.[13]

This is the discourse that Tom articulates at the beginning of this chapter, and the length to which he went to question or suppress his implicit negative attitudes about homosexuality is evident in his hesitant response to my question about whether homosexuality is immoral:

Q: Do you think that the homosexual act is immoral?

A: The physical aspect of it? Hmmm.

Q: Yeah.

A: Immoral for society or immoral for like spiritual outlook?

Q: Just for you personally, yeah.

A: [pause] The questions are getting much tougher, Peter. You can go back to [asking about] life as a child.

Q: I know, I did that on purpose. But you know you're getting near the end when the questions get tough.

A: Do I think it is an immoral act? [long pause] If those two individuals, I don't think I, I don't think I have the right to say that that is an immoral act. I think that that is a spiritual question more than a legal question. Again, you have two people in a loving, caring relationship, and I'm going to tell them that the only way that they can express it, the ways they choose to express themselves to each other is immoral? What's to stop them from looking over here and say, "You know what, well I find that absolutely disgusting over there, what you're doing." It's like, well yeah, but there's a lot more of us than you. Well, does that, does sheer numbers mean that I am wrong? . . . I don't think I have the right to say that that is immoral. It may seem immoral to me, but . . . the way I interpret my religious and my life is different from the next guy. (Tom, forty-seven)

It takes numerous long pauses and several conversational turns before Tom expresses himself, and when he does, it is as if he is having a conversation in his own head. He ultimately denies that his moral intuition is legitimate, instead choosing to espouse a moral relativism that is a clear marker of this discourse.

Libertarian pragmatism combines the value of individual liberty with a refusal to judge the morality of another person's action, as long as it has no negative consequences for others. The discourse is libertarian because the speaker refuses to cast a moral judgment on behaviors that are considered private; it is pragmatic because the belief in individual freedom is predicated upon a specific outcome: that the action causes no harm to others. Informally, the discourse declares, "It's a free country; you can do what you want, as long as you're not hurting anybody."

Applying this discourse to gay marriage, informants constructed it by affirming that lesbians and gays can live their lives any way they choose, by denying that homosexuality is a sin while also expressing some negative attitude about homosexuality, and either by denying that their opinion about gay marriage mattered or by expressing mixed feelings about it. People used libertarian pragmatic discourse to affirm people's freedom to love whomever they want, even though they might not approve of homosexuality:

I see [gay marriage] on TV and stuff like that, like everybody else, but I can't judge them people either. They, that's their lifestyle, that's what they love. They love somebody just as well as somebody else. I'm not, I don't go one way or the other. If that's what they want, then that's what they should have, you know. (Jillian, forty-nine)

I don't know, I really, what's their business is their business. I honestly don't really care too much for it, but I'm not going to have a biased point of view and say it's wrong. That's that person's life, it's not mine. It's not affecting me in any way. (Dylan, twenty-three)

These informants do not think people's sexuality affects them personally, so it is not right to judge them.

Although most informants' negative attitudes about homosexuality remained the implicit, unspoken premise of the discourse, occasionally they were quite explicit. For example, Harvey was an affable, talkative twenty-three-year-old student who had served in the military and had numerous remarkable stories to tell. But his discomfort with homosexuality was evident throughout the interview. When I first brought up the issue of gay marriage, he responded by telling stories that made his homophobia clear:

> When I was in the military, I didn't even see, like homosexuals until I was in the Navy out in California. We went to San Francisco, and I was like, I went to like a Starbucks and like I saw this guy, I saw this girl in line, but she looked like she had facial hair. I kind of thought it was a guy in a dress, and I was just like, "What?" I was like, "What is that?" Or you know, like I'd be on base, and I would get approached by like a guy who's gay, and he'd really try to talk to me, and I'm sitting there like, "This guy's gay."

Never mind that I had merely asked him whether he had heard much about the issue of gay marriage, the presumed shock and horror of having to interact with someone who is not straight appears to be the main point of his answer. This was not just life in liberal California, either. At one point, he recalled an incident in one of his classes:

> A gay guy was sitting there looking across the class, looking at me across the room, looking at me like this [makes face]. Like that's uncomfortable, you know what I mean? Okay, maybe a girl, but that's what we do as far as guys, but when a guy does it, then it's like, I want to beat him up.

The negativity and double standard expressed in this statement are shocking: the way he looks at women is okay, but when a man does it to him, he becomes uncomfortable to the point of violence.

Amazingly, Harvey did not say he opposed gay marriage. Like others who articulated this discourse, he denied having an opinion, even when I asked him directly:

> Like I said, I just don't really even care. . . . It just really doesn't affect me so I really can't just, you know, downplay somebody else who goes there. Like if I go to a club and like somebody sees me talking to like a white female, and then it's like, "Oh you can't do that," it's like, "What am I doing to hurt you?" . . . I got my own things to worry about. Same-sex marriage really isn't one of the things on the table at the moment.

Harvey, who is African American, uses the example of interracial dating as an analogy to explain his refusal to state an opinion. Simply because one does not approve of another person's behavior does not mean it is appropriate to pass judgment.

There is, of course, an important difference between what you feel and what you say. It may be that Harvey, Tom, and others who constructed this discourse really did oppose gay marriage but were unwilling to say so. Whether implicit or explicit, their negative attitudes about homosexuality were built on a long-standing moral rejection of it—one that is probably coded masculine, as Harvey's visceral revulsion at the idea of a gay man coming onto him suggests.

But like with immoral inclusivity, the importance of libertarian pragmatism does not lie in whether or not it masks some unspoken, true opinion about gay marriage; it lies in the social and ideological tension that creates it. Libertarian pragmatism contains within it a justification for not taking sides in a conflict; it allows those espousing this view to be "politically correct" while maintaining their usually implicit negative attitudes about (male) homosexuality.

Although both young and old harbor negative attitudes about homosexuality, the discourse was more common among the parents. In effect, libertarian pragmatism is a result of how the negative attitudes about homosexuality that the older cohort grew up with pull their discourse one way, while a political culture that values equal rights and rejects discrimination against minorities pulls it the other way. That young people also articulate this discourse testifies to the persistent staying power of institutionalized social stigma.

How Cohort Matters

So far, this chapter has described how four discourses are produced because of how individuals' religious and political ideology interacts with their cohort-related attitudes about homosexuality. But how can we be sure that these attitudes are cohort-related? Although it is impossible to rule out other factors that might explain why cohort is associated with these discourses, my research design allows me to conduct a controlled comparison of discourses between matched pairs of parents and children to isolate the effect of cohort from the influence of ideology and parental socialization.[14] Even among family members who share common political and religious beliefs, differences in their discourses emerged because of their divergent attitudes about homosexuality.

Of the ninety-seven individuals I interviewed, sixty-five can be matched with a corresponding parent or child (this is an odd number because two of my student informants are siblings). Figure 4.2 plots all of the sixty-five individuals in a three-by-three table, classified by their political and religious ideologies; it also displays the kinship ties and whether each informant articulated a supportive, opposing, or middle-ground discourse of some kind. If one reads the figure spatially, like a two-dimensional plane, the proximity of matched pairs illustrates several points about how cohort shapes discourse.

First, the importance of ideology is obvious: not only do supportive and oppositional discourses cluster as expected, but even middle-ground discourses are most common among moderates. Second, the basic pattern of generational change is represented in this figure: only one of the thirty-two parents articulated a discourse that is more supportive than that of the student (an unusual case, in which the student supports gay marriage but opposes the rights of lesbians and gays to adopt children).[15] Third, the power of parental socialization is evident in how ideologically similar most children are to their parents; in only four cases does the kinship tie cross more than one ideological line. Indeed, in my qualitative memos comparing each student to his or her parent, I identified only six pairs in which some ideological influence probably accounts for a difference in discourses.

In this chapter, though, I wish to focus on a fourth pattern in the data: the cohort-related difference in gay marriage discourse that exists

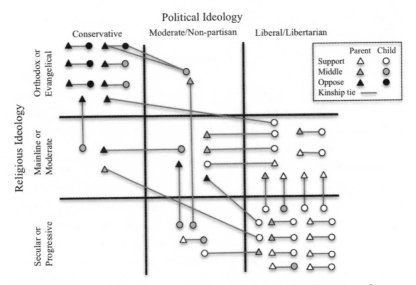

Figure 4.2: Gay Marriage Discourses of Parent-Child Pairs in Two-Dimensional Ideological Space

among ideologically similar kin. Among the eight student-parent pairs who share political and/or religious conservative ideologies, four students articulate middle-ground discourses rather than oppositional ones like their parents. Similarly, five of the sixteen parents who share a liberal/libertarian and/or secular/progressive ideology with their children articulate a middle-ground discourse. Examining the similarities and differences of these matched pairs can illuminate how cohort influences discourse, apart from any other ideological or parental influence.

Comparing liberal parents with their liberal children shows that it is the influence of cohort that distinguishes libertarian pragmatism from unambiguous support. Older liberals are like their liberal children in that they deny that homosexuality is immoral and argue that discrimination is wrong; however, they are like their more conservative age mates when they express discomfort and other negative attitudes regarding homosexuality. Parents who constructed middle-ground discourses did not accept homosexuality unproblematically, like their children, but instead talked about homosexuality as stigmatized and unnatural. Because homosexuality was culturally constructed as a *deviant lifestyle* during the period in which they came of age, they continue to hold negative associations with it.

Consider, for example, Matthew, age fifty-one, and his son, Nate, nineteen. Matthew raised Nate in the same small town in rural Illinois in which he himself grew up; they are both politically liberal atheists who have supportive attitudes about cohabitation, premarital sex, and divorce. Despite all they have in common, they spoke about gay marriage in very different ways.

Matthew's discourse exemplifies libertarian pragmatism. When asked about gay marriage, he responded with few words: "I don't really approve of it, but whatever floats your boat." Like many parents, Matthew expressed discomfort with homosexuality, but he seemed unwilling to say it is okay to limit someone's civil rights. Ultimately, he said he was okay with gay marriage as long as he didn't have to see it: "I'm not completely for [it], but I'm not really completely against it either. As long as they stay away from me and mine, that's fine. I just don't want to get involved in it."

By contrast, Nate enthusiastically supports gay marriage, and he strongly rejects the opposition's arguments:

> It's mostly religious organizations combating the gays, which in my opinion, from a legal standpoint is extremely contradictory to what this country was founded on, you know. We have freedom of religion in this country, and to take the legal standpoint that says the two people of the same sex cannot be married—that's ridiculous because you have no real argument to stand on other than God, and God says, "no." . . . So I'm really curious to hear somebody else's argument about that, about why it's bad rather than just from a religious standpoint. I personally think it's a great idea. I think it should happen, you know, because people should be allowed to pursue their freedoms.

Like many young liberals, Nate is so supportive of gay marriage that he has trouble even imagining a legitimate reason that someone would give for opposing it. Nate expresses tolerant attitudes toward lesbians and gays, denies that there is anything immoral about homosexuality, and rattles off a list of people he knows who are lesbian, gay, or bisexual.

In contrast with Matthew's implicit negative attitudes about homosexuality, Nate's attitude about homosexuality is perhaps best characterized as blasé.[16] When Nate recalled learning that someone in his high school came out as gay, his memory of the conversation conveys how unremarkable the news was:

> I heard somebody mention that he was gay, and it was like, "Oh. That's news to me." "Yeah, he came out a couple months ago." "Oh really? Great. Good for him." But I don't think he was necessarily looked down upon. . . . People were like, "Okay." I think people had their suspicions earlier anyway.

Nate tells this story as though other students already anticipated his coming out, and he describes the act as barely worth mentioning: "Good for him." Although Nate acknowledges that many people in society still label homosexuality as deviant, there is no indication in his discourse that either he or his friends think that.

As with libertarian pragmatism, comparing the discourses of young and old conservatives shows how immoral inclusivity is distinguished from unambiguous opposition because of an attitude difference between the two cohorts. Young religious conservatives are like their conservative parents in that they draw from a common set of religious beliefs to talk about the immorality of homosexuality; however, they are like their more liberal age mates when they say that people should be more tolerant of lesbians and gays. Like young supporters, many young conservatives empathize with lesbians and gays, accepting homosexuality unproblematically as a person's inherent sexual orientation.

Comparing Bethany (age twenty-two) with her mother, Andrea (age forty-five), shows how the two cohorts express different attitudes about homosexuality when they talk about gay marriage. Both are evangelical Christians, and both identify themselves as politically conservative. Their religious faith is extremely important to them, and they both disapprove of divorce and cohabitation. They even agree that homosexuality is sinful. However, they constructed different discourses because of a difference in attitudes about the sin and those who commit it.

Paradoxically, Bethany uses her beliefs about sin as a basis to empathize with lesbians and gays. She is open to the idea of gay marriage because she believes that homosexuality is no worse than her own sins:

> God says that marriage is between a male and a female. You're right, he does say that. You're right, I do believe that. However, just as much as I really can't cast stones at people who get divorced or people who overeat or people who are alcoholics, God says all of those things are just as much of a sin. . . . You want to get married, go right on ahead, it really doesn't bother me. And they want to be entitled to the same views because their level of commitment is more or greater or as equal to the happiest married heterosexual couple and that, you know, I think that's really important when it comes down to it. I mean, heaven forbid if my significant other got into a car crash or something; I wouldn't want it to fall on his great aunt who he never talks to, who is his only surviving family member; I would want that decision to be up to me, and I understand why they're fighting for those rights.

Bethany imagines herself being in the position of same-sex couples who love each other but cannot take care of each other because the relationship is not legally recognized. This empathy is indicative of her overall positive attitudes toward lesbians and gays. When I asked her about her memories of the first time she encountered someone who is gay, she told me about a teacher she had in college:

> Oh, I didn't know gay people were so cool. . . . It was almost like, "Really? One up for you." I mean, so I was more like excited to see someone, to be subjected to someone, who I thought was intelligent, knew what they were doing, had their stuff together, you know. They weren't a bad person, you know, cause I, just as much as I was raised by the Bible, I mean, God, your gut instinct tells you a whole lot about people before you even know it.

It is striking that, given her conservative religious and political background, she would describe such a positive reaction to the first gay person she ever met. She never admits to feeling uncomfortable or questioning her teacher's identity. This may be because she grew up during a time when lesbians and gays were beginning to be portrayed sympathetically in popular culture and mass media. When I asked her about homosexuality's portrayal in mass media, she responded by mentioning *Will & Grace*:

> *Will & Grace* portrayed it, you know, did they have some deep episodes? Yeah, I wasn't a faithful watcher, but as someone who doesn't have, like growing up in high school, I mean that show was like a popular show, and seeing it and having that be my only connection with the homosexuality world, I think it portrayed it in a really lighthearted, not a serious [way].

Thus, media representations gave Bethany some "lighthearted" contact with homosexuality even when she didn't know any lesbians or gays personally. This story is consistent with the parasocial contact hypothesis, which predicts that such media exposure can reduce prejudice against minorities.[17]

Bethany's mother, Andrea, also claims to regard homosexuality as a sin that is no worse than her own. However, her negative attitudes toward lesbians and gays lead her to draw very different conclusions about homosexuality and gay marriage:

> Absolutely, you choose to act upon your impulse. I don't classify it any different than a pedophile or . . . a nymphomaniac, you know. I believe that in your heart and in your mind and your soul, you can be driven to commit and perform and act against another person that is improper, and it's up to you to not proceed with those acts. Specifically, I think that God tells us, if your right hand is going to offend you, better that you cut off your right hand than be damned to hell because you can't stop stealing.

Whereas Bethany imagined lesbians and gays as being exactly like herself, Andrea compared them to thieves, pedophiles, and nymphomaniacs. This contrast reveals Andrea's implicit negative attitudes about homosexuality. Because she understands homosexuality as a deviant behavior, the solution to homosexual feelings is to repress them, and she believes that the institution of marriage should not be altered to accommodate them.

As these comparisons demonstrate, the tolerant attitudes expressed by young conservatives in *immoral inclusivity* and the negative attitudes implicit in *libertarian pragmatism* do not come from political ideology, religious ideology, or parental socialization; they appear to be related to cohort. If this is true, it implies that people's attitudes about homosexuality are rooted in how homosexuality was constructed in American culture when each cohort came of age. But this claim merely begs the question of why different cohorts developed different attitudes about homosexuality during these two periods. In the next chapter, I show that the cohort differences in how informants talk about homosexuality at the micro level can ultimately be traced to the macro-level changes in the *social imagination* of homosexuality that I described in Chapter 2.

Conclusion

Although gay marriage was one of the fiercest battles in the culture wars after 2003, many Americans of all ages remain caught in the cross fire. In particular, older liberals and young conservatives do not align with either supporters or opponents because of how their cohort-related attitudes about lesbians and gays clash with their political and religious beliefs. For older liberals, their belief that equality and tolerance for minorities is important clashes with the implicit negative attitudes that they harbor about homosexuality. For young religious conservatives, their religious belief that homosexuality is a sin clashes with their empathic, tolerant attitudes toward lesbians and gays. In each case, individuals' ideology pushes them to take one position about gay marriage, while their cohort-related attitudes pull them toward the opposite position. The result is a contested middle ground that is influenced by the polarized discourses that anchor the field.

Looking at these middle-ground discourses in conjunction with the supportive and oppositional discourses is a crucial first step in understanding exactly how cohort matters in shaping public opinion about gay marriage. I argue that cohort shapes a person's attitudes about homosexuality because of how homosexuality was constructed in American culture during the period in which each cohort came of age. The students whom I interviewed all grew up during the Gay Rights Period, and they have positive or tolerant attitudes toward lesbians and gays because of what they take for granted. In their lifetimes, lesbians and gays have always been a recognized status group, and politics has always been marked by ongoing conflict over their rights. Even young religious conservatives, whose ideology tells them that homosexuality is a sinful lifestyle, have witnessed the struggles of this group and empathize with them.

By contrast, the older cohort of Baby Boomers whom I interviewed grew up during the Homophile and Resistance periods; they have negative attitudes toward homosexuality because they grew up during a time when homosexuality was understood as a deviant behavior or mental illness. Older liberals, whose ideology tells them to support equal rights for all, still struggle with a deep-seated feeling that homosexuality is a negative social behavior above all else, something to be avoided or repressed.

This chapter's focus on middle-ground discourses reveals much about the nature of the culture wars going on between supporters and opponents. First, it shows that the culture wars are fought not by everyone, but only by certain groups: young liberals and older conservatives in this case. These culture wars are not monolithic struggles between religious and secular, or between liberal and conservative, or even between young and old; the discursive dynamics depend upon the intersection of cohort with ideology. So while young liberals and older conservatives are fighting the culture wars, young conservatives and older liberals (among others) are not—and may even be actively resisting them.

Second, this chapter shows that issues like gay marriage are not inherently polarizing because of people's individual beliefs; rather, culture wars emerge through the discourses of social groups that are dialogically antagonistic with one another. The wide variety of people in our society, with all of their different combinations of status group identities, possess a correspondingly wide variety of life experiences, which culture transforms into a smaller number of repeating discourses. Gay marriage became a battle in the culture wars only when the dialogic antagonism became embedded in dominant religious and political ideologies and amplified by mass media. Thus, there is nothing inevitable about the emergence of culture wars, but the current features of key American institutions allowed gay marriage to become one.

Third, if I am correct that younger cohorts are more likely to support gay marriage because they developed positive attitudes toward lesbians and gays, while older cohorts are more likely to oppose it because they developed negative attitudes regarding homosexuality, then this suggests that the demographic metabolism of society is continually altering the battleground of the culture war, strengthening the ranks of supporters and weakening the ranks of opponents. It is as if the opposing side to gay marriage is suffering heavy casualties, while the supporting side is continually getting fresh recruits. Thus, the victory for supporters may have come from a war of attrition as much as from any tactical maneuver.

Finally, an analysis of middle-ground discourses shows how cohort seems to matter for the gay marriage debate: it shapes attitudes about homosexuality, independently of any influence of political ideology, religious ideology, or parental socialization. Even parents and children who agree with each other ideologically disagree about gay marriage. But upon closer examination, this finding only begs a further question: Why does being in a different cohort seem to shape people's feelings about homosexuality? The provisional answer suggested in this chapter—regarding how homosexuality was understood in mainstream American culture when each cohort came of age—is vague and impressionistic. Even more, it sounds very much like it implies an alternative answer to the question of how cohort matters. Perhaps the real issue is that young people think that homosexuality is innate, genetically caused, and beyond an individual's control, while older people think that homosexuality is a lifestyle choice that can be controlled. The next chapter addresses this question of homosexuality's attribution directly and also points beyond it. It shows that people's attitudes and attribution of homosexuality are only surface-level manifestations of something much deeper and more fundamental to their worldviews: their social imagination of homosexuality.

5

The Imagination and Attribution of Homosexuality

Many social scientists experience a "Eureka!" moment—a sudden epiphany in which the puzzle that had baffled them for so long is suddenly resolved. Mine was more of a "Jackpot!" moment. I was having the kind of interview that made me feel like I had struck gold, however unwittingly. At the time, I observed that my young informants seemed so much more at ease talking about gay marriage than their parents, regardless of their political and religious beliefs, but I didn't know why. What was it about being young that seemed to shape their attitudes and discourses, independently of politics, religion, and family background?

I was sitting in the same Starbucks in which I had conducted many interviews before. Nick, age twenty-one, had finished the small black coffee that I bought him long before I broached the subject of gay marriage. He had already shared with me the story of his conversion to Christianity, a conversion that seemed coerced. Although he had an affable personality, he wore a serious expression on his face, and he seemed to not fully believe some of the things he was saying to me. For example, when I asked him how he felt about cohabitation—a couple living together even though they are not married—he answered:

> I don't find it to be a good thing. I think it, on the surface, it makes a lot
> of sense, you know, try it out before you [commit]. But for me . . . I'm
> going to trust God that he, you know, knows what he's doing. And uh,
> you know, he says it's wrong, and so, and he knows a lot more than I do.

Granted, God is all-knowing, but to Nick cohabitation "makes a lot of sense." Ultimately, Nick rejects his common sense and invokes the religious teaching that it is wrong, on account of the possibility that it would lead to premarital sex. It seemed almost as if he was suppressing what he truly thought on account of what his religious ideology told him he should think.

This pattern of talk continued after I brought up gay marriage. After I asked him if he had a personal opinion about it, he replied:

> Um, yeah. It's hard. I mean if I didn't have, you know, my religious beliefs, I would say I feel like, "You know what, if that makes them happy, then do it." And I had a cousin who's gay, and it's hard 'cause then it comes back to the question, you know, of um, is it like a choice or is it something that they're born with? You know, I don't want to sound like a closed-minded, you know, conservative, like "all gays go to hell" or whatever, anything like that. But I got to, I do think that [marriage] is meant for a man and a woman, and so I don't agree with it. But it's hard for me not to agree with it. But I just, I don't agree with it just cause it's, you know, it's in the Word, and I've just kind of got to go with it.

Nick is clearly inclined to support gay marriage, but he blames his "religious beliefs" for the fact that he has to say he opposes it. Nick was unusual in how little he seemed to really believe what he said; no other religious person whom I interviewed seemed wishy-washy about his or her faith.

At the time, I only sensed that I had hit the jackpot because of how explicitly ideology was pulling his discourse one way, while something unseen and unspoken was pulling it the other way. In essence, Nick's interview was crystal clear evidence for the analysis I presented in the previous chapter, though I still didn't understand what it was about being young that made people feel differently about gay marriage. In retrospect, my feeling of hitting the jackpot came not from his wishy-washy faith, but from the fact that he was giving voice to a realm of knowledge, hidden beneath explicit belief and ideology, that usually remains implicit and unarticulated. Although I could not explain what he was doing at the time, I had sensed that he had some sort of intuition about homosexuality that was at odds with what his ideology defined it to be. He asked the consequential question of homosexuality's *attribution*— whether you are born gay or whether homosexuality is a choice—just like many of my other interviewees. But the meaning of this question (for him and for others) extends far deeper than the purely scientific matter of whether we can identify the "gay gene" or whether conversion therapy works. Nick raised this issue because it taps into the deeper cultural schemas that people have for homosexuality: is it the *people* who are gay, or is it the *behavior* that is gay?

Eventually, I learned how to sort out different aspects of homosexuality's ontology—how to distinguish people's explicit beliefs from their implicit schemas, or their attribution of homosexuality from their imagination of it. As it turns out, the question of homosexuality's attribution—our explicit beliefs about what causes homosexuality—is an important one, but not in and of itself. Whether or not you believe sexuality is caused by nature, nurture, or choice is a surface-level manifestation of a person's deeper *social imagination* of it. In this chapter, I argue that it is this social imagination of homosexuality—not their attribution of it—that explains why cohort shapes people's attitudes and discourses about gay marriage, independently of their ideology. In other words, the fact that support for gay marriage has increased has little to do with the question of whether or not we believe people are born gay; it has to do with the fact that our commonsense understanding of homosexuality—our cultural schema of it—now characterizes homosexuality as an innate part of a person's identity, rather than as a behavior in which anyone might indulge.

How did I come to this conclusion? In essence, I found the explanation from attribution theory lacking (more on this below), and the analogies and metaphors that my informants used to explain their views suggested an alternative. I originally noticed how many people compared gay marriage to interracial marriage and the struggle for racial equality in America more generally. When I began investigating what metaphors are and how they work, I began to hear dozens upon dozens of other metaphors and analogies in my interviews that I had not heard before, and I began to understand how metaphors and analogies give voice to something deep inside a person's worldview that otherwise tends to remain unspoken. It is through these metaphors and analogies that informants expressed their imagination, and the differences between the metaphors and analogies used by the two cohorts help to explain why they differ in their attitudes toward homosexuality and gay marriage.

Attribution Theory

In the social sciences, attribution theory states that people's attitudes about a behavior or condition depend on what they think causes it, especially whether or not it is beyond an individual's control. If people believe that a stigmatized condition—like poverty, homelessness, or obesity—is due to an individual's behavioral choices, then they tend to be less tolerant or empathetic toward the person than they would be if they believed that it is due to genetic, environmental, or other factors the individual cannot control.[1]

Researchers have shown that people's attitudes toward homosexuality and gay rights depend, in part, on whether they think homosexuality is innate—that you are born gay—or freely chosen.[2] Attribution theory therefore offers one plausible explanation for why support for gay marriage increased so rapidly in the United States. Increases in the belief that homosexuality is innate and not freely chosen might cause more people to support gay marriage; moreover, if young people are more likely to say that homosexuality is attributable to biological or genetic factors, then this could explain the pattern of generational change that we have seen in discourse and in public opinion.

There is a fair amount of evidence to support this line of thinking. First, as Chapter 3 shows, it is true that the belief that people are born gay is associated with support for gay marriage. It is also true that the percentage of Americans who say that homosexuality is due to factors beyond an individual's control—and that it cannot be changed—has increased in the past two decades. Moreover, the historical timing is right. As discussed in Chapter 2, the 1991 publication of Simon LeVay's famous study on the neurological difference between gay and straight men was part of the turning point that brought about the Gay Rights Period.[3]

However, despite the evidence in favor of attribution theory, there are also three problems with explaining the change in public opinion in terms of changes in the attribution of homosexuality. First, the association between cohort and attribution is opposite to the expected direction: it is not young people but older people who are more likely to say that homosexuality is innate.[4] Therefore, attributions of homosexuality may be related to support for gay marriage, but attribution theory cannot explain why younger cohorts are more supportive of gay marriage than older cohorts.

The second problem with attribution theory as an explanation for this trend has to do with temporal order and the direction of causation. Attribution theory could explain attitudes about gay marriage only if people develop their beliefs about what causes homosexuality *before* they develop attitudes about gay rights. While this is plausible, it is equally possible that people construct beliefs about homosexuality's attribution after they develop an opinion about gay rights. Evidence in favor of the latter possibility is mounting. Psychologists are finding increasing evidence that people develop moral attitudes quickly and that they develop cognitive beliefs only after the fact as post hoc justifications.[5] It is common for people to construct cognitive beliefs that are consistent with their moral attitudes to maintain cognitive consistency or minimize cognitive dissonance.[6]

The third and final problem with attribution theory as an explanation for the increase in support for gay marriage is that both political liberals and religious conservatives have strong ideological incentives to construct attribution statements that are consistent with their identities and belief systems. There are strong religious-conservative pressures to say that homosexuality is a choice because it fits with orthodox teachings that homosexuality is a sin. Liberals confront similar pressures to say that it is innate, since legal arguments for gay marriage are premised upon the belief that homosexuality is unchangeable and that lesbians and gays are a protected class.[7] So the correlation between attribution and attitude may be spurious, since ideology is associated with both.

Attribution Statements in Discourse

My interviews cast further doubt that the changing attribution of homosexuality could explain the generational change in opinions about gay marriage. In all interviews, if interviewees did not volunteer their views on homosexuality's attribution, I asked them specifically, "What do you think homosexuality is? What do you think it really means if someone identifies themselves as gay/lesbian?" Based on their answer to that question, I sometimes asked one or more follow-up questions: "Do you think people are born gay? Do you think it could be caused by how people are raised? Do you think people choose to be gay? Do you think homosexuality can be changed?"

In general, three patterns of answers emerged that troubled me. First, most of the responses to my questioning defied clear categorization according to the basic innate versus choice framework of attribution theory. Some informants articulated beliefs about homosexuality that were multicausal or context-dependent:

> That's just like a nature versus nurture debate. It's a little bit of both. I, I've met people that think that they're not, that think that they've been gay since they were five years old. . . . I think that some people do choose to be gay. I think that some people do believe that it's a genetic thing. I believe other people think that it's something that was when they were born. I believe it's all those things. (Bill, twenty-nine)

Other informants thought that the answer of homosexuality's attribution depended upon the person:

> There is probably subcategories of, like, the psychologically gay, you know, in their mind they're gay, so they are gay and they are attracted, so it's more of a psychological issue. There's probably, there probably are some cases where there is a gene that just sets them off for the same sex. And then I'm not so sure about this one, but it's kind of almost like what I was saying before . . . it's a source of attention. (Barrett, nineteen)

Many people, like Bill and Barrett, clearly see the innate versus choice dichotomy of attribution theory to be a false dilemma. Still others refrained from using the language common to attribution theory to define homosexuality. Some informants defined it in spiritual terms, like a deception from Satan or a spiritual connection; others defined it as a fad or a desire to attract attention. In all these ways, people's attribution statements failed to conform to the basic framework of attribution theory.

The second pattern of answers that made me doubt attribution theory as an explanation is that many people responded to my questions as factual matters that are beyond their knowledge:

> You know, I don't have an opinion on that. I just thought, I tend to think that it is more of a control, only because my own belief and not really

caring. I think that, you know, but I don't know. It's one of those things that you look at that you really don't know because you are not on that side, so you don't really know. (Maria, forty-five)

Because many people feel that they do not know the factual, scientific truth of what causes homosexuality, some seemed all too eager to agree to my specific follow-up questions and probes.[8] The following exchange illustrates this conversation dynamic:

Q: What do you think homosexuality really is?
A: I think it's something inside of you. A feeling that you just know that's what you were meant to do. I don't know.
Q: Do you think people, do you think people choose to be gay?
A: I don't know, maybe they had an experience and then they liked it, you know. If I didn't have ice cream and I ate ice cream, I would like it. So I don't know. It's hard to say. Little kids always experiment when they're little, so who knows? They don't know any different. So who's to say?
Q: Some people think that, some people think that people are born gay.
A: They could be. It's possible. I think it's possible. (Jillian, forty-nine)

These passages illustrate that the attribution of homosexuality is not a simple question to which people have preformed answers. Because it is a matter that requires deliberate cognitive processing, people not only interpret the question as a factual matter beyond their knowledge, but also can be primed to alter their attributions.

Of course, this may have been partially an artifact of the interview process: as I am a researcher affiliated with a prestigious university, both students and parents alike frequently told me that they wanted to perform well—as if I were grading them. Nevertheless, this points to an important characteristic of homosexuality's attribution that makes it unlikely to be the cause of generational change: it is a cognitive belief that is subject to slow, deliberative cognitive processing—in which people weigh the evidence, learn new information, and ultimately articulate a position. By contrast, the primary animating force of the controversy over gay marriage is the moral status of homosexuality—and moral attitudes are processed quickly and automatically. If dual-process theories of cognition are correct, then these beliefs about homosexuality's cause are arrived at only *after* people's emotional attitudes and moral judgments have already been made.[9] Attributions of homosexuality aren't the cause but rather an effect of what is really driving the change.

The third and final pattern of answers that ultimately made me reject attribution theory as an explanation for the change is that when people did articulate simple, mono-causal attributions of homosexuality, it was typically done dialogically—in a politicized discursive context in which they were arguing against the opposition's rhetoric. In other words, informants usually articulated strong stands about homosexuality's cause as evidence to support their argument or when they wanted to rebut an opposing argument:

> I think homosexuality is a lifestyle choice, not that you are born to. I think that you can make a choice whether you want to live with someone of the same sex or whether you want to try and make a marriage. I mean, I think a lot of us can go one way or the other, and it's the choices we make, not the, not what we're born to. (Sarah, sixty)

> I don't see how preventing gay marriage is preventing people from being gay. But that boils down to whether it's nature or nurture, so that's a whole 'nother debate there. [*Do you have any feelings about that, while we're on the subject?*] I don't think someone would choose to be harassed, to be threatened, to be made fun of, to be hindered. I wouldn't choose something that would hinder me like that. I wouldn't make the decision, "Well, I want to be gay because I would like to be restricted socially and religiously." (Jane, nineteen)

These informants may genuinely believe that homosexuality is what they say it is, but we cannot conclude that from the context. In these passages, attributions of homosexuality are statements made to serve an evidentiary function in support of a claim. They are means to an end.

Put together, these points suggest that attributions of homosexuality matter, but not in the way that attribution theory suggests. First, attribution statements serve a dialogical and ideological function in discourse. When someone declares that people are born gay, that they do not choose to be gay, or that it is a choice, she is both bolstering her preexisting worldview and signaling her social group affiliations. Even firmly held beliefs about attribution function as cognitive shortcuts that structure perception.[10] The reality is that homosexuality, like heterosexuality, is both innate and choice: it is part biologically determined orientation and part behavioral expression of one's feelings.

Second, and perhaps more importantly, attribution statements are manifestations of a deeper, more fundamental cognitive structure—one's cultural schema of homosexuality. Attribution statements are the metaphorical tip of the iceberg: they indicate how people imagine homosexuality, not what causes it. If people are asked what homosexuality is or what causes it, they must first invoke their cultural schema of homosexuality and then try to construct a statement that both expresses and is consistent with that mental image. Attribution statements, therefore, are only the surface-level, visible part of a much larger, invisible construct: the social imagination.

Metaphor Theory

If attribution statements are the visible part of the iceberg—above the surface, and explicit in discourse—then how can we know what is invisible and beneath the surface? One way is through interpreting the metaphors, analogies, and other figurative tropes that people articulate in speech. With respect to gay marriage, the metaphors and analogies give clues as to how the informant imagines same-sex sexuality cognitively; and because language is meaningful only when it is socially, collectively understood, the metaphors and analogies for homosexuality reflect how a society (or at least a social group) understands it. To understand why metaphors and analogies give voice to the social imagination, it is necessary to explain what metaphors are, how they work, and how social scientists interpret them.

A metaphor is a figurative trope in which one subject is described using the language of something else. As cognitive scientists George Lakoff and Mark Johnson have written, "The essence of metaphor is understanding and experiencing one kind of thing in terms of another."[11] Aesthetically, metaphors are prized in poetic and literary composition for their ability to generate novel descriptions and feelings, as when Romeo declares upon seeing Juliet walk to her balcony: "What light through yonder window breaks? It is the east, and Juliet is the sun." The metaphor redefines Juliet as a ray of sunlight and in so doing conveys Romeo's feelings for her in a unique way.

However, metaphors are not just aesthetically valuable; they are socially necessary. Scholars have long observed that our everyday language is inundated (metaphor intended) with metaphors, many of which go unrecognized as such. In their classic book *Metaphors We Live By*, Lakoff and Johnson shed light on (metaphor intended again) this fact, arguing that both our perception and our understanding of the world are shaped by conceptual metaphors. For example, we both experience and understand personalities as warm and cold, relationships as close and distant, and power as high and low. Lakoff and Johnson explain, "Because so many of the concepts that are important to us are either abstract or not clearly delineated in our experience (the emotions, ideas, time, etc.), we need to get a grasp on them by means of other concepts that we understand in clearer terms (spatial orientations, objects, etc.)."[12] In other words, we use metaphors in language to express complex ideas to one another in ways that are easier to grasp (I'll stop pointing these out now); and over time, we often forget that the metaphor exists and simply understand the concept in metaphorical terms.[13]

So how do metaphors work? To analyze how a metaphor works in discourse, one must take into account three levels of analysis simultaneously: the semiotic, the semantic, and the hermeneutic.[14] At the semiotic level, a metaphor substitutes one subject for another, constructing a novel relationship between signifier and signified. For example, to refer to a skilled billiards player as a pool *shark* creates a tension between "shark" and "player," in which some of the attributes of sharks are transferred onto the player. Additionally, the meanings of the metaphor depend upon its semantic context—its use in a sentence. It is one thing to warn, "Don't play that guy; he's a shark," and quite another to victoriously exclaim, "Way to go! You're a shark!" Finally, at the hermeneutic level of analysis, the metaphor generates new cultural meanings and discursive entailments with respect to both subjects—sharks and pool players—such that the meanings of each subject are shaped and modified by the other.

Although the metaphor of a pool shark is cliché, it is an example of a *living metaphor*. For philosopher Douglas Berggren, "the legitimate and vital use of metaphor" creates a tension between signifier and signified, between subject and predicate, between literal and figurative meanings, and between truth and falsehood.[15] This tension produces a new mental image—what Paul Ricoeur calls the metaphor's "iconic moment"—that creates new cultural meanings even as it preserves the two previously separate ones.[16] Creative artists prize living metaphors because of this iconic moment. By contrast, the sorts of metaphors analyzed by Lakoff and Johnson and other social scientists are *dead metaphors*, like "skyscraper"—figurative expressions whose metaphorical tension has been resolved and forgotten, its novel meaning having been thoroughly absorbed into the cultural common sense of a group.[17]

To interpret metaphors sociologically, as we will below, we must reject both their strict literal and their strict figurative readings;[18] we must instead interpret them as expressions both of the public, shared culture of a group and of the internal, cognitive structures of the mind. Reading metaphors literally results in nonsense (sharks don't play pool) while reading metaphors figuratively ignores their sociological, psychological, and political significance (e.g., pool sharks do exploit lesser skilled players for free playing time). To interpret the pool shark metaphor sociologically, we must analyze how the metaphor both encodes and perpetuates cultural meanings of sharks, masculinity, deception, aggression, gambling, and so on.

From this perspective, the social and political implications of metaphors are far-reaching. The political scientist Michael Schatzberg argues that metaphors in discourse constitute a "realm of subjacent politics," a domain of daily life experience and cultural meanings that provide a hidden foundation for political actions.[19] Schatzberg supports this argument by showing how pervasive the metaphors of eating, family, and fatherhood are to the politics of Central Africa. The fundamental cultural understandings of a society are encoded in language, both which shapes how individuals perceive and understand reality, and which individuals use in order to participate in politics.[20]

Applied to the case of gay marriage, the metaphors and analogies that we articulate in language attest both to individuals' cultural schema of homosexuality that is located deep inside their mind and to our collective, cultural understanding of homosexuality in society. If generational theory is correct, the social imagination of homosexuality that was dominant in American culture when each cohort came of age will shape individuals' cultural schema of homosexuality, which will then be articulated metaphorically. Differences in how cohorts use metaphors and analogies to talk about gay marriage can be interpreted as evidence of generational change in the social imagination of homosexuality.

In the analysis below, I first describe the ubiquitous dead metaphors for homosexuality that are used equally by members of both cohorts. These metaphors are so pervasive that they are rarely recognized as such, and my discussion of them illustrates how metaphors can be interpreted sociologically as expressions of the social imagination. Then, I turn my attention to cohort differences in metaphors and analogies; I show that cohorts vary in the frequencies and semantic contexts of the use of certain metaphors. Specifically, the Identity Cohort uses metaphors and analogies that define homosexuality *as identity*—as who you are—more frequently than their parents, and they do so in ways that essentialize homosexuality and trivialize its significance. By contrast, the older cohort uses metaphors and analogies that define homosexuality *as behavior*—as what you do—more frequently than their children, and they do so in ways that emphasize its significance. I argue that these differences in metaphors and analogies indicate differences in how people imagine homosexuality, and that the social imagination is the reason that cohort, independently of ideology, shapes people's attitudes about homosexuality and gay marriage.

Ubiquitous Metaphors: Orientation and Attraction

Because I did not begin this study with metaphor theory in mind, I did not realize that the ways in which I talked about homosexuality in my own interviews were fundamentally shaped by metaphors. Indeed, two of the most common ways of talking about sexuality in American society—as sexual *orientation* and as sexual *attraction*—are dead conceptual metaphors.[21] It is unclear exactly what influence these metaphors have on the ways that we *think* about homosexuality, but they manifest themselves in our discourse in so many different ways that they certainly affect how we *talk* about it.

Sexual *orientation* is a spatial and directional metaphor, implying that sexuality is a spatial field of at least one dimension, that individuals are located somewhere within it, and that they have a subjective viewpoint that accompanies their position. As a phrase, "sexual orientation" came into popular use only after the 1960s; its metaphorical nature has been forgotten, and we now interpret it as a label or category: "What is your sexual orientation?"[22] However, this metaphor appears in language in many subtle ways. My informants used nouns like *direction, way, path,* and *journey* to describe a person's sexuality, and they used verbs like *go, swing,* and *lean* to talk about what individuals do within the domain of sexuality as a whole—which they metaphorically described as *sides, worlds,* or *fields.*

> I feel like, to each his own. If you feel you want to go that way, be my guest. Just leave me out of it. (Katrina, twenty-five)

> If you had that option [same-sex marriage] and you had homosexual tendencies, would you probably go that route faster? Yes. If you had the option and you didn't know where you were tending to lean, it would be another avenue to pursue, but I think that would be good because it would make people figure out what's right for them. (Karen, fifty)

In cognitive terms, the orientation metaphor is significant because we all have the embodied experiences associated with spatial and directional awareness; we can therefore use this language to communicate about an abstract concept like sexuality in terms to which everyone can relate.

Interpreted sociologically, the orientation metaphor appears to be important because heterosexuality and homosexuality function as binary oppositions that anchor the entire domain of sexuality. Most people imagine everyone to be either one or the other, while bisexuality is received skeptically:

> In a way, it's like, pick a side, you know. You're either with us or against us in some sense. [laughter] It's like, come on, you can't have it both ways. . . . Pick a side. Come on, you can't have the best of both worlds, so to speak. (Jesse, twenty-seven)

Many scholars consider binary oppositions to be essential to cognition and culture, and people's skepticism of bisexuality in popular culture has been well documented.[23] People of both cohorts use the metaphors of *exploring* and *experimenting* to explain the sexual behavior of people who identify as bisexual:

> It seems like a lot of bisexuals that I know, when it comes right down to it, they really are heterosexual, or they eventually make up their mind which way they're gonna go. It seems like bisexuals are kind of like experimenting, but eventually they're gonna find a set pattern and probably stay with it. (Emily, nineteen)

Like Emily, many informants argued that people are either straight or gay, and that bisexuals are going through some *journey* or *stage* to *find* their true selves. The orientation metaphor, therefore, may be a cause or an effect (or both) of the tendency to view sexuality in binary, essentialist terms.

The other conceptual metaphor, sexual *attraction*, is a physics metaphor that describes romantic feelings in terms of unseen forces that pull people together. The sociological significance of the attraction metaphor is that it equates human beings with inanimate matter, whose behavior is caused by external forces rather than internal volition. Many of us have the experience of feeling irresistibly *drawn* to a person or *falling* in love, as though we are at the mercy of some alien force bringing us together.[24] Discursively, the attraction metaphor expresses that embodied sensation. My informants used the metaphor in both positive and negative senses: words like *gravitate, tendency,* and *force* convey the idea of attraction itself, while words like *repulsion, resistance,* and *struggle* convey the idea that the external force of attraction is not always a good thing:

> I don't know if you're so much born that way as that's the way you grow up feeling. I don't think you're born with the gene, but it could just be what you yourself gravitated towards. (Tracey, fifty-three)

> Q: Do you think that homosexuality is immoral, like the homosexual act is immoral?
> A: I don't know if it's immoral; it's repulsive to me. (Bernice, fifty-three)

The attraction metaphor appears congruent with attributions of homosexuality as innate or genetic, in that it places a person's sexuality beyond her control. One informant recognized this fact and protested the implication:

> Q: What do you think homosexuality really is? Like if you were going
>   to try and define it?
> A: Attraction to the same sex. Um, well no, I'm not going to define
>   it that way. Somebody can have an attraction to the same sex . . .
>   but not believe in that and not act upon that and be against that.
>   (Paul, nineteen)

As Paul acknowledges, simply being attracted to someone or something is not a justification for action. Unlike the inanimate objects implied by the metaphor, human beings have agency, and conservatives argue that we must choose whether to *give in to* or to *struggle* to *resist* our feelings:

> All of us have the potential of becoming depraved. All of us. It's up to
> us to make the choices of whether we're going to step through that or
> not. . . . Homosexuality is a sin just like everything else, and every person
> understands that's a sin they struggle with. And if they choose, "I'm go-
> ing to get control over this sin," and they don't practice it, then they're not
> sinning because they're controlling that sin. They may struggle with it all
> their life, but they're not sinning. (Dana, forty-eight)

Thus, even if it were scientifically proven that homosexuality has a genetic attribution and is thus beyond an individual's control, such findings would mean little to gay marriage opponents:

> If someone looked at me and said, "I feel that I was born, all my life, at-
> tracted to men," I would say, "I believe you, but I feel that you should turn
> away from this act." (Andrea, forty-five)

These terms, *orientation* and *attraction*, are such common terms used to describe sexuality that we tend to take them for granted; we have forgotten that they are metaphors, not literal descriptions of sexuality. Regardless, these dead conceptual metaphors both reflect and shape our experiences with sexuality, and they have profound sociological impli-cations. The orientation metaphor is congruent with binary schemas of sex and gender, while the attraction metaphor justifies the attribution of homosexuality as innate and unchangeable. Thinking of sexuality in terms of these metaphors may, in turn, shape people's explicit beliefs about sexuality, though to my knowledge this has not been demonstrated empirically.

Homosexuality as Identity

The metaphors of attraction and orientation are so ubiquitous, and used by young and old alike, that they could not explain the cohort differences in discourse identified in the previous chapter, nor the pattern of generational change as a whole. However, my informants used other metaphors and analogies whose frequency and semantic context did vary by cohort. These metaphors and analogies coalesce around two contrasting understandings of homosexuality: metaphors and analogies that express homosexuality *as identity* were used more frequently by students and in ways that construct homosexuality as morally equivalent to other group identities, while metaphors and analogies that express homosexuality *as behavior* were used more frequently by parents and in ways that emphasize its deviance from social norms. I argue that these metaphors and analogies are the key to understanding how cohort shapes attitudes about homosexuality and discourses about gay marriage: they should be interpreted as manifestations of two social imaginations of homosexuality, each of which was dominant in mainstream American culture during the period in which each cohort came of age.

Table 5.1 displays most of the major metaphors and analogies that informants in each cohort used to talk about homosexuality and gay marriage, categorized by their discursive function. Although the relative frequencies with which cohorts articulate each metaphor are suggestive, one cannot draw any conclusions from the numbers alone. This is true for two reasons. First, my sample is unrepresentative of any larger population, so these numbers are not statistical estimates; they cannot be interpreted as the percentage of Americans (or cohort members) who think or talk in a particular way. Second, because any metaphor can be used in a variety of ways to communicate different messages, it is more important to focus on the semantic contexts of their use than their frequency. Thus, in what follows, I describe the semantic contexts in which

TABLE 5.1: Percentage of Each Cohort Using Selected Metaphors for Homosexuality and Gay Marriage

	Students (%) (n = 65)	Parents (%) (n = 32)	Total (%) (N = 97)
Ubiquitous metaphors			
Orientation	42	44	42
Attraction	94	94	94
Behavior metaphors			
Lifestyle	14	47	25
Business (none of your)	12	19	14
Experiment/explore	32	31	32
Identity metaphors			
Race	52	41	48
Heterosexuality	52	34	46
Adjectival metaphors			
Invisible (should not see it)	14	50	26
Unnatural	17	28	21
Rhetorical metaphors			
No big deal	25	8	20
Major acts of deviance	9	19	12

these metaphors and analogies were used in order to show that young and old cohorts use them to communicate fundamentally contrasting understandings of homosexuality.

Students used the two identity metaphors—analogies to *race* and *heterosexuality*—more frequently than parents, and they did so while using essentialist language and invoking a moral and existential equality between majority and minority groups. Students did not deny that there are differences between groups; rather, they used a variety of analogies in their discourse that rhetorically minimized the significance of homosexuality as *no big deal*. Taken together, this pattern of discourse characterizes homosexuality as *identity*—as *who you are*, not what you do. Although sometimes informants used these analogies deliberately as a rhetorical tactic, at other times they were used without any apparent rhetorical motive. I therefore interpret them as expressing the social imagination of homosexuality as identity that was dominant during the Gay Rights Period, when these students came of age.

Almost three-quarters (74 percent) of students compared homosexuality to either heterosexuality or race at some point during my interview, while 59 percent of parents made one or more of those analogies. Rarely do these analogies appear as part of an oppositional discourse: only one student and three parents who used *either* analogy expressed unambiguous opposition to gay marriage. Perhaps more importantly, though, the articulation of these analogies is not an indicator of liberal ideology: for example, ten of the twenty-five informants who self-identified as conservative or Republican used the race analogy.

Although both race and heterosexuality are identity categories, their use in discourse varies somewhat. They are similar in that many informants use them in order to explain homosexual feelings of attraction:

> Q: Where do you think it comes from? Like why do you think some people are homosexual?
> A: I don't really know. I guess wherever our feelings come from. The same place that my feelings about my boyfriend come from. Some people, you know, there's white people who like black people or Mexicans who like white people, or you know, people who like people with blonde hair or people who like people with dark hair. . . . It's what we see that attracts us, I guess. (Claudia, twenty-two)

People also used both analogies to explain their feelings about gay marriage. If homosexuality is like race, then the debate over gay marriage is analogous to the past debate over interracial marriage:

> I think over time it's gonna be seen as the miscegenation laws of, I think eventually it's gonna be seen in that kind of ridiculous light. There's gonna be some people, like, "that law was great," but they'll be marginalized. (Alan, twenty-two)

Similarly, when informants compare homosexuality to heterosexuality, they imagine the controversy over gay marriage in terms of their own heterosexual relationships:

> I really think that if two people are happy, then far be it from me or the government to tell them that their love is wrong. Like, how would anyone else feel if, "No, you can't be married because when you get married, that's a sin. Your love is wrong"? That would be a horrible feeling to me. If I brought home my boyfriend and my mom said, "No, your love is wrong," I think, I don't think that's fair to judge. (Jane, nineteen)

Quite simply, when asked to explain their feelings about homosexuality or gay marriage, many people find both race and heterosexuality to be simple, culturally accessible, and hence widely understood analogies to help them express their opinions.

Aside from these similarities, however, there are important differences. The analogy to heterosexuality is unique because it is the binary opposite of homosexuality. When asked to explain an abstract concept, it is logical to define it by what it is not; so it should be no surprise that *anyone* would compare homosexuality to heterosexuality. What is noteworthy is that the young cohort uses the analogy primarily to describe homosexuality as ontologically and morally equivalent, rather than inferior:

> They're basically the same as everyone else, but you know, have different, they swing differently. You know what I mean. They're people too. They're the same. I don't know how to describe it. They're just like me; they just like guys. (Ron, twenty)

Some informants invoked the heterosexual analogy along with a *species* metaphor to emphasize their fundamental equality:

> Gay people, it's not like they're a different species. They have the same feelings that straight people have towards each other. So, it's still the same feelings they have that would be going through. (Alan, twenty-two)

Thus, the comparison of homosexuality to heterosexuality is sociologically significant in that informants used it to assert an ontological and moral equivalence between gay and straight: it would be wrong to discriminate against someone who is lesbian or gay, just as it would be wrong to discriminate against someone who is straight.

The race analogy is unique also: because of the salience of race in US history and culture, the entire gay marriage debate is refracted through the prism of race. In general, informants compared the prohibition of gay marriage to various moments in the history of racial discrimination, and they positioned gay marriage within the narrative of racial progress. For example, some informants compared the prohibition of gay marriage to slavery and segregation:

> I think it would be another step in acceptance of them, and I think that's something our country should have because, you know, it's always kind of been a battle of race in the country after slavery and everything. African Americans weren't widely accepted. Right now, it's homosexuals aren't widely accepted, and I think it's just another step. (Nate, nineteen)

The analogy of "separate but equal" was invoked frequently when asked about the hypothetical scenario of creating separate civil unions for same-sex couples:

> I would be opposed to it. . . . They tried that before, that with the African Americans and the white people and saying that they're separate but equal, you know. And obviously that didn't work out, you know, that was a big disaster. (Kevin, twenty)

Informants also mentioned the Civil Rights Movement of the 1960s when talking about gay marriage:

> If they're gay and they're in love, let them get married. That, I don't see, it's just, it's discrimination and we should have, I thought we did away with it all in the sixties with the Civil Rights Movement, and we, we didn't have to go through any of that shit again. (Terrence, nineteen)

Interestingly, informants thought that, just like racial progress, true equality for lesbians and gays would be achieved only over the long term:

> I think sooner or later it's going to be legalized. It's one of those issues that we inch forward, that we inch closer to day by day. But it's just, it's just like equality for blacks. It's something that, yeah, they were freed during the

Civil War, but it took them over a hundred years to get on the same status as white people. It's not something that's just going to happen overnight. (Simon, twenty-four)

Last, because I conducted my interviews around the time of the 2008 election of Barack Obama, the idea of a black president served as an analogy for the possibility that gay marriage would be legalized one day:

Q: If you think into the future, like I don't know, twenty, thirty, forty, however many years, do you think same-sex marriage is ever going to be legal in the United States?

A: Yeah, I think so. We elected a black man. I'm serious, nothing surprises me more. I mean, I already told you, I voted for him, but I'm still amazed he made it. (Lindsay, forty-five)

Because of the American cultural consensus that racism, slavery, and segregation are wrong, and that racial equality is a positive value, this analogy provides strong rhetorical support for gay marriage. Logically, if homosexuality is like race, then discrimination against lesbians and gays is wrong because racial discrimination is wrong. The invocation of race is a rhetorically powerful—if logically flawed—argument in support of gay marriage.

Americans imagine race and heterosexuality to be unchangeable aspects of self-identity, so the use of essentialist language—that homosexuality defines who you are—follows logically. About one-third (34 percent) of older informants used some form of essentialist language to talk about lesbians and gays, while 47 percent of younger informants did so. The discursive construction of homosexuality as identity was thus bolstered by the use of the verb *to be* to define homosexuality as a part of who you are:

It's not really a choice, I don't think. It's more of how that person is, what stimulates their brain to want that. It's not a decision; it's not a choice; it's just how they are. (Dylan, twenty-three)

This essentialist language frequently accompanied the attraction metaphor, and it has similar implications: homosexuality is not something you simply choose or that you cannot change. It is not like a *switch* or *light bulb* that you turn on and off:

> I think that it is something that, you feel a certain way, you're not exactly certain why. Some people see that they are different; they can't help feeling that way. I mean, it's not something that you can just turn on and off like a light bulb. (Chris, twenty-two)

Not only do informants who use this essentialist language conclude that you cannot change who you are, but it logically implies a division between those who are *true to their selves*—who are authentically gay—and those who are *lying to their selves*:

> I don't think that you can change completely. You can tell people that you're not gay, or you can suppress emotional tendencies, or you can lie to yourself and other people. But I don't think that you can biologically change the way you feel. . . . You could try as hard as you can, but you can't really change who you are. (Jane, nineteen)

Many young people, even conservatives like Jesse, interpreted the question of whether or not lesbians and gays should refuse to act on their feelings as a ridiculous one:

> Q: What do you think about people who identify as gay or lesbian but choose not to have homosexual relations?
> A: Well that doesn't really make any sense. I mean, in a way, it'd be like, well I like women, but I don't want to get down. . . . I think that's kind of denying yourself in a way. I don't think that's the right thing to do either. (Jesse, twenty-seven)

If one imagines homosexuality *as identity*, stigmas and religious prohibitions against homosexuality prevent people from acting authentically in the world. The idea that legalizing gay marriage would encourage people to be gay was also interpreted as ridiculous, except in that it would help make it easier for those who are "truly" gay to be *open* about who they are, or to *come out* of *the closet*:

Q: Do you think that, like, legalizing same-sex marriage would encourage more people to be gay?

A: To be more open about it maybe. Um. [pause] Not necessarily like to encourage them, like for wrong reasons, but like to, maybe like open their eyes and like see who they really are. Like some people may be more open about their relationships if there was same-sex marriages. (Jeremiah, nineteen)

For these informants, legalizing gay marriage would be a recognition and validation, not of deviant behavior but of people's inner selves.

Finally, informants who imagined homosexuality as identity were not oblivious to the stigma of homosexuality, so when they did address the ways in which it was different from heterosexuality, they tried to delegitimize the stigma by trivializing the difference. Young informants in particular compared the difference between heterosexuality and homosexuality to the most insignificant differences among people that they could think of:

It's not my personal, you know, my personal opinion that we should tell people, "Well no, I don't agree with it, you shouldn't get married because I don't feel the same way that you do." I mean that would be like saying, "I like Play-Doh and you like Legos. I'm sorry we can't play together because you like something else." (Chris, twenty-two)

Twenty-five percent of students made such a trivializing statement, and eight percent of parents did so. In no case did the informant who made such a comparison oppose gay marriage. Informants articulated these analogies for rhetorical reasons, because they perceived that gay marriage opponents get *bent out of shape* about homosexuality. To them, homosexuality is truly *no big deal*:

I don't really see why this has to be a big deal with everybody, you know. It's like two people love each other, they want each other, you know, to be secure for the rest of their lives. . . . It's not like we're saying everyone should get married, or people should marry animals and all this weird stuff. It's just so, uh, like a guy and a guy want to get married, that shouldn't be a big deal if that's how they are. (Terrence, nineteen)

Interpreted sociologically, these metaphors and analogies both indicate and articulate the social imagination of homosexuality *as identity* that has been increasingly dominant in American society since 1993. This imagination of homosexuality interacts with the informant's political and religious ideology in discourse about gay marriage. If an informant is politically liberal, imagining homosexuality as identity will shape a discourse of *unambiguous support*. By contrast, if an informant is a religious conservative, imagining homosexuality as identity results in the discourse of *immoral inclusivity*. All seven informants who articulated this discourse are young conservative Christians; six of the seven articulated at least one analogy to race or heterosexuality, and five of the seven articulated at least one trivializing analogy. These informants agreed that homosexuality is a sin, but they trivialized the sin and argued that their sins were no worse than anyone else's sins:

> I'm not going to condemn, you know, homosexuals acting on their urges any more than I'm going to condemn someone stealing a candy bar from the convenience store down the road. (Kyle, twenty-three)

Young religious conservatives articulate the discourse of immoral inclusivity to reconcile their imagination of homosexuality as identity with their religious belief that homosexuality is a sin. It is because they imagine homosexuality as identity that they do not articulate an oppositional discourse, like their elder counterparts.

Homosexuality as Behavior

In contrast to the identity metaphors and analogies that students used in discourse, the parents used metaphors of *lifestyle, invisibility,* and *nature* more frequently than students—metaphors that characterize homosexuality as *behavior*—as *what you do*, not who you are. They also more frequently compared homosexuality to *major acts of deviance*, like stealing and alcoholism, and therefore rhetorically emphasized the significance of homosexuality. As with the younger cohort, sometimes these metaphors and analogies were made consciously and sometimes apparently unconsciously; regardless, they give voice to the social imagination of homosexuality as behavior that was dominant in American society when Baby Boomers came of age.

First, almost half (47 percent) of all parents used the *lifestyle* metaphor to talk about homosexuality and gay marriage, while only 14 percent of students did so. The lifestyle metaphor defines homosexuality as an array of practices and behaviors that, perceived as a unified whole, distinguishes a way of life. The word characterizes homosexuality in terms of actions, not feelings:

> If that's their lifestyle, and they want to find the ideal partner for them, and to be equal, really, I think that's what it is. I think they want to be acknowledged for who they are and for us to be happy for them that they found their mate. . . . I can't say I condone it, but like I said, I was raised that that's just not the right way to be. Girls are supposed to be with guys, guys are supposed to be with girls. (Debra, fifty-seven)

This quote is illuminating because the informant uses essentialist language ("to be") in a way that refers to behavior, not identity. Discursively, the lifestyle metaphor translates the identity aspect of sexuality into a behavioral one. This discourse is thus closely related to the attribution of homosexuality as a choice, and it prompts informants to make analogies to other *life choices*:

> There may be certain people out there that lean that way, okay. But life is about choices. I mean, it's like alcohol. When I was younger, like I said, I drank, but when I got married, moved up here, realized drinking wasn't the smartest thing to do. It was going to create problems. . . . Sometimes those choices at the start are very tough, very hard to carry through on those choices. But it's choices. (Vincent, forty-eight)

Conservative Christians were especially likely to speak of homosexuality as a behavior because religious prohibitions against homosexuality are prohibitions against sinful behavior, not feelings or identity. In orthodox religious discourse, homosexual acts are sins, and people choose whether to commit them or to *struggle* to *resist* them. The analogies used by older conservatives to explain their views on homosexuality—*gluttony, smoking, alcoholism, drug use, stealing,* and *criminal sexual behavior*—indicated the severity of their disapproval:

> There's a delusional thinking that they were born that way, that they were born gay. . . . That's like saying I was born a crack addict or I was born a drunk. Maybe predisposed to an environment that allows you to have an addiction; and that addiction could come in the form of alcohol, drugs, or sexuality. So it's a choice that you choose: you can choose to be homosexual, you can choose to be lesbian. (George, fifty)

Conservative Christian discourse clearly represents homosexuality in behavioral terms—as a sinful lifestyle—and it even strengthens the behavior/identity dichotomy by urging people to refrain from sinful behavior, even if they have an innate inclination to sin. For example, if I was born with a predisposition to addictive behavior, it does not logically follow that I should go gambling at a casino, nor does it excuse such behavior. To "hate the sin and love the sinner" is to show love and compassion to the person by preventing him from engaging in immoral behavior that, as they understand it, is harmful to his self or his soul:

> I do believe God is all-loving, infinite love. Where we may condemn a sin or a way of living, I believe God has more love than we can ever understand, and he will still love them no matter what. Our job as Christians is to try to show as much of that infinite love as we can to others, no matter who they are, no matter what their lifestyle is, no matter that they are still sinning or still living a lifestyle that is not acceptable to us. (Pablo, fifty-one)

This view on sinful behavior is reinforced by a theological belief that people are created in God's image, and that God does not intend for people to be homosexual. Informants use metaphors of *wiring, planning,* and *design* to convey the idea that human beings are created by another agent who intends for them to function in a particular way. Similarly, metaphors of *deception* and *temptation* by Satan or other evil forces are used to explain feelings that deviate from God's plan:

> I believe in the Bible, I believe in our creator, who said that that's not how he, that's not how he wired us up. And I don't believe he, I think

[homosexuality] is the greatest deception of our age. I'm convinced of it. And [the Bible] said, "Even believers will be deceived in end times." (Theresa, fifty-five)

Two of my older informants actually spoke from their personal experience of resisting and renouncing past homosexual feelings and behaviors as proof of their moral duty and ability to resist temptation.

Although the orthodox religious discourse is the most obvious manifestation of this behavioral imagination of homosexuality, there is a secular variant. In secular discourse, *nature* replaces God; homosexuality is compared to a *mistake, handicap,* or *disability* instead of a sin; and a rhetoric of *invisibility* replaces a rhetoric of struggle and resistance. The *nature* metaphor is a complex one, in that it lends itself equally well to both the behavioral and identity dimensions of homosexuality, and it is overwhelmingly used in the negative: homosexuality is *unnatural.* Ultimately, the view that homosexuality is unnatural is grounded in the logic of evolution and the act of sexual reproduction: same-sex sexual behavior cannot lead to the reproduction of the species, so even a "gay gene" that was created by nature and that predisposed a person to homosexuality would be a *mistake*:

> I personally think that it's, if you can be born with a defect—missing fingers, missing toes—why can't you have something go haywire with the chemicals that make you who you are? (Stephanie, fifty)

Although this metaphor implies that homosexuality is wrong and could foster negative attitudes about it, some informants made analogies to *handicaps* and *disabilities* to argue for greater acceptance of lesbians and gays. This particular variant of the nature metaphor is consistent with the imagination of homosexuality both as identity and as attributable to factors beyond an individual's control:

> [Lesbians and gays] are not just designed to piss you off or to get your church upset or anything like that. It's not that. It's not like saying, "Okay, I'm going to have a Down syndrome child." They have an extra chromosome, that's why that child is Down syndrome. There's reasons for things. (Ariel, forty-seven)

In some ways, then, the nature metaphor inspires tolerant attitudes toward lesbian and gays. However, most informants who described homosexuality as unnatural, or as a mistake of nature, did not support gay marriage: only six of the twenty informants who articulated this metaphor constructed a supportive discourse.

The natural/unnatural dichotomy was reinforced by other binary adjectival metaphors, such as *healthy/unhealthy* and *functional/dysfunctional*, which informants used to describe the larger context—whether that be a person's life, her family, or her society as a whole:

> My wife works with preschoolers, and she has kids coming in there sometimes that have same-sex partners with just really a lot of psychological problems. . . . Even with a healthy relationship with two same-sex individuals, it would be, I think, more of the exception than the rule that they would have children that would function in a way that would be healthy for society as a whole. (Stan, fifty-nine)

For many people, not only is homosexuality unnatural, but it is also unhealthy and dysfunctional for individuals, families, and society.

Last, 50 percent of older informants used metaphors of *invisibility* to express their feeling that one should not have to see or confront homosexuality in any way, while only 14 percent of younger informants did so. No student who used this metaphor supported gay marriage, though several parents did. These informants argued that lesbians and gays should have equal rights because their sexual orientation does not make them less human; but they said they did not want to *see* it, and they did not want it *in their face*:

> I just don't want to see it. I don't want to see you kissing anybody. I just don't like to see that kind of stuff. I just don't feel comfortable with that. (Debra, fifty-seven)

Some informants expressed this feeling by talking about how lesbians and gays *rub*, *cram*, or *throw* their sexuality in people's faces:

> I don't like it being thrown in my face all the time, 'cause just like, even though I, you know, am a heterosexual, I don't feel like it's necessary that

I throw that in your face all the time, too. So that's how I feel about that whole thing. . . . I feel like any sexual situation is just, or any relationship needs to be private; it shouldn't be thrown in people's face like it is. (Elaina, twenty-two)

Like the nature metaphor, the invisibility metaphor is complex, an adjective that can modify both identity and behavior. These informants are imagining homosexuality in behavioral terms, and nonreligious informants express disapproval for lesbians and gays only when they cannot be mistaken for straight. By contrast, *coming out of the closet* shows how the invisibility metaphor applies to identity. Both are parts of the larger metaphor of invisibility, but they carry opposite cultural and political implications.

The insistence that sexuality remains invisible is also related to a *business* metaphor that deems one's sexuality private, not public. In modern Western culture, business is a private domain to be protected from unnecessary interference by the government or outside parties. Supporters of gay marriage used the business metaphor to express the right to privacy and to explain why they thought it was wrong to prevent lesbians and gays from having the same rights as heterosexuals. However, informants also used the business metaphor to claim that it is improper for lesbians and gays to speak or act openly about their sexuality:

I don't have any problem with, you know, I figure people's sexuality is their business. I don't want to, you know, I don't want to know about their sex life. I really don't care. . . . A lot of them are kind of radical and they're in your face about it. It's like, I don't care, I just, I just don't care. That's just, if you want to have sex with a particular person, as long as it doesn't involve animals or kids, hey, you do whatever, whatever makes you happy. Behind closed doors, you know. I've always found it interesting that they, most gay people say they just want to be an accepted part of society, but then "we want, we want special rights, we want this, we want to be looked at as like a minority almost, like we need affirmative action for gays," you know. Why should that have any bearing? You know, it's your sex life, it's supposed to be private, it's behind closed doors. (John, forty-seven)

This demand that sexuality be rendered invisible creates a double bind for lesbian and gay activists. These informants are, by and large, supportive of gay rights, but they view open expressions of sexuality and political demands for equal rights negatively.[25]

Interpreted sociologically, the metaphors of lifestyle, nature, and invisibility indicate and articulate a social imagination of homosexuality *as behavior*. This imagination of homosexuality was dominant in American society during the period in which Baby Boomers came of age, and the imagination of homosexual behavior remains the primary source of stigma and homophobia directed toward lesbians and gays. Like the imagination of homosexuality *as identity*, this imagination shapes people's attitudes and interacts with their political and religious ideologies to produce specific discourses about gay marriage. Imagining homosexuality as behavior is consistent with conservative religious ideologies that classify homosexuality as a sin, and they shape a discourse of *unambiguous opposition*: of the seventeen informants who articulated this discourse, sixteen articulated one of the metaphors or analogies above. By contrast, many political liberals who imagine homosexuality as behavior articulate a discourse of *libertarian pragmatism*. Seven of the eight informants who articulated this discourse described homosexuality as unnatural, as a lifestyle, or as something that should be invisible. Faced with a contradiction between their imagination of homosexuality and the liberal political belief that one should be tolerant and extend equal rights to minorities, they try to avoid stating an opinion by denying that it is any of their business:

> The whole gay thing and stuff, I really don't understand it, but at the same time, I think that, I guess I can understand why people want to be, they want to have the recognition. I don't think that it bothers me that much. I mean, it's the other people's business, it's not mine. It doesn't affect me, you know. (Maria, forty-five)

For liberals who imagine homosexuality as behavior, the business metaphor allows them to deny that their opinion about gay marriage matters and thus avoid expressing negative attitudes about lesbians and gays—an action that would be inconsistent with their ideology.

Conclusion

With metaphor theory and the tools of metaphor analysis in hand, we can now return to Nick and the "Jackpot!" moment with which I started the chapter. Nick's discussion of gay marriage is characterized by a blatant conflict between his explicit ideology and his implicit imagination. That he imagines homosexuality as identity is evident in the metaphors and analogies he uses. For example, he told stories about his gay cousin and invoked the heterosexual analogy to explain his feelings about homosexuality:

> Q: Do you think that homosexuality can be changed, you know?
> A: That's a tough question. I mean, can you make a gay person straight?
> Q: Yeah, like if your cousin was like, "I don't want to be gay anymore."
> A: I don't know. . . . If someone were to say, if I were to say "I don't want to be straight anymore," I don't think I could make myself like men. . . . I have heard of people, um, going from being gay to um, you know, they call themselves recovering homosexuals, and they have, you know, wives or whatever. But uh, I don't see how that could be possible. But I mean, I'm, it could be.

In this quote, we see clearly how his imagination of homosexuality as identity makes the idea of someone becoming "not gay" seem like nonsense, and how that conflicts with conservative Christian beliefs that one can become a "recovering homosexual."

The influence of the social imagination is also evident in his statement about homosexuality's attribution:

> I think maybe in some instances, it could be a choice. But I do think, um, there's definitely, could be, you know, a genetic link to it. I mean, I know they do studies on rats with it. They talked about that in psychology. And my cousin even said, he's like, "You know, why would I ever choose to be this way?" Um, and so I do think, I do think some people are probably born to be, um, attracted to men.

Nick's genetic attribution of homosexuality is informed by factual learning and constructed through deliberate cognition, but the story he tells about his cousin and the presence of the attraction metaphor suggest that the social imagination of homosexuality is being expressed also. It is worth emphasizing again: it is not that the attribution of homosexuality does not shape discourses about gay marriage; rather, it is only one manifestation of the deeper cultural and cognitive structures of the social imagination.

Nick's case is unusual in how pronounced was the conflict between his implicit imagination of homosexuality and his explicit religious ideology, but he was by no means alone. Members of the Identity Cohort, regardless of their political or religious beliefs, all came of age during a period in which homosexuality was culturally imagined to be part of your identity—part of who you are—like your race or ethnicity. So from their point of view, the question of gay marriage seems not all that different from the question of interracial marriage, and the idea that you should prevent two people from finding true love and happiness because of something so trivial as your sex seems patently absurd to them. It is not so much that they *disagree* with the logic of gay marriage opponents; it is that they don't even *understand* it. This sentiment—a sheer lack of understanding—was repeated by many, many students whom I interviewed, especially the liberal ones:

> I really don't get why people are so against that. The ones that I see that are so against it are just, it's mainly religious. It's a religious thing, they don't like gay people in the first place, you know. So of course they don't want them to get married. They're all saying how it's a sanctity issue and it's a man and woman thing. I'm like, "Why? Why does it have to be?" I don't understand that. (Betsy, twenty-four)

Conservative students were somewhat different in that they were immersed in conservative social networks where oppositional discourses are dominant; but even still, many of them had difficulty explaining how they felt about gay marriage because their implicit understanding of homosexuality fit poorly with the explicit religious teachings that homosexuality is a sinful behavior.

The opposite, of course, was true for older liberals and conservatives. For older conservatives, their implicit understandings and explicit beliefs about homosexuality are clearly compatible. If you imagine homosexuality as behavior, then there is no inherent, logical reason why the institution of marriage should be changed to accommodate it, and the idea of legitimating deviant lifestyles inside one of society's oldest institutions might understandably upset or anger you. This is why many older conservatives felt that *they* were the ones being attacked:

> It's a distortion of the way God originally made things. And you know, a lot of times, it's like, well, it's kind of like the way the Jews went about condemning Jesus in front of Pilate. . . . They insisted that they wanted him crucified, so they got the crowd stirred up and they thought if they could . . . make themselves noisier or louder or demand more or threaten more, then somehow they could justify that action. It seems to me that a lot of that tactic is practiced today by the homosexual community. Because it seems to almost be a militant-type thing, that anytime you talk in a way that's not supportive, then you're against it. And then, of course, you're anti-gay or anti–everything else. (Stan, fifty-nine)

This compatibility between imagination and belief fuels the opposition to gay marriage. By contrast, the incompatibility between older liberals' imagination of homosexuality as behavior and their explicit political beliefs of equality for minorities makes many of them want to avoid the issue altogether. The discourse of libertarian pragmatism articulates their desire to stay out of the fight.

In summary, although discourse about sexuality is thoroughly marked by conceptual metaphors (orientation, attraction, the closet), there is a unique cohort-related pattern of metaphors that gives voice to distinct generational imaginations of homosexuality. Identity metaphors—which characterize homosexuality as who you are—are used more frequently by the Identity Cohort and in semantic contexts that create a moral equivalence between gay and straight. Behavior metaphors—which characterize homosexuality as what you do in your lifestyle—are used more frequently by Baby Boomers and in semantic contexts that create a moral dichotomy between gay and straight—where homosexual behavior is unnatural, is sinful, and should be invisible. These metaphors give voice to the informants' imagination of homosexuality, which was shaped by the period in which they came of age and which influences attribution statements, attitudes, and other explicit statements about gay marriage. It is not attribution theory but the social imagination that explains the generational change in attitudes about gay marriage.

Of course, not all old people and young people think and talk in the ways described above. Many older Americans have changed their attitudes about gay marriage and now support it, while many young Americans remain opposed. In Chapter 7, we will analyze the discourses of some of these individuals to find out whether or not these cases are compatible with the story of generational change being advanced here (spoiler alert: they are; the interesting question is *why* they are). For now, the main idea is simply this: discourses about gay marriage are shaped by the interaction between a person's explicit ideology and her implicit imagination of homosexuality, which is expressed (obliquely and often unconsciously) through metaphors and analogies. Because the social imagination of homosexuality has changed over time, the period in which a person came of age caused different cohorts to develop different imaginations of it—hence, the cohort and period effects in public opinion.

But what about marriage? The question of gay marriage is not only about homosexuality; it is not just another gay rights issue. As my previous comments suggest, marriage is an important social institution, fundamental in many ways to the structure of family and society as a whole. Moreover, as a way of organizing intimate relationships and sexual behavior, marriage is both religiously and culturally meaningful to people. In the next chapter, I will turn my attention to how my informants talked about marriage—not gay marriage specifically, but (heterosexual) marriage in general. As we will see, the issue of marriage plays an unexpected role in the dynamics of the debate. Although we are used to contrasting the *religious meanings* of marriage with the *secular rights* of marriage, there are other, arguably more important, understandings of marriage at play.

6

The Imaginary Marriage Consensus

So far, this analysis of gay marriage has centered on the "gay" part of it; but the "marriage" part matters too. For many people, the controversy over gay marriage actually had more to do with the meaning of marriage than anything about homosexuality per se. For them, gay marriage isn't like other gay rights issues, like the right to serve in the military or protection from employment discrimination. The controversy over gay marriage went much deeper—into issues pertaining to the very meanings of family, kinship, and the reproduction of the species.

Take Emily, for example. A nineteen-year-old psychology major, Emily had long wavy brown hair that kept falling over her left eye as we talked. Her dark eye liner and purple V-neck sweater contrasted with her pale white skin, all of which gave her a sort of mysterious air. But she was open, friendly, and thoughtful as she explained to me why she simply could not support gay marriage, despite having several gay friends.

Emily was raised in a very religious household—her family converted to Catholicism when she was a child, and even though she did not identify herself as a traditional Catholic, the belief system clearly influenced her. For example, when I asked what the word *marriage* meant to her, she invoked the Gospel of Mark: "Two persons coming together to become one. There, I will take a very, very Catholic standpoint [laugh]." She described her views on cohabitation as "old-fashioned," and her feelings about divorce reflected more than the typical disappointed resignation to the idea: "I view marriage as something that is sacred. So I personally don't believe in [divorce] and I would do everything in my power to avoid a divorce." Simply put, Emily generally accepted the Catholic teaching that marriage is a covenant with God and therefore much more profound than a legal agreement between two people.

When I asked her about gay marriage specifically, she immediately brought up the conflict in her social world:

I have friends of mine who are like gay and lesbian, and so I've heard like that side of the fence also. You know, I go to Catholic Church and it's this kind of thing, they are definitely opposed to it. I guess I would say my own opinion for it is, um, I don't think that it's right for like gays and lesbians to try to change how the church thinks about it, but if they can change the state's way of thinking about it, fine, let them.

In general, Emily supported equal rights for lesbians and gays, but her religious views on marriage simply precluded her from unambiguously supporting gay marriage:

Personally, just the way I was, you know, the way I view marriage from like a biblical standpoint, it's between one man and one woman because the purpose of marriage really is to propagate the species. I mean not just for convenience or whatever. I mean, obviously love is important, but I mean, the real reason for the institutionalization of marriage is that two become one flesh.

Emily acknowledged that same-sex couples love each other, live together, and should be entitled to the same financial and legal benefits that come with marriage; but the inability to procreate meant that there was an unresolvable contradiction at the core of the idea of gay marriage. When I asked her about a "civil union" alternative to gay marriage, she affirmed that that is what she supports. Because marriage carries deep theological meaning in Catholic dogma, even pro-gay Catholics could not fully support gay marriage.

Ironically, the religious meanings associated with marriage prompted many avowed atheists to come to the same conclusion as Emily—support for civil unions, but not gay marriage—except that the atheists perceived the religious meanings of marriage to be unwanted encroachments into what they thought should be a secular institution. For instance, Edward, a twenty-year-old math major, was very pro-gay but had this to say when I asked him about gay marriage:

I'm a really big fan, and I support and I agree with the idea that—the most prevalent one is the one that Obama and Biden have actually said [in the 2008 election]—they support granting rights to same-sex couples, they support creating an institution where a same-sex couple and a hetero-sexual couple have exactly equal legal standings, but they don't think that the, they don't agree with the idea of same-sex marriage. . . . Marriage is not a governmental thing. The word *marriage* is a religious thing, and so when they say they are in favor of same-sex civil unions, they're in favor of heterosexual civil unions as well. . . . The government shouldn't be al-lowed to mess with the word *marriage* at all, same-sex or heterosexual.

Emily would find little to disagree with in Edward's position here—a paradoxical alliance between two people with essentially opposite views of marriage. In contrast with the deep spiritual significance marriage held for Emily, when I asked Edward what the word meant to him, he said: "Marriage, to me, as an atheist—it's a tax shelter."

For Emily, Edward, and many others, there's something about mar-riage. Or rather, several somethings; but those somethings are different depending on who you are and how you think. At one level, there is a tension in the gay marriage debate that comes from the fact that mar-riage is simultaneously a religious and secular institution in the United States—an ambiguity that is deeply embedded in our marriage laws. But at another level, there is a tension in the debate that comes from the fact that marriage means so much more to most people than just the legal rights and benefits that had been historically denied to same-sex couples. For most of us, marriage means love, commitment, and life-long aspirations of togetherness, and the legal fight over gay marriage was about granting social recognition to the lesbian and gay relation-ships that have those characteristics. When my informants talked about gay marriage, those tensions in the meaning of marriage had significant effects on the discourse, making the battle over gay marriage different from the battle over other gay rights.

Just like with homosexuality, we must contend with the difference between what we explicitly say about marriage when we argue about it and how we implicitly imagine marriage when we converse about it. In the political public sphere, we immediately become defensive when we hear the other side politicize marriage in some way—and we insist that marriage is either a religious institution or a secular one in order to ward off ideological encroachments from our opponents. But outside of those politicized contexts, when we are talking with friends and family about our own relationships, the discourse about marriage happens on a different level—one that is more concerned with how marriage fits into our lives and loves, our spirituality and social life, our aspirations and fears.[1] In these contexts, we are engaged in what Habermas calls *communicative action* that is oriented to mutual understanding, and it is our depoliticized, implicit understanding of marriage that shapes this discourse.[2]

When it comes to marriage, this chapter shows that the dynamics of the social imagination are opposite from what they are with homosexuality. Instead of fundamental cohort differences in the imagination of marriage, we see striking similarities. There is a basic cultural consensus in American society about what marriage means in everyday life that exists beneath the surface-level disagreements about whether marriage is a religious-exclusive-traditional institution or a civil-inclusive-modern one. The generational change in support for gay marriage, then, comes from an unusual combination of cohort-based *differences* in the imagination of homosexuality and cross-cohort *similarities* in the imagination of marriage. This shared understanding of marriage—the *imaginary marriage* consensus—legitimated the fight over gay marriage for supporters and opponents alike and, when combined with new understandings of homosexuality, provided both the cultural logic for supporting gay marriage and the final rationale for Justice Anthony Kennedy's opinion that legalized it throughout the United States.

Marriage: Legal Denotation and Social Connotation

One recent study perfectly illustrates what is so special about marriage and how it differs from other gay rights issues. In 2010, the sociologist Long Doan and his colleagues presented a nationally representative sample of Americans with a short vignette about an unmarried cohabiting couple and randomly varied the names of the couple to make the couple either heterosexual (Brian and Jennifer), lesbian (Heather and Jennifer), or gay (Brian and Matt); they then asked survey respondents how much they agreed or disagreed with granting the couple various formal rights (like insurance benefits) and informal privileges (like holding hands in public).[3]

When they analyzed people's responses, what they found was surprising on two levels. The first surprise was that heterosexual men and women did not discriminate when it comes to formal rights: they approved of giving the same-sex couples equal access to family leave benefits, hospital visitation rights, inheritance rights, and insurance benefits. However, they did discriminate when it comes to informal privileges: whether or not it is okay for the couple to tell others about their relationship, hold hands in public, and kiss in public. Thus, overall, the study showed that Americans tend to support equal rights for lesbians and gays while they simultaneously denied them practical, everyday equality.

The second surprise was that heterosexuals seemed to regard marriage more as an informal privilege than a formal right: heterosexuals' responses about whether or not the same-sex couples should be allowed to get legally married were similar to their responses about holding hands in public. For marriage and these informal privileges, heterosexual Americans were more supportive of heterosexual couples' access to them than same-sex couples' access to them. In short, although straight Americans adopted egalitarian attitudes when it comes to formal rights, they did not when it comes to informal privileges—and they treated the question of gay marriage as if it were a privilege, not a right.

This study shows not only that same-sex couples continue to face every day prejudice but also that the American public imagines marriage to be about much more than a grab bag of legal rights and benefits bestowed upon them by the government. So what is marriage about, if not just the legal rights and benefits that are at stake in a court of law? What makes gay marriage special? Some of it comes from the *legal denotation* of marriage: the explicit debate about whether marriage is (or should be) defined as a religious-exclusive-traditional institution or a civil-inclusive-modern institution. The rest of it comes from the *social connotations* of marriage: the implicit and taken-for-granted understandings of how marriage fits in with society and what implications it has for your everyday life.[4]

With gay marriage, three large issues pertaining to the legal denotation of marriage are at stake: who has authority to grant and recognize marriages, whether or not the relationship must be exclusive to opposite-sex couples, and whether or not the institution can change over time. The first issue has to do with the fact that, in the United States, both government and religious figures have the authority to perform marriages: there is no legal difference between civil and religious marriage ceremonies. Unlike in many European countries, religious figures in the United States are empowered to act as civil marriage officiants, which means that, as long as they complete the appropriate paperwork, American couples can choose either a civil ceremony or a religious one; if they opt for a religious ceremony, they don't need to do both. Whether your wedding ceremony is performed by a priest, a clerk in the county courthouse, a celebrant in Las Vegas, or your best friend who impulsively decided to become an ordained minister online, the resulting marriage is perfectly valid—as long you do the paperwork.[5]

It is true that the state will not recognize a marriage if the appropriate legal standards are not met (e.g., marriages between minors or in polygamous groups), and it is true that religious institutions like the Catholic Church can refuse to perform marriage ceremonies or recognize marriages if they fail to meet its standards; so it cannot be said that there is *no* difference between civil and religious marriages in the United States. However, because this one-way erosion of the boundary between church and state gives religious figures the legal right to perform civil marriage ceremonies, the debate over gay marriage inevitably appears as a threat to the marriage policies and practices of religious institutions.

The second and third issues relating to the legal denotation of marriage will be taken together: they deal with whether or not marriage requires an opposite-sex couple—the "traditional" one-man-one-woman marriage—or whether marriage can be modified to be inclusive of same-sex couples. It is widely believed that marriage has always been between one man and one woman, and rhetorically "traditional" marriage means "heterosexual" marriage; same-sex couples need not apply. For practical purposes, in the United States it has always been common sense that a man could only marry a woman and vice versa; it was so widely understood that it didn't even need saying. And after the outlaw of polygamy in the nineteenth century, only a relationship between an opposite-sex *couple* could be called a marriage.

Of course, anthropologists have documented a wide array of kinship arrangements beyond heterosexual monogamous marriages, and there is historical evidence of same-sex unions recognized in early European, Christian societies;[6] but even when we restrict the claim to modern Western societies, scholars have shown that the idea of "traditional" marriage is more accurately thought of as a cultural ideal (with pronounced racial and class overtones). Marriage and family relationships in nineteenth-century America were more about the means of economic survival than anything: wealthy white families could afford to base marriage on mutual affection, but marriage in poor and rural families was mainly about agricultural production and survival, while slaves were legally denied the right to marry. In the early twentieth century, the combination of industrialization, urbanization, and the rise of consumer culture generated a new *companionate* marriage ideal, in which romantic love replaced economic survival as the primary logic for marriage and family formation. The post–World War II booms—in babies, housing, and the economy—represent both the ultimate fulfillment and the last gasp of the companionate ideal. The 1960s and 1970s witnessed the rise of the *individualized* marriage ideal, characterized by greater access to birth control and divorce, lower fertility rates, more diverse family forms, and new attitudes about everything from premarital sex to the household division of labor.[7]

Thus, "traditional" does not mean just one man, one woman but also implicitly signifies a "nuclear family" that lives independently in a household largely separate from extended family and the domain of work.[8] The ideal of traditional marriage is built partly on nostalgia for the 1950s family form that was historically unique, only briefly a reality, and then only for some Americans.[9] By contrast, the diversity of family forms and relationships that characterize contemporary households—including single-parent families, remarried couples, step families, and cohabiting couples—suggest that the reality is best characterized in terms of multiple "modern" families.[10] True, none of these variations in the past and present realities of marriage presumed the existence of a same-sex couple, so even if we admit that there is no such thing as "traditional marriage," we must also concede that gay marriage constitutes a fairly revolutionary break with history.

Related to this debate about how exclusive "traditional" marriage is of same-sex couples is the debate about whether humans can fundamentally change the institution of marriage. If marriage is religious and God-given, then no; but if marriage is civil and changeable by popular democracy, then yes. As a sociological matter, the answer is easy: Marriage is socially constructed—it has changed many times in the past, and it will change many times in the future. Contemporary, modern marriages are drastically different from what they were even 150 years ago. But many argue that marriage, philosophically, theologically, and even biologically, is unalterable, despite what humans do.

For the religious orthodox, marriage is an institution created by God that human beings may tinker with but not fundamentally alter. For example, the Catechism of the Catholic Church declares, "The vocation to marriage is written in the very nature of man and woman as they came from the hand of the Creator. Marriage is not a purely human institution despite the many variations it may have undergone through the centuries in different cultures, social structures, and spiritual attitudes."[11] In this view, foremost among the unalterable properties of marriage is that it provides the environment for the procreative reproduction of the species and thus of society as a whole. For those who believe that the fundamental definition of marriage is neither created nor changeable by humans, gay marriage is fake marriage. States and societies—which are fallible—may decide to call same-sex relationships "marriages," but that does not mean that they are really, truly marriages.

Not everyone who feels this way is religious; many who are more in tune with biology than theology come to the same conclusion. People who believe in the inherent wisdom of nature and evolution observe that opposite-sex monogamous relationships are adopted by species throughout the animal kingdom; therefore, they reason, marriage may be a "naturally" superior type of social arrangement for the reproduction of the species. At its core, whether based in theology or biology, this belief ultimately boils down to a matter of faith: the voluminous track record of actual human modifications to marriage may be written off as evolutionarily dysfunctional or spiritually inauthentic—the familial version of false consciousness.

These three issues, taken together, amount to a high-stakes, explicit disagreement over the boundaries of marriage, and whether or not a relationship between a same-sex couple counts. In the political battle over gay marriage, opponents fiercely defend the religious-exclusive-traditional definition of marriage, while supporters emphatically define marriage in civil-inclusive-modern terms. Each side must attack the opposite definition of marriage while advancing their own because to concede the definitional point would be to concede the battle. But of course, as the astute reader has already recognized, marriages in the

United States are both religious and civil, exclusive and inclusive, traditional and modern in various ways. So the rhetorical battle must be fought, but it cannot be won by argumentation alone.

It should be observed at this point that both the rise of individualized marriage in the 1960s and 1970s and the challenge to heterosexual marriage emerged in the lifetimes of the parents whom I interviewed, whereas the students came of age after those changes. Broadly speaking, attitudes about marriage and family have changed dramatically during the lifetimes of the parents.[12] Therefore, it would be reasonable to expect to see generational differences in the two cohorts' attitudes about marriage, just like we saw in their imagination of homosexuality. In fact, scholars have documented cohort differences in attitudes about premarital sex, gender ideologies, and definitions of family.[13] But as we will see below, I find little evidence of cohort differences in how my informants talked about marriage. I suspect that this can be attributed to the fact that many of the cultural ideals of companionate marriage have persisted, even as more visible changes, like the rise in access to contraception and divorce, have changed the reality of marriage.[14]

In the shadows of this contentious, explicit disagreement about the legal denotation of marriage, then, there is an implicit agreement about the social connotations of marriage: we generally share a common understanding of what marriage means in practice, in our daily lives. In other words, the heat and light created by the fight over the definitional boundaries of marriage obscure a deep cultural consensus that lies at its heart. The bulk of this chapter is devoted to outlining what these imaginary social connotations of marriage actually are and why they are just as important to the gay marriage debate as the high-profile disagreement over marriage's legal denotation. But as a preview, a few observations about the unusually high esteem in which marriage is held in mainstream American culture will illustrate what the imaginary marriage consensus looks like.

We celebrate marriage in our society to an unreasonable degree—unreasonable because much of our anxiety about marriage is based on the fact that we fail to live up to the lofty standards we set for it. According to sociologist Andrew Cherlin, the United States' extraordinarily high rates of both divorce *and* marriage are due to the fact that, compared to other Western nations, we place higher value on two contradictory ideals: marriage and individualism.[15] Simply put, most Americans aspire to marriage but are unwilling or unable to moderate our individualistic tendencies enough to make marriage a lifelong commitment. If we expect our own marriage to be the epitome of a fulfilling relationship and our most cherished social bond, and we expect our spouse to be our eternal true love and perfect soul mate, then we are bound to be disappointed when the day-to-day trials and tribulations of our real marriage fail to match the fairy tale. Divorce is the obvious resolution to a problem of social cohesion in an individualistic culture— when a disappointing relationship gets in the way of our own happiness and aspirations.

It would be illogical to fault individual Americans for our collective delusion; we get our cultural ideas about marriage from the perfect romances we see in the media, from the sacred values promoted by our religious leaders, and even from the law itself. In his majority opinion in *Obergefell v. Hodges*, Justice Kennedy begins with a paean to marriage and its virtues throughout human history:

> From their beginning to their most recent page, the annals of human history reveal the transcendent importance of marriage. The lifelong union of a man and a woman always has promised nobility and dignity to all persons, without regard to their station in life. Marriage is sacred to those who live by their religions and offers unique fulfillment to those who find meaning in the secular realm. Its dynamic allows two people to find a life that could not be found alone, for a marriage becomes greater than just the two persons. Rising from the most basic human needs, marriage is essential to our most profound hopes and aspirations.[16]

That Kennedy characterizes marriage in such glowing, romanticized terms is striking and stands in sharp contrast to the cynical view of marriage that one might encounter on the late-night comedy circuit. In fact, it is this romanticized characterization of marriage that provides Kennedy with his warrant for ruling that the Fourteenth Amendment of the Constitution guarantees lesbians and gays access to marriage:

> As the State itself makes marriage all the more precious by the significance it attaches to it, exclusion from that status has the effect of teaching

that gays and lesbians are unequal in important respects. It demeans gays and lesbians for the State to lock them out of a central institution of the Nation's society. Same-sex couples, too, may aspire to the transcendent purposes of marriage and seek fulfillment in its highest meaning.[17]

The US Supreme Court ruled that gay marriage must be legal, not just as a matter of nondiscrimination on the basis of sex or gender, but also because they consider the freedom to marry to be one of the fundamental liberties that the US government must guarantee to all its citizens.[18] This is but one example of how our laws, our tax code, and our political system are premised upon the glowing, idealistic social connotations of the meaning of marriage, but there are many more.[19]

In the battle over gay marriage, these social connotations played a decisive role in both the battle itself and the terms of its resolution. When I listened to my interviewees talk about gay marriage, I heard them arguing vociferously about whether or not marriage is defined as a religious-exclusive-traditional thing or as a civil-inclusive-modern thing—and thusly, whether or not gay marriage is something they opposed or supported. But more importantly, I heard them all implicitly agree upon the legitimacy of the battle itself. Nothing in our shared imagination of marriage—its high cultural value, its embodiment of love, commitment, and sexual attraction (but not procreation), its symbolic validation of the relationship, the legal and financial stability it provides—ruled out the possibility of expanding it to include same-sex couples. Because of this shared understanding, both proponents and opponents alike acknowledged the legitimacy of the pursuit of marriage by lesbian and gay couples.

The Contested Legal Definition of Marriage

It should be no surprise that, when asked explicitly about gay marriage, people cited their beliefs about marriage as part of their rationale for holding one opinion or another:

Q: So you've heard a little bit about the same-sex marriage controversy?
A: I have, yeah. I'm opposed to it. I'm opposed to them calling it marriage, and I'm opposed to legalizing it. I mean, if they want to have a, some kind of a legal agreement where they can share benefits or

whatever, that's one thing. But I mean, to call it marriage is not right. Marriage should be between a man and a woman. (Sarah, sixty)

I have no problem with it whatsoever, I think it's beautiful. Like I said, love is blind. . . . I think that anyone and everyone, you know, no matter what sex, what race, what color, you know, whatever. If you get married because, like I said, if it's just only for men and women, isn't that just saying that that's just because you know, just so they can have children? I mean, that's not the meaning of marriage, I don't think. (Paula, twenty-three)

Both opponents like Sarah and supporters like Paula justified their feelings about gay marriage by citing their views of marriage. In the quotes above, the sex of the couple is the main axis of disagreement, but for others, whether or not marriage is a religious or a civil institution and whether or not marriage can be changed by society was the primary axis of disagreement.

This divide between those who defined marriage in religious-exclusive-traditional terms and those who defined it in civil-inclusive-modern terms emerged in dialogical antagonism with the opposing side. Both supporters and opponents tried to refute the definition of marriage that was the premise of the other side's arguments as a way to justify their own position:

Even though it may be a possibility that it would be legalized, I hope it never will be. I hope the Christian Church will always fight to insure that it's always, marriage is marriage. It's got man and woman, and even though that may sound a little narrow-minded, it was not made up by man. It was made up by God, and that's where it comes down to. If you want to call it a lifestyle, if you want to get them equal rights as in pay, as in insurance benefits and stuff, fine. I got nothing wrong with that. Just don't call it marriage. (Pablo, fifty-one)

Just as Pablo refutes the supporters' definition of marriage as something that is civil and modern, so too did many supporters refute opponents' definitions. Thus, for partisans in the culture war, the explicit definition of marriage was simply one more weapon in their discursive arsenal to wield in the heat of battle.

That said, the definition of marriage paled in comparison with the significance of homosexuality in shaping the discourses about gay marriage. Aside from six informants (including Emily and Edward) who said they supported civil unions instead of gay marriage, I found little evidence from my interviews to suggest that people's definitions of marriage "made the difference" for them. For most people, the main controversy over gay marriage was about homosexuality, and marriage was a secondary point. For this reason, the disagreement over the explicit definition of marriage was not really the main reason marriage mattered in the debate.

Another reason that the explicit definition of marriage warrants less attention than the social connotations is that people rarely invoked those aspects of the definition of marriage when they were talking about marriage *in general*.[20] Unless we were talking about gay marriage specifically, people rarely talked about marriage in terms of religious versus civil, exclusive versus inclusive, traditional versus modern. For example, when asked what the word *marriage* means to them, only five out of the seventeen people who opposed gay marriage said "man and woman," and none of them used the word *traditional*. Similarly, barely half (twelve of twenty-three) of the informants whom I classified as having orthodox or evangelical religious beliefs used any sort of religious or spiritual language when answering that question.[21] Therefore, to fully understand the significance of marriage in the gay marriage debate, we need to look beyond the narrow, contested definition to the broader, social connotations of marriage.

The Imaginary Marriage Consensus

In general, there is a cultural consensus among people in both cohorts about what marriage means, a consensus that ultimately validates the fight over gay marriage. Before bringing up the issue of gay marriage in any of my interviews, I asked my informants two broad questions that were designed to give them an opportunity to tell me how they imagined marriage. I first asked, "What does the word *marriage* mean to you?" I followed that question with, "What are some characteristics of a good, strong marriage?" Comparing the themes that students and their parents brought up in their answers shows both similarities and differences in how the cohorts understand marriage.

Figures 6.1 and 6.2 show the themes that emerged in response to each question, sorted by the percentage of students articulating them. Visually, significant differences in how parents and students imagine marriage stick out if you track the two types of bars as you move from top to bottom in each chart. In general, there are few differences in the

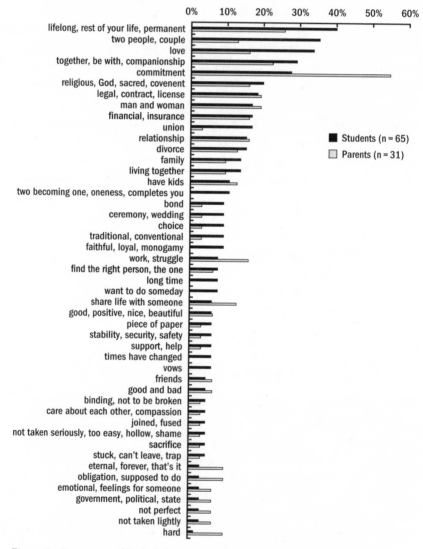

Figure 6.1: Percentage of Each Cohort Mentioning Themes for Meaning of Marriage
Note: Only codes with four or more mentions are shown.

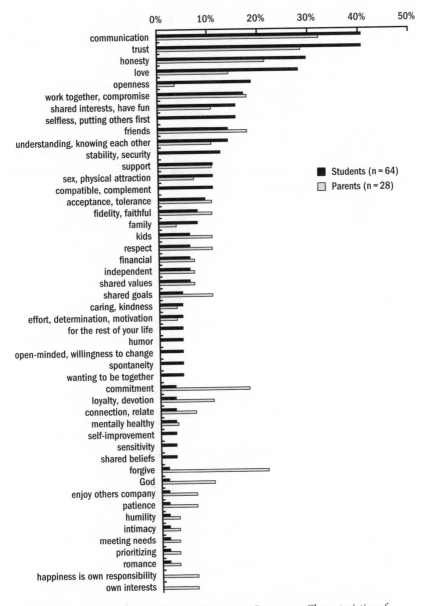

Figure 6.2: Percentage of Each Cohort Mentioning Important Characteristics of Marriage

meanings and characteristics of marriage identified by each cohort: thirteen of the top fifteen meanings and eight of the top ten characteristics named by each cohort in response to each question are shared. Regardless of age, Americans imagine marriage as a lifelong commitment between two people (man and woman, or any couple) who love each other and want to be together, and they variously describe it as a religious institution and a legal contract with financial implications for the couple. Americans believe that you need communication, trust, honesty, and love to make a good, strong marriage; you need to be able to compromise, to enjoy doing things together, to be friends, and to understand one another.

The following comments are typical and illustrate the kinds of answers that people gave when asked, "What does the word *marriage* mean to you?"

> A union of equals. Love and compassion. It's like, pretty much your best friend, in a sense. Somebody you want to spend the rest of your life with. You don't necessarily need to, but you want to, so you do. (Denise, twenty)

> Marriage, huh, that's interesting. Well, I suppose that ceremonial commitment that people make with each other. They decide to celebrate to the world, "here, we are going to be a couple" and recognize themselves as a couple, recognize themselves legally, be able to have the benefits, the retirement package, those kinds of things you kind of expect. Trying to build a life so that it becomes two people building a life together and having the same interests, you know. (Maria, forty-five)

Now some typical responses to "What do you think are some of the most important characteristics of a good, strong marriage?"

> I think good characteristics would probably be, two people who know how to work through their problems. I think there has to be a great deal of love between the two individuals. You know, they have to be able to work with each other. I think a lot of good marriages probably are, you know, trying to get two people who complement each other—you know, one makes up for the other's weaknesses. (Alan, twenty-two)

Communication, one, number one thing. Trust, you know. Spontaneous, sometimes you gotta be spontaneous to just, you know, keep your partner interested. Love, and just take care of them, of each other. (Demarcus, twenty-three)

To the extent that there are major differences in how the two cohorts imagine marriage, they seem to reflect age differences that come from life experience, rather than cohort differences that come from their formative years. Only a few students whom I interviewed had ever been married or even engaged, while all of the parents were speaking from direct personal experience with marriage; thus, themes of conflict, work, and forgiveness figure more strongly in parents' discourse about marriage, while students used more idealistic terms.

In both figures, *commitment* stands out as the number one meaning of marriage for parents and as a characteristic of a strong marriage that parents mention much more frequently than students.[22] It is not that students don't recognize the importance of commitment, but parents had more direct experience of how much commitment it takes over many years to sustain a relationship through thick and thin:

Well, the word *marriage* to me is basically kind of synonymous with commitment. And commitment is really, has its basis in, not in feeling, but in decisions or in actions, in demonstrations. And so to me, marriage is more of a demonstration of your faith and commitment to another person. Now, the only problem with that is we're imperfect. And to make something good in an imperfect world, you have to work at it. And to me, that takes a lot of work, I mean, a lot of devotion to looking at the other person's side of things, learning patience, and learning to develop sensitivity. (Stan, fifty-nine)

Stan's firsthand experience with marriage informs his explanation of why commitment matters in marriage—the hallmark of an age effect in discourse.

The prominence of commitment in parents' discourse is especially meaningful when considered in tandem with other differences in the discourses between parents and students. Parents' emphasis on commitment was amplified by the fact that *work (struggle)* and *hard* were themes that emerged disproportionately in their discourse; *forgiveness, patience,* the insistence that *happiness is one's own responsibility,* and that you need to make time for your *own interests* are important characteristics of a good, strong marriage. By contrast, students were unique in mentioning numerous idealistic themes in their discussion of marriage: students alone mentioned themes of *two becoming one (oneness, completes you),* and *faithfulness (monogamy, loyalty)* as meanings of marriage, and students alone named *selflessness (putting others first)* and *compatibility (complementarity)* as characteristics of a good, strong marriage. Since parents have reckoned with the messy day-to-day realities of marriage to a degree that students have not, students are freer to imagine marriage in more romantic terms.

Beyond these differences, the overwhelming similarities between the two cohorts suggest that students and parents would have no trouble communicating about marriage across generational boundaries. Because both cohorts imagine marriage in similar terms, they share a common cultural understanding of what marriage means, how it fits into people's relationships, and how it fits into American society. Even polarizing disagreements about whether marriage is a religious-exclusive-traditional institution or a civil-inclusive-modern one can be carried out on a common ground of mutual understanding.

The remainder of my interview protocol on marriage reinforces this conclusion and shows just how deep the marriage consensus goes. Although I had prepared numerous questions on divorce, most informants talked about it in remarkably similar ways, even when they expressed different opinions about it in the abstract. For example, although many religious conservatives oppose divorce for religious reasons and many secular liberals support it because it provides an individual with a new chance at happiness, they shared the same understanding of divorce as failure—something regrettable, something to be avoided by hard work if at all possible, but a safety valve that should be available when other options have been exhausted:

Q: How do you feel about divorce?
A: That's touchy. I believe that it grieves God. I believe it was not his plan. I believe that people get into marriage, some people get into

marriage, looking for something and thinking that marriage will fix it, and when they find they don't, they realize they've bitten off more than they can chew and they may get themselves in an abusive situation, and I do not believe that God wants anyone to be in an abusive situation. And in those cases, I believe he's more concerned for their well-being and he can cover any failures in your life, even divorce. (Dana, forty-eight)

Q: How do you feel about divorce?

A: Mm, I mean I don't like it, but if you know, you're in a marriage and you just can't, you've tried every single thing, every you know, like if you've gone through therapy and you've tried to work out your issues, and if that still doesn't work and you're just feeling unhappy, then I mean, yeah, I guess divorce is the next, next way to go. But people just, you know, it feels like people don't even try anymore. Like they just, like I said, it's so easy to get, you know, that little paper saying that you're divorced and you can just do whatever you want. So people take advantage of it. (Natalia, twenty-two)

Dana, an older conservative, expresses her religious opposition to divorce before justifying it, while Natalia, a younger liberal, expresses her tolerant support of it before condemning it. Divorce was a necessary evil for most of my informants.

Another manifestation of the cultural consensus on marriage can be seen in their regard for media representations of marriage. Almost all informants said that marriage was portrayed in an unrealistic manner, if it was portrayed at all. Whether the media romanticized and glorified or trivialized and degraded it, my informants agreed that they fail to represent marriage accurately:

I think it's not portrayed very well . . . I think a lot of times people kind of make fun of it, or you know, they make it seem like, "Oh, you're married, your life sucks, you know, it's so much more fun to be single and do whatever you want." And then I also think that they tend to kind of raise your expectations of it at the same time. Like, I think people get married and they expect for everything to be perfect and, you know, to have a great

sex life and a great romantic life and great friendship, but I think people
don't realize that that's really not how reality works. (Carolina, twenty)

Carolina's comments articulate the conventional wisdom that marriage
is in trouble and that the mass media are partly to blame for its current
problems. Of course, this popular imagination of "the media" is itself a
cultural construction, but whether or not it is really true is beside the
point: the fact that almost all informants spoke about the media like
Carolina testifies to a common understanding of what marriage means
in our society.

Does the cultural consensus extend to how Americans talk about sex
in marriage? This question matters because the role of sex in marriage
affects the gay marriage debate in two ways. First, marriage has historically provided an important institutional context for procreation, but
procreation became less central to the idea of marriage throughout the
twentieth century. Second, the issue of sexual attraction matters for marriage because some opponents argued that there was no reason to allow
gay marriage since lesbians and gays could already marry people of the
opposite sex. Thus, the extent to which procreation and sexual attraction
to one's partner are essential to our understanding of marriage makes
the prospect of gay marriage more or less logical.

When I directly asked eighty-four of my informants how important it
was for a married couple to have children, only seven (8 percent) said it
was important, without any qualification—and then only three of those
seven insisted specifically on heterosexual procreation. The overwhelming majority (77 percent) of informants said that having kids was unnecessary, that it was a personal choice, or that it was okay if a couple did
not have kids. Sheila's comments are typical:

If you don't want to raise children, then you shouldn't. No one should
bring in a child because of pressure, because, um, they'll know it—that
they weren't wanted or whatever. And I think you both need to want children, and if one doesn't, then you have to get through it, because a child's
going to be affected. (Sheila, fifty)

Even informants who personally wanted to have children and believe
that having children would be important for their own marriage did not

want to insist that procreation is important for everyone. Both on this issue and on other matters, like the role of religion in marriage, the overwhelming sentiment expressed was pragmatic: every person and every relationship is different, so different marriages need different things in order to be healthy and successful. This pragmatic attitude toward procreation certainly does not disqualify lesbians and gays from marriage.

The same was true for people's views about sexual attraction in marriage: most people imagined sexual attraction to be essential to the notion of marriage and rejected the idea that one should marry someone to whom one is not sexually attracted. I explicitly asked eighty informants about how important sexual attraction is to marriage, and 65 percent of them said unambiguously that it was important or very important. Many others offered more nuanced responses—that it depends on the individuals, or that it was a good thing but that other things were more important—but only four people (5 percent) said that sexual attraction is unimportant.

People's talk about sexual attraction made it clear that most people understood it to be a characteristic that distinguished marriage from other kinds of relationships:

> Obviously if there is no flame, there's no, there has to be a certain amount of attraction to the person because obviously if you don't feel anything towards them, you know, what's the point of getting married to them? I mean, you have to like them both personality wise, but also physically to some extent. (Chris, twenty-two)

> I don't think anybody's going to be interested in the relationship if they're not attracted to the person. I personally couldn't ever marry somebody that I didn't, I wasn't attracted to. It's, it just freaks me out. Like the idea of the arranged marriage? Oh, that would kill me. (Gina, twenty)

The comments from Chris and Gina show that the American cultural understanding of marriage—based on a companionate marriage ideal that renders procreative and arranged marriage ideals as deviant—includes sexual attraction as an essential ingredient. Some informants even added religious justifications to this cultural understanding of marriage in order to explain why they thought sexual attraction is important:

> I think it's important, because otherwise, why not just be in a friendship with the person? I think marriage is just, kind of, I'm quoting something, but I've heard someone say it's friendship on fire. Um, it has that element of passion and sexual attraction that aids in two people being close with each other. And I could go at it from a biblical perspective, too, and say that, you know, once two people have engaged in sexual activity, they become one flesh. According to the Bible, you know, they become close with each other, develop that lifetime bond. So it's important. (Hannah, nineteen)

Many people said that sexual attraction was important, if only at the beginning of a relationship, and that as people aged and the relationship changed, sexual attraction became much less important. But still, it almost seemed to go without saying for my informants that sexual attraction played some role in starting and defining a marriage. To suggest that lesbians and gays who are attracted to members of the same sex should get married to members of the opposite sex, then, would be nonsense.

I also asked about the role of sexual attraction in marriage in a different way. After interviewing people about gay marriage, I asked those who were not opposed to it how they would feel about a marriage between two individuals of the same sex who were heterosexual and thus not sexually attracted to each other. The reactions of those sixty-one individuals indicate that they viewed mutual sexual attraction as essential to marriage: over one-third indicated that they found the idea absurd, either by laughing or by using terms like *weird, awkward,* and *stupid* to describe it. Many people seemed confused by the question and asked clarifying questions, and the most common opinion that informants expressed about the idea was to question why anyone would do such a thing at all. Richelle's response is typical:

> Okay, let me get this straight. There's two people, same sex, want to get married, but they're not attracted to each other? [*Yeah*] I'd ask them why they're going to get married then. If you're not attracted to each other, obviously you don't care for each other. Why are you getting married? That don't make, no, that wouldn't make no sense. Don't get married if you're not attracted to each other, have nothing in common, or anything else. (Richelle, forty-seven)

Although some people like Richelle rejected that kind of relationship as a marriage, almost one-third of respondents were willing to support the idea of a same-sex heterosexual couple getting married:

> I don't know. That happens in the heterosexual world all the time, so I mean, I don't think there could be much done to stop it. . . . I don't see why they would exactly, but I don't really see a problem with it. Like I said, it doesn't really affect me. If it's for something like insurance purposes, I don't blame them for trying to get it. I mean, I don't know. It's kind of weird. (Gina, twenty)

Gina was not the only person to observe that heterosexual couples already get married for reasons other than love, but some people interpreted this phenomenon—like people getting married for reasons of insurance or citizenship status—as trying to cheat the system:

> That's kind of a loophole. I think that's filthy. That's not love. Marriage is about love. That's a, they're obviously abusing the word *marriage* and the idea and concept of it and using it for financial reasons. . . . You know, if they're really close friends, they're already helping each other by sharing a flat or whatever. I think, yeah, that's kind of a joke. I wouldn't like to hear about that. (Trey, twenty-one)

Clearly, my informants view sexual attraction to be an essential ingredient to an authentic, true marriage—one that is more than a mere "piece of paper."

Although people reacted to my question in different ways, there was a common theme. The intent of my question was to "breach" one of the accepted social norms about marriage to see how people would respond, and the reactions of my informants confirmed that we do have an unspoken assumption that marriage implies sexual attraction. Just as most Americans have a hard time imagining arranged marriages in other societies that are not based on love, so too do they have a hard time imagining marriage without some implied sexual, romantic component to the relationship. Sexual attraction is one of those unspoken connotations of marriage, so the controversy over gay marriage cannot be written off by denying lesbians' and gays' feelings for their partners.

In sum, the ways in which my informants talked about marriage, apart from the contentious issue of gay marriage, were remarkably similar across lines of cohort and ideology. Beneath the explicit disagreement over whether marriage is a religious-exclusive-traditional institution or a civil-inclusive-modern one lies a shared imagination of what marriage means in practice. Not only are there clear similarities across cohorts about the meaning and important characteristics of marriage, but there is broad agreement that procreation is not one of them, though sexual attraction to your choice of partner is. In practice, Americans imagine marriage to be both a highly valuable form of social relationship and one that is adaptable to the needs, desires, and preferences of all different kinds of people; it is an institution whose imagined characteristics require no modification to accommodate same-sex couples beyond its narrow, legal denotation.

The Coming Reinstitutionalization of Marriage

The debate over gay marriage was shaped by generational change in the imagination of homosexuality and generational stability in the imagination of marriage. The lack of generational change in how Americans imagine marriage—not as it is legally defined, but as it relates to our everyday lives—provided lesbians and gays with both a cultural justification for why they would seek the right to marry in the first place and a firm institutional position within which gay marriage could be fit. The elements of the intergenerational consensus about the social connotations of marriage that I describe above mark the contours of the position that gay marriage now occupies within the institution.

Marriage used to be a bastion of *heteronormativity*—the ways in which social institutions and social interactions assume, privilege, and perpetuate heterosexuality as normal and natural in society. Now, marriage is a bastion of both hetero- and *homonormativity*: both opposite-sex and same-sex couples are included.[23] Because of our cultural consensus about what marriage means for people's everyday lives and relationships, the institution required no cultural revision to open it to lesbians and gays. The legalization of gay marriage, therefore, elevates homosexuality to the level of a normalized, institutionally recognized sexuality, though still not equal with heterosexuality and perhaps at the expense of transgender, queer, and nonbinary sexualities.

Paradoxically, the legalization of gay marriage may challenge social scientists to rethink the future of the institution. Back in 2004, Andrew Cherlin argued that marriage in the United States was going through a process of *deinstitutionalization*—meaning that the cultural consensus about the norms, meanings, and practices relating to it as well as its overall importance to American society were weakening. As evidence, Cherlin cited the rise in the divorce and cohabitation rates, the rise of out-of-wedlock births, and the controversy over gay marriage. Looking toward the future, he predicted that marriage would never "re-institutionalize"—that is, regain the strength that it had as a social institution in the early twentieth century.[24]

Although I agree with Cherlin that we will never go back to the past, I do think it is possible to go back to the future. This chapter presents some evidence that the case for the deinstitutionalization of marriage may have been overstated. The marriage of the twenty-first century will certainly not look like the companionate or procreative marriages of previous centuries, but there certainly appears to be an intergenerational consensus about the place of marriage in American society. Marriage may, in fact, be in the process of *reinstitutionalization*—now with homonormativity and gender equality.[25]

The re-institutionalized American marriage of the twenty-first century is open to any couple, regardless of sex or gender; it is one where egalitarian gender ideologies work just as well as traditional ones; and it is still valued symbolically, legally, and politically, more than other family arrangements, even though it remains one option among many for forming families.[26] The reinstitutionalized marriage may not be the institution that organizes sexual activity, reproduction, or the generational social contract, to the extent it did back in our great-grandparents' days; but it does remain important to all of those things, and it continues to provide the cultural ideal for individuals who aspire to long-term, loving, committed relationships together.

If anything, the opening of marriage to same-sex couples will likely increase the value and importance of the institution to American society. Making marriage less exclusive has the potential to increase the numbers of people who marry, who aspire to marry, and who reap socially prescribed benefits from marriage. Although in economics the value of a good is directly proportional to its exclusivity, marriage is not a commodity to be bought and sold on the market: its value comes not from scarcity, but from the cultural, legal, and political arrangements in society that grant privileges to those who opt in. Allowing lesbians and gays to opt in might have cheapened the institutionalized marriage of the nineteenth century, but the generational change in attitudes that I document in this book means that the twenty-first-century reinstitutionalized marriage probably will be revalorized instead.

This raises the question of whether or not American marriage in the twenty-first century will be *consensually* inclusive: will the idea that marriage can be between any two individuals, regardless of sex or gender, become part of a new cultural consensus about the social connotations of marriage, or will it remain part of the contested denotation? Will gay marriage ever be universally accepted? The next chapter provides the likely answers to these questions by examining the "exceptions" to the main pattern of generational change documented in the rest of this book—by considering why some members of each cohort are immune or resistant to the dominant social imagination that characterized the society in which they came of age.

7

Narratives of Attitude Change and Resistant Subcultures

One of the staunchest opponents of gay marriage I interviewed was a twenty-year-old student named Taylor. When I interviewed him at his campus student center, he wore a green Aéropostale shirt and blue jeans; he was heavy-set, sported shaggy brown hair, and had slight brown stubble on his upper lip and chin. He looked young, and he came across as unassuming and calm, but his rhetoric was anything but.

He was almost comically anti-gay. He said the kinds of things that you might expect to hear in a satire of homophobia, but he was not joking. For example, when I asked him what effects legalizing gay marriage might have on society, he didn't just slide down the slippery slope; he raced down it:

> If we allowed gays and lesbians to get married, like our society would become pretty much a society to where you could do whatever you want. Like where would we stop then? I mean, it's like if we legalize marijuana, I mean, what's to stop us from legalizing heroin? Or let's just do wrong things and get away with it. Or like prostitution, I mean, wouldn't we allow prostitution then, I mean if it makes people happy? I mean, if people are getting married, and they are the same sex, I mean wouldn't we just allow . . . everything then? I mean, where would be the point where we would draw the line? . . . If I can marry a boy, why couldn't I marry a cow?

It would not surprise the reader to learn that Taylor's father shared his opinions and that he identified as a religious conservative. It was clear to me when I was talking to him that he had learned this rhetoric from his religious community.

Conventional wisdom suggests that Taylor's homophobia was born out of ignorance: that he never knew anyone who is gay, and that if he did, he would become more tolerant.[1] But in Taylor's case, this would be wrong. Instead, Taylor's homophobia had been reinforced by his personal encounters with gay men. When I first asked him about gay marriage, he immediately brought up these negative experiences:

> I know that Massachusetts, I think, you can get married there in Massachusetts. I don't like the fact that you can do that. And so whenever anybody ever tells me that they're married I'm like, "No you're not. You're only married in Massachusetts. You're not married here." Cause I had an old boss who was married to a guy. [*Really?*] Yeah. I didn't even know that, like, I didn't think he was gay until I started working there. And it was really weird cause I didn't think that the place I was going to work at was all gay guys and two straight girls. I didn't know that.

After inquiring further, Taylor explained that being surrounded by gay men at work was uncomfortable for him:

> I felt weird and out of place because I've never worked with so many gay guys before. Like I've worked with one or two, where they're the minority. But I was the minority now, and they had these little things where they always had like their inside gay jokes. . . . All the gay guys there were very moody. Like sometimes they'd be happy and other times they'd be like real crabby and "Oh no you didn't." and I'm like, "I didn't do anything." And so that's why I got fired, because there was just too many times like that where they were like really moody and I didn't do anything wrong.

It is easy to imagine a situation in which someone might be fired for being a bad fit in the workplace. The fact that Taylor was relatively oblivious to how his own personality likely contributed to this conflict nevertheless does not change the outcome. The raw, unreflective animosity toward gay men that Taylor expressed was unusual among my informants.

What makes Taylor's case sociologically important is that there are millions of young Americans like him who are just as opposed to gay marriage as their elders, despite the fact that they know and have encountered many lesbians and gays in their lives. Likewise, there are millions of older Americans who are just as supportive of gay marriage as their young, liberal counterparts. People like Taylor do not fit the generational narrative advanced so far in this book, and these exceptions appear to undermine generational theory as a whole. Can generational theory account for the fact that so many people are out of step with their cohort?

In this chapter, I analyze the exceptional cases—the young opponents and old supporters of gay marriage whose discourses do not fit the main pattern described in the rest of the book. In particular, these exceptional cases embody three main challenges to generational theory. After explaining them in theoretical terms, I turn to a conceptual framework in the sociology of knowledge that can help us make sense of how people can hold worldviews that are out of step with those of their mainstream counterparts. After analyzing their discourse, I argue that these individuals are exceptions that prove the rule: they actually strengthen, not weaken, the explanation that generational theory provides for the rapid increase in support for gay marriage in the United States.

Back to the Generation: Attitude Change, Period Effects, and Resistant Subcultures

As we saw in earlier chapters, the influence of generational change on how people talk about gay marriage appeared because of how their imagination of homosexuality interacted with their political and religious ideologies. The students who imagined homosexuality as an identity articulated discourses of unambiguous support or immoral inclusivity, depending upon whether they were secular liberals or religious conservatives. Similarly, the parents who imagined homosexuality as a behavior articulated discourses of libertarian pragmatism or unambiguous opposition due to the same ideological impulses. I have argued that these cohorts imagine homosexuality in those ways because they reflect the cultural understandings of homosexuality that were dominant during the periods in which they came of age.

So far, this story fits the generational change narrative closely: old people keep the views they developed in their formative years, and young people are oblivious to the past. However, this simple account is incomplete. It perpetuates the stereotypes of young and old, and it ignores both the old liberals who are just as supportive of gay marriage as their younger counterparts and the young conservatives who are just as opposed to gay marriage as their elders. This more complicated picture presents three significant challenges to generational theory: the reality of attitude change among older adults, the presence of period effects (not just cohort effects) in public opinion, and the insulating effects of resistant subcultures all apparently limit the power of generational change.

First, the fact of attitude change among older adults challenges generational theory because it includes an assumption that the attitudes formed during a person's impressionable years will be durable and resistant to change over time—in other words, that the cohorts will carry their distinctive worldviews with them as they age. By contrast, both period effects and age effects are characterized by intra-cohort attitude change. Thus, if older adults are changing their attitudes about gay marriage, this weakens the argument that cohort replacement is responsible for the change in public opinion.

The persistence hypothesis—that attitudes formed while coming of age persist across the life course—has been documented and confirmed in many cases, but it is not a universal law.[2] In fact, some scholars have shown that attitude change among elders is much more common than we usually think.[3] But the reality of attitude change does not mean that the persistence hypothesis is wrong; instead, the durability of our worldviews depends upon which aspect we are talking about. Some beliefs are easily changed—for example, because they are subject to factual correction (Pluto is not a planet) or because we have not built social identities around them (vegetarians would be more resistant to learning that eating meat is good for your health than nonvegetarians)—while others are much harder to change (as a child of the eighties, I will always believe it to be unsafe to go for a bike ride without my helmet).

The second, and related, challenge to generational theory is that attitude changes show up in public opinion data as period effects, which pose a challenge to generational theory because they compete with cohort effects as explanations for change in the data. If a period effect occurs at the same time as a cohort effect—as it did with gay marriage—then the fact that older Americans are becoming more supportive over time means that the distinctive views of young cohorts account for less of the change in public opinion.

As described in Chapter 3, this might be a problem from a quantitative perspective, but not from an interpretive perspective. The same historical and social changes logically affect people differently, depending on their stage in the life course: they would cause young cohorts to develop distinctive worldviews while causing older cohorts to question their prior assumptions and recalibrate their moral and attitudinal dispositions. For example, if an event like the terror attack of 9/11 caused Americans of all ages to increase their level of patriotism, this could be a period effect that wears off over time for older Americans and a cohort effect that endures for young Americans who came of age at that moment. If there were such a shift in public opinion, it would not be wrong to interpret the period effect as part of the process of generational change. Therefore, neither the presence of period effects in public opinion data nor attitude change among older cohorts necessarily undermines the theory of generational change.

Third, generational theory must contend with the sheer cultural complexity of contemporary societies, which includes the presence of resistant subcultures that are either different from or entirely opposed to the mainstream culture of a society. Generational theory assumes that young cohorts are influenced by the Zeitgeist, but it is relatively silent about the fact that cultures are not monolithic wholes; they are instead internally fractured, multiple, inconsistent, and changing. Simply put, in every era, there are extensive networks of dissenters, outcasts, and deviants of all stripes, and if you come of age in one of those subcultures, you are unlikely to exhibit the characteristic mind-set of "your generation."

As discussed in Chapter 1, part of our solution to this problem lies in the distinction between what Mannheim called the "generation location" and the "actual generation" (or social generation): not all members of a cohort are alike, and it takes a certain kind of experiential encounter with history to make one a part of the actual generation. In this chapter, we see further evidence of the importance of this distinction: today's young religious conservatives are just like the liberal activist youth of the 1960s in that they are immersed in social networks who imagine homosexuality in ways that are out of step with dominant culture. Generational theory allows for the fact that a given society contains widely disparate subcultures that are situated and animated within networks of like-minded peers; we just have to explicitly state the exclusions and limitations of our story of social change. Who is part of the cohort but not part of the generation, and why?

Glaeser's Sociology of Understanding

The work of social theorist Andreas Glaeser offers a rich framework for working through this challenge. In particular, his book *Political Epistemics* advances a "sociology of understanding" that is compatible with the theory of social imagination advanced here, and it is based on a case study of the worldviews of East German Stasi (secret police) officers both before and after the collapse of the Berlin Wall.[4] The effects of a unique historical period (the collapse of communism), the question of attitude change (or the lack thereof), and the unique mind-sets of resistant subcultures (the Stasi) are all part of Glaeser's case, so it provides a model for analyzing the challenges that these factors pose to generational theory.

Glaeser is interested in how people understand the social world—the kinds of understandings that exist and how they are either supported or challenged by people, ideologies, and experiences in the world. He argues that it is through processes of validation that understandings are either reinforced or undermined. Glaeser identifies three types of validation: *recognition* comes from interactions with other people and the extent to which they share the same understandings; *corroboration* comes from the consequences—positive or negative—of our actions in the world based on a given understanding; and *resonance* comes from the compatibility or incompatibility of a given understanding with the rest of our belief system. For example, if I understand homosexuality to be a deviant behavior, that understanding will be validated to the extent that my social networks, experiences, and ideologies affirm this understanding, and it will be challenged to the extent that they do not.

Glaeser's analysis of his case shows that, even as the flaws of East German socialism were becoming all too obvious to everyone and increasingly fatal to the entire socialist experiment, the Stasi officers and other party officials failed to comprehend them. They were not oblivious to the flaws and shortcomings; rather, they misunderstood them (misinterpreted them, I would argue) because of their immersion in Communist Party social networks, their adherence to the party's official ideology, and the fact that their positions as members of the secret police skewed their experience of East German society. Each type of validation reinforced the other, making their misunderstandings of the problems facing East German socialism so impervious that it took the sudden, complete collapse of the state to get them to realize it.

Although all social and political understandings, whether mainstream or deviant, can be analyzed by tracing these "dialectics of validations," Glaeser's framework is especially useful here because it can help us understand the deviant cases—the worldviews of those older liberals who are just as supportive of gay marriage as their younger counterparts and of those young conservatives who are just as opposed as their elders. For these groups, we can analyze how their social networks, ideologies, and experiences with lesbians and gays created attitudes about gay rights and gay marriage that are or were out of step with the mainstream at a particular point in time. But not all older liberals who support gay marriage have always supported gay rights; some tell stories of attitude change that give clues about the mechanisms of social influence that can cause people to change.

In the end, I argue that the analysis teaches us new lessons about Glaeser's sociology of understanding and about generational theory. With respect to Glaeser's theory, the data show that the processes of validation—recognition, resonance, and corroboration—do not just happen; they result from active processes of interpretation. It takes work to create and to change understandings, so no personal encounter, ideology, or evidence will automatically result in a particular understanding. For example, as we will see, intimate personal contact with lesbians and gays can either lead to attitude change or not, depending upon the "interpretive community" in which individuals live and depending upon how much they rely on a given ideology to help them interpret that personal contact.[5] The resistant subcultures in this chapter, then, function effectively as interpretive communities that provide their members with the cognitive and cultural resources to defend a preexisting understanding of homosexuality; by contrast, the parents who change their attitudes about gay marriage are more open to reimagining homosexuality on account of new encounters and experiences.

With respect to generational theory, this chapter shows that the attitude changes, period effects, and resistant subcultures that appear to contradict the theory are actually part and parcel of it. In other words, we should actually *expect* to see these "exceptional" cases in the process of generational change because the forces that are powerful enough to cause it are rarely felt only by a single cohort or a single interpretive community.

Bulwark of Opposition: Orthodox Interpretive Communities

Only 9 percent of the students I interviewed unambiguously opposed gay marriage, but the discourses of those six individuals hold important clues about the future of the opposition. They suggest that, even as cohort replacement causes support for gay marriage to become increasingly widespread in the population, there will eventually be a "ceiling effect" where support for gay marriage levels off. This is because religious conservative networks form the basis of a resistant subculture that is relatively immune from the secularization of American society—and even thrives from it.[6] People immersed in orthodox subcultures imagine homosexuality differently, interpret the rise of gay marriage as evidence of the moral decline of society, and therefore resist the generational change happening around them.

In Glaeser's language of validation, imagining homosexuality as deviant behavior *resonates* with the religious ideology that defines homosexuality as a sin. The power of this religious ideology was discussed in Chapter 4, and little else needs to be said about it, save for the fact that an orthodox religious worldview appears to be a necessary ingredient of opposition among young people. Without a strong orthodox ideology, my young informants would not have unambiguously opposed gay marriage; and as the discourse of immoral inclusivity illustrates, sometimes even the ideology wasn't enough. What appeared to distinguish young conservatives who oppose gay marriage from those who did not was in the realm of *corroboration* and *recognition*: young opponents interpreted their personal encounters with lesbians and gays in ways that were consistent with ideology, whereas conservatives who articulated middle-ground discourses reevaluated their ideology when their personal experiences contradicted it.

As with Taylor above, it is tempting to presume that young opponents have no personal contact with lesbians or gays. However, four of these six students reported having either a family member or a close friend who is openly gay, so only one student who opposed gay marriage reported *no* meaningful contact.

The students with gay friends and family members interpreted their contact in the framework of their religious ideology, which caused them to express feelings of both love and sadness about them: they believed that their friends and family members would suffer because of their sinful actions. For example, Hannah is a nineteen-year-old music enthusiast who attends a nondenominational church weekly and whose conservative identity is shaped by her faith; the story she told about a close friend coming out to her is indicative of this interpretive process:

> To me, it's a really sad story. Um, he was a singer in the [music] group that I played with, and it's really sad because he still identifies with Christianity as his religion. You know, he really loves God, but he just, he feels like he's struggling. Well, he wouldn't define it as, some days he defines it as struggling, some days he defines it as this is just who he is. But he is a homosexual who still identifies himself as a Christian. And um, we've known each other since probably about sixth grade. His church did stuff with my church, and so like, he's a really dear friend to me.

After I asked Hannah how she felt about his coming out, she said:

> It wasn't a surprise. Like I said, we always had suspicions. I was just surprised that he still, at times, wanted to justify it. That's what really surprised me. [*Like how does he try to justify it?*] By saying that sometimes he doesn't know, like he says that he prayed to, like, be rid of these feelings, but it never really happened, so maybe it's okay for him to be like that. And I disagree with that. I told him that it's probably because he really wasn't like surrendering his deep-down desires to God. So I don't think that he really did pray with a sincere heart about it. I think he just kind of said, "God, if I'm wrong, then take these feelings away." I don't think that's really the way to do it.

As Hannah continued her story, she did not accuse her friend of simply making a "choice" to be gay, noting that nothing about his personality changed when he came out. So to some extent, she takes for granted that he probably always has been gay, and she laughed that her boyfriend doesn't get mad when she hangs out with him on that account. Nevertheless, she still interprets his gay identity in orthodox terms, reasoning that her friend simply didn't pray hard enough to be rid of his homosexual feelings.

Hannah was not the only young conservative to rationalize and resist a friend's coming out. In a quiet booth at a modern, stylish McDonald's, Ron, age twenty, recounted the still fresh details of his friend's coming out to him only a week earlier:

> We were talking, I don't know, and he said, "I love you." And I didn't think anything of it, 'cause you know, I've had friends that say, "I love you, man. . . ." About ten minutes later, he was like, "You know, I meant that as a friend." And I was like, "I didn't even remember you saying it, but sure, yeah, I know." And then he's like, "I have something to tell you. I feel bad"—or I feel like, I don't know exactly how he worded it, but he felt, bothered him, I guess. And then he told me he was gay.

Ron explained that they were still friends and that he wasn't surprised by his coming out because other people had speculated about his orientation. Nevertheless, he discounted his friend's coming out like Hannah did, but on practical rather than ideological grounds:

> I told him, I don't think he's gay from what he tells me. . . . For jokes, I asked him what his porn percentage, or porn ratio was, and he said, "70–30 girl." And I was like, "It's not a hard decision; you're straight," you know. But the thing is he likes, he's attracted to them. He just doesn't like their personalities, their personal, like the way they act. And I said, "I just think you've had a poor experience with women, or girls; you haven't dated a woman. . . . I just think you're confused," you know. And now it's accepted to be gay, so more people are, I think, trying it.

Like Hannah, Ron reported having a close relationship with his friend when I interviewed him, and he also disbelieves that his friend is really gay. In their religious worldview, the fact that homosexuality has become more accepted in society merely increases the likelihood that people will "try out" a gay identity. So the fact that close friends and family members identify as lesbian or gay does not necessarily challenge their ideology; it reinforces it.

In many ways, religious ideology trumped all for these young conservatives. Even having a close friend come out to them failed to shake their religious interpretation of homosexuality or their opposition to gay marriage. To Ron, the fact that his friend reported a 70–30 "porn ratio" is *corroboration* that homosexuality is something that is freely chosen and able to be resisted; to Hannah, her friend did not offer up genuine prayers to not be gay, an interpretation of the event that *resonates* with her ideology. Finally, Taylor's negative experiences with his coworkers constitute *recognition* that homosexuality is indeed a sin that causes people to do bad things.

In contrast to the students who articulated a discourse of immoral inclusivity, these individuals found resonance, corroboration, and recognition in their real-world experiences with homosexuality that preserved their religious worldview. It was preserved in part because of their interpretive community: they were surrounded by family members, friends, students, and churchgoers who shared their ideology. In other words, the recognition that they created came not just from lesbians and gays whom they encountered, but also from the straight people who make up their social networks.

For example, Paul is a nineteen-year-old psychology major who is thoroughly immersed in conservative, religious networks: he attends a nondenominational church in Rockford with his family on Sundays and during the week for small group activities; he met his girlfriend there; he attended a private religious school through middle school; and although he transferred to a public school for high school, he reported that "most of my friends were outside of school through church" and from his previous school. The only gay person he reported knowing is a "friend of a friend," and when I asked him where he had heard about gay marriage, the first source he mentioned was "friends and family." Simply put, Paul's social life is dominated by religious conservatives, so it is no surprise that his social worldview reflects it.

Having such a firm grounding in religious networks empowered these students to stand up against the influence of secular society and secular culture. For example, Haley (age nineteen) attended a religious school throughout middle school and high school, and she reported being shocked when she started college:

My best friend, she and I went to our first class together and it was like a shocker. Like this isn't what I'm used to, they're not even in my age group, and the teaching curriculum is drastically different. I'm used to having the teachers that would pray with you at the end of each class or just willing to go with you that extra effort. And I remember our first class, the teacher said, "I don't care if you fail." And we went, "What? You don't care?"

When I asked her if she felt these different experiences in college changed her at all, she responded:

I think that it grounded me in what I already was. Like I feel so much stronger. And I'm so much more decisive about what I believe in and how I feel about issues, that if nothing else, I think it strengthened me in what I believed in.

Thus, it is not as though Haley and the other orthodox conservatives lacked exposure to mainstream society and culture; rather, their immersion in conservative networks gave them the power to resist secular influences.

In sum, these young religious conservatives oppose gay marriage unambiguously because their imagination of homosexuality is the same as their parents'. They live in a social world that is not very different from that of their elders, and their worldview is dominated by orthodox religious understandings. The shared ideology of their interpretive community causes them to interpret their experiences with lesbians and gays in a way that preserves the preexisting worldview, and as a result they are able to resist the generational change that affected the rest of their cohort.

Being Pro-Gay before It Was Cool: Subcultures of Inclusivity

The situation of many older liberals is analogous to that of young conservatives. Although some parents who support gay marriage reported that their attitudes had changed over the course of their life (more on that below), others could not remember (or did not report) a time in which they were opposed to gay rights. These parents were the products of a different counterculture—from the 1960s and 1970s—that advocated tolerance and support for all who are looked down upon by society.

Among the twelve parents who unambiguously supported gay marriage, seven reported that they have always been supportive of gay rights—or at least have not been opposed to them. On the surface, they appear to have little in common: they vary in age, religious background, and even political affiliation. But they all professed to having a long-standing moral belief that it is wrong to discriminate against people who deviate from social norms. For some, the source of this belief was ideological, while for others it grew out of experiences and personal contact with those who experienced discrimination firsthand.

For example, David was born in 1958 to a family of Catholic Democrats, and although he was too young to remember much about the Civil Rights Movement himself, he reported that the lessons he learned from his family were heavily influenced by the times:

> My parents, they just, back in 1968 or 1970, you didn't really talk about homosexuality; it just wasn't talked about. . . . But you had this understanding that you accept people for who they are. It's, you know, the content of their character, not the color of their skin.

When he went to college, he witnessed discrimination firsthand when his student newspaper, backed by student government, refused to run an advertisement for a gay rights group on campus. Ever since then, he reported having been supportive of gay rights.

Other older supporters grounded their views in their religious ideology or in larger moral principles. Ruth, a fifty-nine-year-old Jewish office worker, had been active in the women's liberation movement during college, and she justified her support for gay marriage in religious terms:

> It doesn't offend my religious beliefs or whatever. I think that any institution or any connections that bring people closer together are good. . . . As far as my religion goes, the important thing in the world is repairing the world. We call it *tikkun olam*, which means repairing the world. That is our obligation: making the world a better place, not fighting with people.

Ruth was not alone in interpreting gay marriage as a moral good because of how it fostered love between people. Karen, age fifty, also supports gay marriage for moral reasons. She repeated several times during

my interview with her that she has a "live and let live philosophy"—
something she attributed to her father. Her discourse was full of moral
reasoning: she rejected prejudice of all kinds as wrong, she thought it
wrong for people to impose their beliefs on others, and she emphasized
the importance of all individuals being able to live their lives as they
choose:

> I have several friends throughout the years that have been gay and I
> do believe in a live and let live philosophy. You gotta live your life for
> what you want it to be, not for what somebody else says it should be.
> And it irritates me when I hear prejudiced comments about minorities,
> about gays, about anybody who's different than the person making the
> comment.

When I asked Karen if she thought legalizing gay marriage would have
any effects on society, she responded affirmatively:

> I would certainly hope that one of the effects would be more understand-
> ing of others that are different, and that maybe it might have an impact
> as well on other prejudicial situations. Too often Americans look at other
> people and they see the outside shell, and they don't bother to get to know
> the people because that shell isn't matching their own. And it bothers me
> to know that people aren't valued based on what their shell says.

As Karen's comments indicate, the moral language that supporters
used was dialogically linked to their interpretation of the opposition.
Implicitly or explicitly, they characterized their opponents as morally
wrong for what they perceived as prejudice against lesbians and gays.

Last, most of the older supporters of gay marriage reported having
significant personal contact with lesbians and gays, but since most of
that contact came later in life, it appeared to reinforce, not cause, their
support for gay rights. Mary's experience illustrates this. Despite growing up in a Republican household, being in a family who opposes gay
marriage, and being fiscally conservative, Mary labeled herself "an inclu-
sionist" and was very vocal in her support for gay marriage. Born in 1955,
she came of age in the early 1970s in the hippie counterculture, and her
general tolerance for deviance seems rooted in that experience. When

explaining her views on gay marriage, she reported that her "best friend growing up is gay now" and that witnessing what she went through reinforced her worldview:

> Her life has been so much harder because of the stigma of being gay. And she even lives in California where supposedly they're more accepting out there. And I think, you know, that's just such a raw deal, you know—she's a nice person in every way, but . . . she's had a much harder life because of it. So for me, any time you exclude in any way, shape, or form, it's self-serving and against my spiritual belief.

Although Mary was unusual in reporting that someone so close to her came out as a lesbian when she was so young, she was typical among older supporters in that her personal contact validated a larger moral philosophy.

Counterintuitively, then, many older supporters of gay marriage have much in common with young opponents: both groups found strength to resist the mainstream imagination of homosexuality in the powerful moral ideologies that were valued by people in their interpretive communities. Their understandings of homosexuality were validated by their personal connections (recognition), their belief systems (resonance), and their interpretations of encounters with lesbians and gays (corroboration); so even when confronted with a culture that opposes it, their understanding remained the same. The big difference between the two groups, of course, is that American culture has finally caught up with the views of these older liberals, while young religious conservatives who remain staunchly opposed to gay marriage because of their immersion in orthodox religious communities are now being left behind.

Narratives of Attitude Change among Older Liberals

Not all older supporters of gay marriage claimed to have always been proponents of gay rights. Five parents who currently support gay marriage unequivocally explained that they have not always been tolerant of homosexuality and told stories about why they changed their minds. These narratives of attitude change cannot be interpreted as literally true because our memories and the stories we tell always morph somewhat to serve our present purposes or fit our current self-concept. Yet, these stories nonetheless provide insights into how and why older cohorts come to change important aspects of the worldview they adopted when they were younger. We can see evidence of all three types of validations in these stories: personal contact with lesbians and gays, evolving belief systems, and changing life experiences all caused them to change their minds about homosexuality.

Unsurprisingly, contact with lesbians and gays was one of the most prominent themes in parents' stories of attitude change. Because these parents came of age during the sixties and seventies, when relatively few lesbians and gays had come out, they can easily recall a time before they knew anyone personally who identified as gay; but as coming out became more common, they began to meet gay men and lesbians, and the issue of homosexuality became personalized for them. For example, Bonnie, age forty-six, contrasted her ignorance when she was younger to her attitudes now, which she attributed to her children:

> I didn't even know [homosexuality] existed until I was hit upon by a woman, and it just blew my mind because I didn't know what the heck was going on. And I was appalled, but that's because it was like an experience out of the blue that I didn't know would ever exist, you know. As I got older, you know, and as my kids grew up, I got a lot more accepting of it because they had a lot more homosexual friends, and actually I've gotten along with every one of them I've ever met better than a lot of the straight friends.

Bonnie's case appears to be one in which children resocialize their parents: by exposing Bonnie to their gay friends, her children taught her to be more tolerant and supportive of gay rights. She also seems to have sought out new knowledge about the issue as well, because she reported that her views about homosexuality's attribution have changed, too. When I asked her if she thought people choose to be gay, she responded:

> No, not at all. I used to think that at first. I thought there was something mentally wrong with them and they just did that because they were like being the ultimate rebel. But no, now I don't believe that at all. I've

educated myself a little bit more on it, and I know that, no, it's not by choice. I know there's a lot of gay people that choose to try not to be, and that's very harmful to them mentally and probably physically, too. No, it's definitely in your body, in your mind, in your hormones, whatever.

Strikingly, Bonnie seems to have learned enough about homosexuality that she flips my question around: not only does she reject the premise of the question—that people choose to be gay—but she argues instead that the element of choice causes lesbians and gays to try to deny their true feelings.

In addition to personal contact with lesbians and gays, change in a person's broader ideology also appears to be a reason why older adults' attitudes can change. Laura, age forty-nine, is very supportive of gay marriage, and her response to my initial question about gay marriage did not give even the faintest whiff of legitimacy to the opposition:

I'm very pro–[gay marriage]. You can't tell someone how to love. And I don't think that because two men want to get married that makes them unhuman. How do you label affection, caring, and love just by body parts? I do not think so. I'm very pro. Marry who you want to marry.

Laura has not always felt this way, though. She was raised Catholic, but she reported having undergone a spiritual transformation, which caused her to reject the labeling of different sexualities and adopt a totally different way of thinking:

My sexuality is just me. It doesn't have a label. . . . If I want to say it has a label, it has my label, it has my imprint on it. And it may be totally different from that other person's imprint, but if that sexuality wants to get together with my sexuality, then there's an exploration there of everything we have together. . . . It's just two souls coming together.

If that sounds a bit new agey, you are not far off. She attributed her change in attitude to her exposure to alternative spiritualities. Despite that change, she acknowledged after my questioning that the negative moral judgment of homosexuality that she learned as a young Catholic has stayed with her:

Q: Do you think that there are particular elements of sexuality that you would describe as right or wrong? . . . To draw an analogy to the Christian upbringing, right, that being raised a Catholic, you were taught that homosexuality is wrong . . . I'm wondering if you have feelings about right and wrong in terms of the way you think about sexuality.

A: I think I did more before because of how I was raised. You know, because I'm, I remember I used to think "Oh, that's wrong," but that was somebody else's idea planted in me. And so now I try not to think that way. And I'm not going to lie, it comes up. You know, but I tell myself, "Whoa, I can't be the judge of that."

Thus, despite the fact that Laura was one of the most emphatic supporters of gay marriage I interviewed, she acknowledges that her old worldview still haunts her. But her current support for gay marriage comes from a much larger shift in her ideology, rather than from a specific incident.

Finally, apart from personal encounters and shifting worldviews, some informants attributed their support for gay marriage to the simple accumulation of life experiences and the new perspectives that they gained as they age. For example, Natalie, born in 1948, was one of the oldest informants I talked to, but she supported gay marriage for many of the same reasons that young students did: she was critical of religion, she dismissed opponents as closed-minded, and she asserted flatly, "gender doesn't matter to me; it shouldn't make any difference." But she has not always been supportive of gay rights; in fact, she recalled having very negative attitudes toward lesbians when she was younger:

I didn't like these dykey gals, you know. I was very much against it. It just, I guess the threat, or I don't know why. I just did not like it. But now, of course, my viewpoints are very much different. . . . [*Why do you think your feelings about it changed?*] Because I got to know the people, and they're actually, you know, human beings. It's not just sexuality. When I was going to college, everything was hormonal. You know, for me, as you get older, you lose that. I have lost that hormonal crap, and you look at the person as just, you know, a person, and you don't look at the sexuality. Just what do they have inside?

Natalie attributed her change of attitude to her maturation, especially the suppression of "that hormonal crap." Logically, if everyone became more tolerant about sexuality as they got older, this would be an example of an age effect, but there is relatively little evidence of that happening. In Glaeser's terms, Natalie might have become more tolerant of homosexuality if her experiences in the world increasingly failed to *corroborate* her understanding of homosexuality as deviant.

Not every parent who had undergone an attitude change ended up fully supporting gay marriage at the time of my interview with them; some appeared to be in the midst of a change. These parents ended up constructing some type of middle-ground discourse, but they included narratives of attitude change that closely resembled those above. The stories differ only in that they feel incomplete. They therefore offer further testament to the ongoing process of attitude change experienced by older adults.

For example, Gerald is a sixty-year-old Catholic, an enthusiastic Democrat who took liberal positions on almost every issue that I asked him about. Like David above, Gerald grew up in a liberal family and recounted stories of supporting African Americans during the Civil Rights Movement. However, he could not bring himself to totally support gay marriage:

Q: Would you be in favor of legalizing same-sex marriage?

A: I would struggle with it, my past. In theory, I would struggle with it, but I want to say, if that comes up in Illinois, I don't think we have voted on that issue yet. I think I would say yes. I would want to say yes. . . . That's the last remaining issue that I would struggle with. And that's based more on an old belief than where I want to be. You know, every decision you make in life isn't necessarily white and black overnight. You struggle with them.

Gerald was unique in how open he was about the fact that the moral values he grew up with were holding him back from being as supportive of gay marriage as he wanted to be. Gerald did not claim to have any friends or family members who identified as gay, but because he is involved in liberal political groups, he had met other lesbian and gay activists. Perhaps a more important source of his attitude change, though, is his work with people with disabilities. He reasoned analogically that society's resistance to accommodating people with disabilities was similar to its resistance to homosexuality. He remarked that gay marriage would be "the last sign of being whole and accepted" for lesbians and gays and remarked on the importance of accepting people who are different:

> In my life, I see friends love being the renegade, love being the Jimmy Dean, you know, "Yeah, look at me, you know, I'm pro-this and I'm the only one that thinks this way." And you love being the rebel. But after a while, you don't want to be the rebel. You want to just have, you just want to feel that when you sit down in a restaurant, someone doesn't stare at you, you know. That's the problem [facing] people with disability. . . . So I think that it's changed my opinion of people that are different for one reason or another.

Gerald's empathy for people with disabilities helps him imagine what it must be like to be gay, and he rejects the traditional Catholic teaching that homosexuality is wrong. Although he had not yet become a vocal supporter of gay marriage, it seems that it would only be a matter of time.

In sum, many older liberals reported changing their minds about homosexuality and gay marriage for various reasons. Unlike the older liberals who reported having always been supportive of gay rights, these individuals recalled a time when they thought about homosexuality differently and did their best to explain the discrepancy between their current views and their prior ones. Whether their narratives are literally true is less important than the fact that they are consistent with Glaeser's theory: they show how the dynamics of recognition, corroboration, and resonance can lead to new understandings of homosexuality and gay marriage.

Conclusion

The stereotype of young people as liberal, tolerant supporters of gay marriage is just as bad as the stereotype of old people as out-of-touch, bigoted opponents, and the voices presented in this chapter speak to that truth. In our study of generational change in public opinion about gay marriage, to ignore these people would be to perpetuate the stereotypes. Yet, they present us with a puzzle: how are we to understand the evidence of generational change presented in the rest of this book in light of the fact that so many young people are just as opposed to gay marriage as their parents and that so many old people are just as supportive as their children?

The presence of period effects in public opinion data, the reality of attitude change among older cohorts, and the presence of resistant subcultures all constitute direct challenges to generational theory. A reasonable critic might examine this evidence and reject generational theory as a social scientific explanation for the changes in public opinion about gay marriage. The generation concept may be intellectually stimulating, but as an explanation for social change it has apparent weaknesses.

If we equate cohort with generation, and if we fail to account for all the differences among people in the same cohort, thereby characterizing cohorts as monolithic wholes, then such a conclusion would be justified. But this book shows this to be an untenable position. Thinking carefully about the data presented in this chapter in light of the generational theory discussed in Chapter 1 shows that these apparent challenges to it are not fatal; indeed, they are presupposed by it. Considering all of the cases in which the pattern of generational change appears not to hold ultimately strengthens the theory as a whole. These are the exceptions that prove the rule.

Let's start first with the resistant subcultures—the old liberals who have always supported gay rights and the young religious conservatives who are just as opposed to gay marriage as their elders. If we equate cohort with generation, then these exceptions are clear evidence that generational theory is wrong. But a cohort is not a generation. What Mannheim called an "actual generation" is only a subgroup of a cohort, which raises the possibility that other subgroups of a cohort will fail to be influenced by the forces of generational change. This is exactly who these two groups of informants represent: older supporters of gay marriage during the 1960s and 1970s were just as out of touch with mainstream American culture and public opinion as young opponents are today. This should not be interpreted as a slight against either of these two groups; rather, these groups constitute resistant subcultures—networks of people who either consciously resist or unconsciously avoid the influence of the Zeitgeist.

As discussed above, Glaeser's sociology of understanding provides an excellent framework for analyzing how these resistant subcultures manage to sidestep generational change. These subcultures are, in effect, interpretive communities who find validation for their deviant worldviews all around them: in the people who surround them, in their ideologies, and in the corroborating evidence that they observe in the world. For older liberals, their personal contact with lesbians and gays, the lessons they learned from the Civil Rights Movement, and their broader ideologies of affirmation allowed them to maintain a pro-gay worldview during a period when less than 15 percent of Americans tolerated homosexuality. Likewise, for young conservatives, their immersion in networks of orthodox conservatives, their religious ideologies, and their interpretations of their contact with lesbians and gays allow them to maintain an anti-gay worldview during a period when tolerance of sexual diversity is the norm. Both groups bucked the cultural common sense of their times, and in doing so failed to be part of the actual generation that defined most of their age mates.

Now, what about the narratives of attitude change and period effects? The stories told by older supporters of gay marriage clearly indicate that the worldviews people develop while they are young are not set in stone. Even with respect to matters that we usually think of as deep and enduring—religious beliefs, views on gender and sexuality—people can and do change. This is problematic for generational theory, which presupposes some degree of attitude stability over the life course. If worldviews are subject to change, then any distinctive characteristic of a generation can dissolve over time. However, evidence of attitude change among older cohorts does not by itself mean that the hypothesis of attitude stability is false or that cohort differences would disappear. In reality, people of all ages change their opinions all of the time—but the people who change their attitudes in one direction are balanced by the people who change their attitudes in the other direction.

What is special about generational change, then, is not that no attitude change happens; it is that some significant event occurs that causes the balance to shift—such that people's attitudes start changing in the same direction. During such periods, older cohorts and middle-aged cohorts experience the shift as something that causes them to reconsider a previously settled matter. By contrast, cohorts who are coming of age experience the shift not as a shift at all, but as just the way the world is; the most naïve among them might even assume that the world has always been that way. Thus, both cohort effects and period effects can emerge from the same stimulus but affect people differently depending upon their stage in the life course.

These narratives of attitude change (and the period effects they indicate), therefore, should count as evidence not against generational theory but for it. One might reasonably be skeptical of any claim of generational change that was somehow strong enough to shift the fundamental worldviews of young cohorts who are coming of age but too weak (or too isolated) to affect anyone older. For example, just as much as older cohorts complain about young high school students' lives being dominated by social media, older adults are adopting the same technologies and are guilty of as many gadget-induced sins as the youth.

In sum, I argue that the period effects, the stories of attitude change, and the resistant subcultures in the gay marriage debate are consistent with expectations derived from generational theory. As long as we do not mistake the generation for the cohort, and as long as we distinguish the historical and cultural processes of generational change from the people who are affected by them, the analysis presented in this chapter provides additional insights into how and why public opinion about gay marriage changed so quickly across all groups in society. Moreover, the stories suggest some important limits to how much public opinion is likely to change: those who are immersed in orthodox religious communities are no more likely to begin supporting gay marriage as they are to change their views on abortion. Orthodox religious communities will continue to serve as a bulwark of opposition to gay marriage for the foreseeable future.

Unfortunately, the evidence of generational change presented here is merely a snapshot in time; to truly know whether and how much people's attitudes have changed, one would need to compare their views at different points in time. Nevertheless, as a snapshot, their views do convey a sense of direction and of momentum, of where people are coming from and where they are going. Moreover, the snapshot clearly depicts the cultural environment of the time and place. In 2008–2009, when these informants shared their stories with me, we were nearing the precipice of a dramatic change. Most people—including myself—did not know just how close we were to it, though we all perceived that we were moving toward it. The train of history was in motion, and people's voices indicate their thoughts about where we are, where we have been, and where we are going.

Conclusion

Moving beyond Generational Mythology

When you think into the future—twenty, thirty years, forty years, whatever,
down the road—do you think same-sex marriage will ever be legal in the
United States?

That was me back in 2008. Of the seventy-five people to whom I
asked that question, only three said no. A few said maybe, but almost
everyone—young and old, liberal and conservative, religious and
atheist—said yes.[1] Two things are interesting about this. One is just how
wrong my question was. When I first began this research, I figured I
would be able to make my whole career studying public opinion about
gay marriage and how it evolved over time; I had thought that giving
people a forty-year window to think about was reasonable. The last thing
I expected was that I wouldn't even finish this book before the issue was
settled—a mere seven years later. Indeed, the policy question animating
the book changed midstream from "Will gay marriage ever be legal?" to
"How did it happen so fast!?" I got left in history's dust, just like we all
will at some point or another.

The other interesting thing about this is that my respondents saw it
coming. Most of them didn't think it would happen quickly either; but
almost everyone saw the writing on the wall:

I'll never know, cause I probably won't be around. [laughs] I think that
it's inevitable, and once you go down that road, unless something drastic
would occur, you know, like Christians would get serious about their faith
and serious about disciplining, unless that happens, yeah, we're definitely
on that road and that's just a matter of time, whether it be ten, twenty,
thirty, or forty years. But I think definitely it's inevitable, because sin is

pervasive and it's kind of like cancer. You know, you have fast-growing cancer and slow-growing cancer, but eventually cancer wins out if it's not treated. (Stan, fifty-nine)

Yeah, I do [think it will be legal]. 'Cause I think about all the things that happened in the past, as far as like, you know, slavery and women's rights and things like that. We've overcome that. Yeah, it took forever, but it happened, so I think this is just another thing that it'll happen over time, you know. (Denise, twenty)

For religious conservatives, legalized gay marriage was a symbol of the moral decline of society; for secular liberals, it validated their faith in that famous quote popularized by Martin Luther King Jr.: "The arc of the moral universe is long, but it bends toward justice."[2] At the time, both my informants and I sensed that society was heading in the direction of gay marriage, as if on a moving train. It felt like slow movement, and at times it felt like it temporarily reversed course; but the overall trajectory stayed the same.

Generational change is that way. Because of the demographic metabolism—the continuous replacement of older cohorts with younger cohorts by death and birth—society is constantly changing. And when young cohorts come of age in a society that is significantly different from that in which their elders grew up, the accumulated worldviews and behaviors of the population change, too. To the extent that the worldviews and behaviors that people adopt during their formative years remain relatively stable throughout their lives, the distinctiveness of young cohorts accumulates until it reaches a critical mass. This is where that feeling of slow, inevitable change comes from. Of course, nothing is inevitable, but generational change is the engine of the moving train that propels society toward some unknown future.

By way of conclusion, I will first comment on the issue of gay marriage and its future. Although it seems unlikely that the legal status of gay marriage is going to change anytime soon—because of that engine of generational change—the political battleground on which the fight over gay marriage took place is changing in significant ways. Then, I will return to the problem of generations and explain three major lessons that we can draw from this book—lessons that can help us begin to solve the problem of generations. In closing, I will say a few words about why I think it is worth all the trouble to do so.

The Future of Gay Marriage

As of this writing, the future of gay marriage in the United States looks secure. This is true for legal, political, and generational reasons. Legally, eliminating gay marriage would be a multistep process across different branches and levels of government that, taken together, appears highly unlikely. It would require the US Supreme Court to first overturn its earlier rulings and then reject alternate legal rationales that could be used to argue that gay marriage bans are unconstitutional.[3] Although it is not uncommon for courts to overturn earlier rulings, this action would then require each state to determine whether or not to recognize gay marriages. And with every passing year, it becomes increasingly unlikely that states would reinstate their gay marriage bans, for both political and generational reasons.

Politically, we seem to have moved on. It was surprising that gay marriage was a nonissue in the 2016 election; if ever there were a moment for a nationwide backlash, it would have been during the first election after *Obergefell v. Hodges*. This is not to say that there was no backlash or resistance. In the ruling's wake, numerous state legislatures passed religious freedom laws that allow private businesses to refuse service to lesbians and gays, and the US Supreme Court agreed to hear a case on the limits of religious freedom in 2017.[4] Other conservatives turned their attention to the issue of transgender accommodations in public settings, capitalizing on fears of men entering women's restrooms to pass legislation that both targeted transgender Americans and restricted gay rights.[5] Although gay rights remain fiercely contested, a sustained, direct campaign to repeal gay marriage appears unlikely.

Because of generational change, and because we have no evidence that people are becoming more opposed to gay rights as they age, the proportion of Americans who support gay marriage continues to increase. The 2016 data from the General Social Survey show that support for gay marriage increased 2 percentage points over 2014 data. Similarly, in the two years after *Obergefell v. Hodges*, Gallup and the Pew Research Center measured an increase of support of 4 to 5 percentage points.[6] As the demographic metabolism continues to churn away, the gains of the gay marriage generation grow increasingly secure; it would take a significant change in how Americans imagine gay marriage to halt and then reverse the trend.

It is worth emphasizing too that the imaginary marriage consensus also bolsters the future status of gay marriage. Because both young and old generally agree on what marriage means in practice—that it is about love, friendship, commitment, and sexual attraction, but not procreation—the institution is unlikely to be altered significantly by opening it to same-sex couples. If anything, the opening of marriage to lesbians and gays should strengthen its status as an aspirational ideal for new generations: precisely because no one is excluded, the institution will more fully embody the inclusive values of young cohorts. Paradoxically, gay marriage may hasten the revitalization, not the demise, of marriage.

In essence, future Americans are likely to look back on this period of history and wonder what all the fuss was about. Because the social imagination of homosexuality shifted so significantly, young cohorts coming of age in a society in which gay marriage is legal are going to find it increasingly difficult to imagine a reason why anyone would have ever opposed it in the first place. This is the significance of the imagination: the logic of supporting or opposing gay marriage begins from fundamentally different starting points—different cultural schemas of homosexuality—and the opposing argument seems like nonsense if you cannot even understand the opening premise. Once upon a time, it was young people who supported gay marriage who seemed to be talking nonsense; in the near future, it will be the elders who are thusly judged.

That said, support for gay marriage probably never will be universal. As we saw in the last chapter, orthodox religious ideologies form a bulwark of opposition, and Americans in such communities are likely to maintain a vibrant counterculture against the mainstream acceptance of it. However, as gay marriage becomes a taken-for-granted fact of life to more and more Americans who never lived in a society without it, opposition to it will become increasingly confined to those religious communities that are most resistant to secular culture.

The legalization of gay marriage appears to mark the end of an era. This quarter-century battle in the culture wars appears to be over. The everyday significance of marriage has been affirmed, even as its legal definition has been fundamentally altered. In generational terms, did the Gay Rights Period, which began in 1993, come to an end in 2015? If so, what is the nature of the new period beginning in 2016, and how will the cohort coming of age during this new period imagine homosexuality, marriage, and the politics of gay rights?

It is still too early to know for sure, and the answer to this question will depend on what people do. After all, generations are not born; they are made. And they are made by young cohorts through interaction with each other, with other cohorts, and with the bigger constellation of social structures that surround them. Whether or not this new cohort will be more tolerant of other nonbinary sexual and gender identities is unclear. On one hand, the legalization of gay marriage has (perhaps unintentionally) reinforced the sexual binary between hetero- and homo-, and the fact that we imagine sexual orientation to be an inherent part of a person's identity may further marginalize people who identify as bisexual, transgender, and queer ("Aren't you just gay?"). On the other hand, the legalization of gay marriage might serve as a new analogy for future struggles: new generations may reason that we ought to be more tolerant of bisexual, transgender, queer, and other nonbinary identities, just like we became more tolerant of homosexuality.

Still another possibility for this new period is that little will change. Because lesbians and gays still do not have equal rights in many states when it comes to matters like employment and housing, the fight for gay rights may continue more or less unabated. Alternatively, gender and sexuality might be displaced from the forefront of American political consciousness as we contend with issues that become more salient, like economic inequality, global warming, and terrorism. If the conflict over gay marriage was indicative of the "post-materialist values" that become politicized in societies with relatively high levels of economic stability, people who face very real threats to their very "existential security" may simply stop caring about the politics of sexuality.[7]

Predicting the future is in many respects a fool's errand in the social sciences. Because of our free will and our ubiquitous irrational behavior, there are few general laws found in the social sciences that compare to the regular laws of the natural sciences. And yet, the study of demographic processes like birth and death, coupled with the insights of generational theory, allows us to be better forecasters than we otherwise might be. It is for these reasons that I will confidently make the very narrow prediction that gay marriage will be an integral part of American society throughout the twenty-first century. What happens beyond this is anyone's guess.

On Solving the Problem of Generations: Three Lessons

As for generational change, this book leads us to a more realistic way of studying and talking about it. In the academic community, in the media, and in society at large, what passes for discourse about generations today ranges from mildly deficient to egregiously wrong. Much of this is understandable, and maybe even inevitable: because of the intractable nature of the five key challenges of generational theory discussed in Chapter 1, it is difficult to scientifically analyze and account for the interconnected cultural, historical, and demographic processes implicated in the idea of generations. Nevertheless, this study reveals three major lessons for those who want to move beyond the generational mythology that dominates popular discourse and to take real steps toward finally solving Mannheim's problem of generations.

Lesson 1

Generations are not cohorts; they are cohort subgroups who respond to generational triggers and who make their own destiny. Therefore, we should devote our attention to understanding generational triggers and how diverse social groups respond to them.

The fundamental flaw in the mythology that drives how we currently talk about and conduct research on generations is the equation of cohort and generation: we treat all people who are born during a certain period of time—the cohort—as if they were all alike and therefore part of the generation. Social scientists fall into this trap to the extent that they consider cohort replacement a theoretical and methodological equivalent of generational change; we cannot pretend to measure generational change by measuring cohort replacement. In analyses of cohort replacement, the cohorts "count" only as empty vessels that are passively born and die at particular times; but the generations (and generation units) that emerge within cohorts are actively influencing each other and their elders. These groups and this type of social change can't be counted in birth rates and death rates.

This book has demonstrated that there is a significant difference between cohort and generation: a generation refers to those members of a cohort who share a common social and cultural exposure to specific historical conditions, which causes generational distinctions to emerge. Not all members of a cohort experience history equally; the generation refers only to those people whose lives are shaped directly by it and who contribute to the making of a new social world. This reality is complicated further still: even members of the generation differ significantly from one another in the ways that *generation units* respond to their shared experiences. Thus, a generation is composed of many distinct communities of people, each of which is defined simultaneously by the *same* sociotemporal encounter with history and *different* reactions to it. The four discourses described in Chapter 4, like immoral inclusivity and libertarian pragmatism, are indicative of generation units, while the "exceptions" described in Chapter 7 illustrate the more fundamental distinction between cohort and generation.

When we talk of people as a generation, then, we are attributing to them both an age and a shared experience of society, and despite the stereotypes that are associated with particular generations, those stereotypes would apply only to one generation unit within the generation, not to the generation as a whole (and still less to the cohort as a whole). For each and every generation unit that embodies a stereotype, there will be one that violates it—because all generation units respond differently to their shared experience, and the stereotype is, at best, only the expression (the *entelechy*, as Mannheim called it) of a single generation unit. The current rhetoric about generations that traffics in these stereotypes, therefore, is not just factually wrong; it is morally dangerous because it symbolically annihilates the experiences of other generation units and other members of the cohort.

Currently, the most flagrant example of all the problems with generational mythology is the rhetoric about Millennials—which is quickly being replaced by an equally vapid rhetoric about iGen (or Generation Z). Almost all academic and popular discourse about Millennials falls into the traps of the mythology just mentioned: it describes a cohort, not a generation; it fails to distinguish among different generation units; and the stereotyping of these young cohorts amounts to a kind of *generationism*, in which all young people are labeled and prejudged according to whichever stereotype a person holds about the mythical group. All of this might be a little more excusable if the cohort were even real in the first place; but the temporal boundaries of the Millennial cohort are completely arbitrary, have no meaningful historical referent, and are based on the pulse-rate paradigm of generations that has no defensible social scientific evidence to support it. Marketers and business consultants can make fortunes by convincing their clients that they do not understand young people, and indeed the profit that can be made is probably one of the primary drivers of the discourse. But in reality, the Millennial Generation is nothing but a crudely fabricated Rorschach blot onto which older cohorts project their anxieties about social change.

To begin to finally solve the problem of generations, then, we must first reject the pulse-rate view of generations as cohorts, including any and all discourse about Millennials, iGen, and the like—unless clear historical, demographic, and cultural evidence can be marshalled to document their existence as real, distinctive groups.[8] These discourses impede clear understanding of generational change because they are built on a theory of generations that is not just wrong, but also obfuscatory and misleading.

Once we do this, we can begin the much harder work of distinguishing the cohort, the generation, and the generation units, and charting their social dynamics. To do this, we should start by focusing on *generational triggers*: the kinds of events, trends, and changes that can cause generations to emerge from the cohorts who are coming of age. Logically, the imprint paradigm that guides Mannheim's theory is opposite from the pulse-rate paradigm: whereas the pulse-rate paradigm begins with the assumption that a new generation exists at a certain time and then looks for evidence to match it, new generational research should start by identifying possible triggers or evidence of generational change and then asking whether, why, and how a new generation emerged. For example, it would be pure generational mythology to characterize iGen as the generation of Digital Natives; but it is sound social science to examine the evidence and triggers that might cause a generation of Digital Natives to emerge, and then to seek to understand who is part of the generation and why.[9]

Lesson 2

The worldview of a generation is not vastly different from that of other cohorts or the fraction of the cohort that is not part of the generation. Therefore, we should conduct research and think more deliberately about how schemas, beliefs, attitudes, and other cognitive "stuff" relate in a more or less coherent way.

This lesson follows somewhat from the previous lesson. Whereas we are tempted to attribute to Millennials a vast array of beliefs, attitudes, and behaviors that are different from those of their elders, the imprint paradigm of generations suggests that a new generation would differ from their elders and from others only in minor, domain-specific ways that are caused by specific generational triggers. For example, there may be some overlap among the cohorts who came of age with smartphone technologies and the cohorts who came of age with an African American president; and some of those people may be Millennials. But there is no reason to expect those triggers to have the same pattern of effects on the same people in a way that would cause a generation's entire worldview to differ. Simply put, these are different generations, composed of different generation units, with different temporal boundaries, caused by different triggers, and characterized by different distinctive cognitive, cultural, and behavioral traits.

This book shows how precise one must be when specifying which aspects of a generational worldview are different and how they came about. In Chapter 5, I showed how different imaginary schemas of homosexuality, as articulated in metaphors and analogies, were at the root of cohort differences in attitudes about gay marriage; and these different imaginations of homosexuality were rooted in the historical periods described in Chapter 2. Notice that it is not every attitude, belief, value, or orientation about homosexuality that differed between the cohorts; the cultural schema of homosexuality varied independently of people's moral judgments about it. Moreover, Chapter 6 showed that there were no significant cohort differences in the imagination of marriage that were related to discourses about gay marriage. Thus, this book shows that generations are not distinguished by wholly different, irreconcilable worldviews; all it takes to make a generation is a *single* change in a *single* mental construct about a *single* topic.

This is not to say that this difference in the imagination of homosexuality is unrelated to other changes or that it could not have ripple effects throughout a person's worldview, but this possibility should be investigated, not assumed. For example, the sociologists Michael Hout and Claude Fischer have demonstrated the existence of generational change in Americans' religious identities, such that young cohorts are much more likely to identify as nonreligious.[10] It is highly plausible that this is related to gay marriage, such that these are just two manifestations of the same generational change. It is also possible that these changes are linked to a broader, more libertarian cultural shift that has caused people to become more sexually liberal and more supportive of marijuana legalization.[11] However, establishing this would require historical research, longitudinal data analysis, and cultural, interpretive research to determine whether and how such changes are part of the same generational process.

Future research on generational change should investigate the structures of people's belief systems in order to determine how something like a new generational worldview might cohere. New research methods in sociology are beginning to show promise in this area: by modeling belief and attitude statements as networks or by clustering groups of people according to patterns of attitude similarity and dissimilarity, we can see how strongly or weakly various cognitive elements are associated with one another among groups in a population.[12] When combined with research on the impressionable years hypothesis, this is a crucial step in determining the characteristics of a generational mind-set.

That said, it may be the case that the concept of a "worldview" is misleading to begin with. I continue to find it meaningful and important, especially in the context of generational theory, as it connotes the sort of taken-for-granted understandings of the world that young people develop during their formative years.[13] However, the label obscures more than it reveals. There is a lot of cognitive "stuff" that, taken together, makes up people's minds, and the idea of a worldview fails to differentiate among any of it. To speak of a generational worldview at all, then, may be part of the mythology.

Lesson 3

The time of generations is not chronological; it is not measured in years or decades and is neither a linear progression nor a repeating cycle dictated by phases of the life course. Instead, we should conceptualize generational history in terms of social time—how time is made meaningful by human behavior.

History doesn't just happen; history is made. People make the revolutions, wars, technological innovations, and economic booms and busts that cause new generations to emerge. This statement of the patently obvious nonetheless has counterintuitive implications for how we think about historical time and generational change.

In sociology, it is commonplace to observe that our units for measuring time are cultural constructions; yet, in the analysis of generational change, we oftentimes attach special significance to cohort birth years or to decades.[14] As Chapters 2 and 3 have shown, the temporal boundaries distinguishing one historical period from another are often ill-defined and span multiple years; moreover, the age at which members of young cohorts come of age varies, so it can be difficult to identify generational boundaries based on birth year. In reality, new generations are defined by the intersection of social-historical time and a particular type of "fresh contact" with society that is characteristic of late adolescence and early adulthood. Given the imprecision of these temporal influences, combined with the fact that new generations respond to human events, we must remember that our usual way of defining generations in chronological terms is at best an approximation.

Likewise, it is certainly not a novel idea that the history of humankind does not follow a narrative of ongoing progress; events both good and bad—progressive and regressive—can define generations. The common belief that each new cohort will be more progressive than the last reflects an optimistic hope more than anything else. The same is true for narratives of decline.[15]

The harder lesson this book teaches on generational time is that the cyclical model of generations—based on the life cycle and the demographic inevitability of birth, aging, and death—is also wrong. While it is true that generational change is *indexed* to the phases of the life course—as the coming-of-age process and the demographic metabolism of cohort replacement show—it is not *determined* by it. In order for coming-of-age processes and cohort replacement to create generational change, something else is required: the changes created by people and social institutions that cause young cohorts to imagine society differently than their elders. These changes are not inevitable, so neither is it inevitable that the succession of cohorts will also be a succession of generations.

The pulse-rate paradigm that generations emerge at semiregular or fixed intervals, like every fifteen years or every twenty-two years, is built upon this flawed premise. The most famous applications of this paradigm, which have attempted to explain hundreds of years of history as a product of this generational succession, incorporate additional fallacies.[16] Life expectancies, the ages at which people go through life course transitions, and the number and length of life stages that people go through vary significantly from one society to another and have changed drastically over time; so it is simply implausible that new generations emerge at fixed intervals of time over hundreds of years of history.

In reality, both historical time and generational change are manifestations of human activity. This book illustrates this fact clearly. Chapter 2 showed how changes in the social imagination were part of the larger political and cultural battles over gay rights and representations of homosexuality in the public sphere. There was no inevitable force guiding the evolution of our attitudes and understandings; instead, changes emerged from court cases, from social movement activism, and from the organizational and institutional changes in mass media. Additionally, the discourses of the gay marriage generation described in Chapters 4 and 5 show how young generations themselves make their own history. They are not passive vessels that are forced by history to move one way or another; they are active participants in creating the generational change.

Thus, social scientific research and popular discourse about generations should reverse the order of their first premises: it is not chronological time that defines social behavior, but social behavior that defines chronological time. Generations do not follow the flows of chronological time; they are a product of social time, and we must use chronological time as merely a convenient language for talking about generational dynamics. Everything that humans do involves time, but our language and theory of time should put human activity at the forefront.

This is not as abstract as it sounds. One way in which we already do this is when we consider short-term and long-term time horizons. The perspectives and consequences of human actions are what define these two different measurements of time. In our society, we often prioritize short-term thinking and its consequences over long-term thinking, but sometimes we accept immediate tactical defeats and setbacks in the interest of long-term strategy. In this book, many actions of the lesbian and gay movement seem as though they were oriented toward long-term generational change: for example, the coming out strategy that was pioneered first in the 1960s and later institutionalized in National Coming Out Day. As a short-term tactic, it was risky and painful: it brought significant social stigma and the possibility of personal harm on the individual. But as a long-term strategy, it succeeded in transforming relations between gay and straight America.

However, even if activists were targeting the minds of future generations in their strategies, how many of them would have wanted or planned for the transformation to happen the way it did? My interpretation of the history of gay marriage is that the pivotal moment in the battle happened between 1987 and 1992—years before the Defense of Marriage Act outlawed gay marriage, a decade before Massachusetts first legalized gay marriage, and over two decades before it was legalized in all fifty states. How many activists counted all of the defeats they endured along the way as part of their plan? Few, I suspect.

Because of cohort replacement, generational time tends to be long-term, slow, and gradual; the temporal pace of other kinds of social change that get our attention is short, fast, and dramatic. Because we usually explain why things happen according to their immediate antecedents, thinking about (or deliberately creating) generational change requires us to adopt a view of time that is sensitive to complex chains of events, long-term unintended consequences, and indirect or path-dependent causes of change. Thinking about time in human-centered ways can offer insights that we might otherwise miss if we fetishize calendar years and eighteenth birthdays.

Another example of the benefits of putting social behavior at the center of our concept of time can be seen in the work of historian Fernand

Braudel. Braudel is perhaps most famous for his concept of the *longue durée*, which we might characterize as the history of epochs and civilizations, but he also called for social scientists to think in terms of *conjunctures*—a medium-term unit of time that the concept of a generation exemplifies.[17] The periods and turning points described in this book are, in effect, particular configurations of human activity that are distinct from those before and after; but these conjunctures appear as only minor shifts in an otherwise stable world marked by the enduring social, economic, political, and cultural structures of the *longue durée*. Thinking about generations in terms of Braudel's theory of time not only helps us to properly historicize social events in multiple time horizons, but also helps us to ground our understanding of time in its social context. By contrast, measuring generational time primarily in years and decades obscures the social forces that truly define history.

There is a paradox, however, at the heart of generational time: generational change is a product of social time, not an automatic artifact of chronological time; but once it begins, it can escape human control and become an autonomous force. Chronological time amplifies social time: once generational change is set in motion, it takes on a temporal and demographic inertia—the power of cohort replacement—that resists human efforts to control it. Like Frankenstein's monster, generational change is a human creation, but it is animated by the cosmic forces of the universe: birth, death, and the ongoing march of space-time.

The reality of generational time, then, brings us to the frontier of where socially constructed, historical time meets biologically predestined, physical time. Just as we insist that generational change happens in socially constructed time, we must also insist that it draws much of its power from transcendent time—from time that predates and surpasses our social structures. We are not free to characterize generational change as biological and historical inevitability, but neither are we free to characterize it as a purely social construction.

In our future discussions of generational change, we should direct our attention to this messy frontier, where human-created social change meets the demographic metabolism. We would benefit greatly from more historical case studies of how human activity mixes and melds with the demographic rhythms of life to produce both intended and unintended changes in the worldviews, behaviors, and communities of people. Properly historicized studies of generational change can illuminate more fully the ways in which time and society mutually influence and constitute one another.

Generational Change: Powerful and Profound

Although we began this book with the problem of generations that Mannheim articulated almost a century ago, in truth concern with generational change goes back much further. Philosophers have long understood that there is something profound about the demographic metabolism—the ceaseless remaking of society through death and birth, combined with the forces of economic, technological, political, and cultural change. Auguste Comte, who was perhaps the first to make the case that there must be a science of society—a "social physics," as he called it—wrote in 1839 that "the chief phenomenon in sociology . . . [is] the gradual and continuous influence of generations upon each other."[18] Comte, like others who have dared to imagine a world without death, realized that society would become stagnant and ossified if social change slowed to a crawl.[19]

Generational change must be one of the most powerful and profound—yet least understood—types of social change there is.[20] Because death is inevitable and because birth furnishes society with fresh minds that comprehend the world anew, unencumbered by the habits, routines, and biases of the aging populace, the potential for widespread change is ever present. This does not mean that change is inevitable; through socialization and culture, the elders of society continuously mold younger cohorts in their own image, thus applying an equally potent brake on the engine of social change. However, technological innovations, historical events, economic changes, and political developments furnish young people in their formative years with unprecedented and unpredictable materials for cognitive and cultural sense making, which translate into worldviews and behaviors that are distinctive and new.

Beyond mere cohort replacement, then, we must strive to understand more completely the many and varied mechanisms of generational change that cause members of young cohorts to depart from the well-worn paths of life and habits of mind set out for them by their elders. Alternatively, we might adopt the opposite point of view: how, in the face of the seemingly omnipresent and overwhelming potential of change, does society manage to reproduce so much of itself over time?[21] Whether one adopts social continuity or social change as the point of reference, there remain many enduring mysteries about how different cohorts and different generations manage to remake the social world in predictable and unpredictable ways.

These questions are not merely academic ones; they strike at the heart of the social dynamism that causes every individual, at different phases of the life course, to question her place in the world—first as rebellion against the old and tired teachings of elders by young people striving to find themselves, and finally as the ponderings of aging seniors who cannot help but marvel at the differences between the current world and the one they hold in memory. The study of generational change is therefore of immense practical significance. Thinking seriously about this topic can help us more accurately understand our own positions in the currents of history, how each of us is but one individual among billions who are continuously being rocked by social currents that both transcend us and yet are made collectively by us. We owe it to ourselves to reject the generational mythology that continuously leads us astray and instead to delve more thoughtfully into the complex reality of generational change.

I am convinced that the endeavor would be worth our time and energy—much more so than when I first began this research. At the outset of this project, I had only the vaguest intuitive sense that something important was going on that caused my students to think differently about gay marriage. Ten years later, I believe that I am beginning to truly understand generational change. It works slowly, quietly, and in numerous ways through the vital connections linking history with culture, culture with cognition, cognition with interaction, interaction with social structure, and social structure back again with history. It works invisibly and imperceptibly within the deep structures of culture and through the schemas of the unconscious mind, but it also works visibly and obviously in both the mundane and the exceptional events of life. Every birth, every death, every new invention, every political upheaval, every "first"—all of them have the potential to change society in ways small and large, short-term and long. Solving the problem of generations can help us to finally understand how change happens.

ACKNOWLEDGMENTS

It has been an incredible privilege to write this book. It would be impossible to thank everyone who has supported me along the way, but some special thanks are in order. First, to the students and parents whose voices are found in this book, I learned a tremendous amount from you, and I am grateful that you took the time and effort to share your experiences and your view of the world with me.

Special thanks also go to Pam Oliver, Lew Friedland, Myra Marx Ferree, Mustafa Emirbayer, and Kathy Cramer. Collectively, you gave me the guidance and mentorship, the inspiration, the exhaustive criticism, and the advice and support that I needed to launch this project. Special thanks also go to the graduate students at UW–Madison: I could not have asked for a better set of peers who taught me so much and challenged me to work harder and smarter.

I want to thank everyone who helped behind the scenes to make the collection and analysis of my interviews possible: Evan Armstrong, Doree Brinson, Jim Brinson, Carrie Coetsch, Rachel Cusatis, Shelley Fite, Rachel Hart-Brinson, Bill Hollander, Daniel Kappel, Natalie Neals, Aaron Niznik, Lauren Olson, Maggie Phillips, ML Tlachac, and Rebecca Turcotte. Thanks to the University of Wisconsin, Northern Illinois University, and Rock Valley College for allowing me to carry out these interviews, and thanks to the National Science Foundation and the anonymous reviewers for supporting this research with a Dissertation Improvement Grant (MSN116987).

After graduate school, my faculty and staff colleagues at UW–Eau Claire and Grinnell College provided friendship, mentorship, and support to me as I worked on this book. In Eau Claire, my colleagues in Sociology have been more supportive of me than I deserve, and they are a model department for how to support junior faculty. I am grateful to my colleagues in Communication/Journalism for giving me the opportunity to indulge the communication and media studies part of my brain. This book would not be what it is without this cross-disciplinary engagement.

Also at UW–Eau Claire, I want to thank ORSP for their financial and intellectual support of my research. For the opportunity to get feedback on my ideas from stellar students and scholars, I want to thank the UWEC Honors Program, the UWEC Psychology Department, the Politics, Culture, and Society Brownbag at UW–Madison, and the Sociology faculty and students at the New College of Florida. Matt Desmond, Pam Forman, Kate McCoy, and Brian Powell also deserve special thanks for their encouragement, support, and collegiality.

At NYU Press, I want to thank Ilene Kalish for her guidance and oversight of this book's production, and Maryam Arain for her thorough answers to all of my questions. Thanks also to the reviewers for their careful reading and thoughtful feedback on earlier versions on this manuscript. In the publication of the scholarly articles that preceded this book, I want to thank the editors and anonymous reviewers for those journals, who helped me refine and clarify my understandings of gay marriage and generational change.

Finally, I want to dedicate this book to six people who have inspired this work, maybe more than they know: to my Mom and Dad, to Rachel and Matt, and to Jacques and Jack. In their own ways, intentionally or not, they taught me what marriage truly means and what the fight for gay marriage is ultimately about. As I have been so blessed in my life because of them and countless others, I hope this book contributes in some small way to ensuring that future generations will have those same blessings.

APPENDIX

Studying Public Opinion with Qualitative Interview Methods

When I first began this research, I knew just enough about the history and statistical evidence that existed at the time to hypothesize that public support for gay marriage was increasing due to generational change. What fascinated me most about the literature on generational change was the implied but unspecified role of culture in the creation of distinctive generations. So I decided to conduct interviews with two cohorts of Americans and listen for evidence of generational differences in how they talked about gay marriage. I wanted to find the cultural foundations of different cohorts' attitudes, as they expressed them in discourse.

INTERVIEWING
Selecting research participants and designing effective interview questions are essential to uncovering evidence of cultural influence in individual interviews. One cannot haphazardly talk to people and expect to identify cultural differences in how they view the world; instead, interview questions designed to tap into the typically taken-for-granted aspects of culture and a strong comparative method for analyzing similarities and differences are necessary.

I chose my research sites and sample selection method for the purpose of comparing two cohorts who differ in attitude about gay marriage but who are otherwise culturally similar.[1] I recruited students from two different colleges in a single metropolitan region, and once I completed an interview with a student, I asked for permission to contact one of their parents for an interview. This strategy would allow me to look for cohort differences between young and old while controlling (at least partially) for the influence of parental socialization.

I selected the northern Illinois region for my research site because it was close to Madison, Wisconsin, where I was living, and because gay marriage was illegal, but not unconstitutional, there—which made it a real possibility that gay marriage could be legalized there through judicial action. Northern Illinois was also attractive because it contains a cross section of rural to urban residential environments, with all the accompanying demographic diversity, and a shared regional culture. The people of Chicago, its suburbs, the midsized city of Rockford, and the countless small towns are diverse in terms of class, race, and political and religious ideology.

I chose a regional public university—Northern Illinois University in DeKalb—and a community college—Rock Valley College in Rock-ford—as recruitment sites. On each campus, I posted flyers on bulletin boards offering thirty dollars in exchange for an interview "about current social and political issues." I specifically mentioned "marriage, sexuality, family, and politics" as the topics of the interview, but I refrained from mentioning anything about gay marriage specifically because I did not want knowledge of my primary research objective to color the rest of the interview. In order to be eligible for the study, students had to be between the ages of eighteen and thirty (born between 1978 and 1990, members of the Identity Cohort) and have at least one parent between the ages of forty-five and sixty-three (born between 1945 and 1963, members of the Illness or Lifestyle Cohorts) living in the upper Midwest. Ultimately, I interviewed sixty-five students and thirty-two parents between September 2008 and April 2009. Demographic characteristics of the respondents are listed in Table A.1.

I prepared an interview guide to use as a general template for each interview. I began with basic demographic questions—easy questions to get informants talking. I then asked them about their life history—focusing especially on childhood, adolescence, and early adulthood—and their current media consumption habits. The heart of the interview contained a series of questions on marriage and relationships, same-sex marriage (the phrase I used in interviews), and homosexuality. I wound down each interview with a discussion of the 2008 presidential election. Each interview lasted between seventy minutes and three hours.[2]

For most informants, I asked the questions about marriage and relationships before the topic of gay marriage came up, so unless the infor-

TABLE A.1: Demographic Characteristics of Informants

		Students ($n = 65$)	Parents ($n = 32$)
Student's school	NIU	55	63
	Rock Valley	45	37[a]
Age (median)		21	50
Gender	Female	40	69
	Male	60	31
Ethnic identity	White non-Hispanic	72	81
	Black	11	3
	Hispanic white	12	6
	Mixed (white/other)	5	10
Parents' education	High school diploma	—	31
	Associate's or professional degree	—	28
	Bachelor's or master's degree	—	41
Political ideology[b]	Liberal/libertarian	48	50
	Moderate/mixed/nonpartisan	34	19
	Conservative	18	31
Religious ideology[b]	Secular/atheist/progressive	49	31
	Mainline/moderate	29	41
	Fundamentalist/evangelical/orthodox	22	28

Note: Values are percentages unless otherwise noted. Although I purposefully refrained from asking about sexual preferences or behaviors, one student voluntarily identified as gay and three students voluntarily identified as bisexual. Two heterosexual-identified parents admitted having homosexual feelings and/or experiences in the past.
a. One parent had two students in the study, one at NIU and one at RVC; the student from RVC contacted me for an interview first.
b. Ideology was determined in the coding process by combining self-identification, expressed political and religious views, and life history information.

mant had been alerted ahead of time (I explicitly asked informants not to tell anyone else about specific topics), I was able to learn about how my informants thought about marriage and relationships in a nonpoliticized communication context. I had just gotten married the previous summer, and many informants, especially parents, noticed the wedding ring on my finger; so this created a conversational opening for myself and my informants to exchange stories, advice, and musings about marriage.

Several types of questions proved effective at tapping into informants' cultural understandings. Throughout the interview, I asked purposefully vague questions because they give people freedom to answer in any way they want and because the task requires them to conjure up their basic cultural understandings of the topic in order to formulate a response. Examples include "What does the word *marriage* mean to you?" and "How do you think marriage is portrayed in the media?" In the part of the interview about homosexuality and gay marriage, hypothetical scenarios proved to be effective at getting the informant to imagine gay marriage and use his or her cultural schemas to formulate answers: "What kinds of effects would legalizing same-sex marriage have on society, if any? Would it have any effects on children?" Breaching questions were also effective because they challenged the taken-for-granted understandings of different groups: "What do you think about people who identify as gay or lesbian but don't have sexual relations with people of the same sex?" Other questions required them to take the role of the other: "Why do you think some gays and lesbians want the right to marry?"

Each of these question types was designed to require the informants to draw on specific aspects of their worldviews in order to answer them. This style of questioning mitigates some of the obvious problems with the method of qualitative interviewing. It did not matter as much if they were giving me their "true" opinion about gay marriage (as if such a thing existed) since I was more interested in finding out what was behind their opinions. Moreover, because people often try to give the answers they think the interviewers want (social desirability bias), asking a variety of different kinds of questions that probe different aspects of their experiences and understandings makes it harder for them to do so consistently (and easier for the analyst to spot).

CODING AND ANALYSIS

All of the transcription, coding, and analysis was done manually—a process that was laborious and time-consuming but also generated a deep familiarity with my interviews. In addition to interview transcripts, I also used the notes I took during each interview, a short summary/

reflection that I wrote after each interview, and memos comparing each parent-child pair to guide my analysis. In general, my approach to coding and analysis followed the grounded theory tradition and was guided by Herbert Blumer's injunction to become as intimately familiar as possible with my data.[3]

In the first stage of analysis, I coded each interview transcript in three ways while listening to the audio recording.[4] I first coded the entire transcript using *question-response codes*, so that I could analyze whole sections of dialogue that emerged in response to the specific questions on my interview guide; this type of code allowed me to see how particular questions elicited various kinds of responses. I also created *deductive codes*, labeling specific passages that contained things I was interested in, such as their opinion about gay marriage, their religious beliefs, and their attitude toward premarital sex. At the same time, I created *inductive codes* for keywords or other ideas that seemed important in some way. Occasionally, I made *annotations* in the transcript next to passages that seemed important or that I thought meant something that was not obvious.

For the second phase of coding, I had two distinct tasks. One was inductive *axial coding*: given that I had deductively identified passages in the interview transcripts that pertained to specific things I was interested in, I then coded those passages inductively to classify exactly what they said about them. The other task was a less systematic sense-making exercise of identifying the similarities and differences between discourses and the people who articulated them. This task was essentially comparative and interpretive: trying to distinguish whether the different ways people expressed themselves corresponded to real, substantive differences (and to what we might attribute those differences) or to mere idiosyncratic variability in speaking styles. This second phase of analysis formed the basis of the analysis presented in Chapters 4 and 7.

Chapters 5 and 6 came from the third phase of analysis. Having documented similarities and differences in discourses about gay marriage and the people who articulated them, I still had not yet determined why they varied by cohort. Since I had noticed what seemed to be differences in the analogies parents and children used to explain their feelings, I returned to the sections of the interview transcripts that pertained to homosexuality and gay marriage and created codes for every metaphor and analogy that informants used to talk about these topics. I also did this manually, and although I am sure that I failed to recognize dozens of metaphors, I also learned that automation would be of limited use. The simplest two-letter words, like "be" or "go," can be metaphors in one semantic context but not another. After I manually coded the transcripts, I used text search queries on metaphors that could be easily identified, like "closet" and "lifestyle," to make sure that I did not miss any instances of their appearance. I then coded each informant as having used the metaphor or not.

For the analysis in Chapter 6, I did not code for metaphors or analogies because I could not come up with a reason to do so: the key differences in how informants talked about marriage seemed to be related to life experience or related to explicit religious or civil definitions of marriage. Instead, I used inductive axial coding of responses to questions that were designed to tap into the informant's cultural schemas of marriage: "What does the word *marriage* mean to you?" and "What do you think are some characteristics of a good, strong marriage?" After coding these passages to reflect as much variety as possible, I then merged, revised, and deleted codes to account for synonyms, errors, and redundancies in the code list. To the extent that there seemed to be any semantic difference between two codes, I kept them separate. For example, although "honesty" and "openness" imply the same thing as characteristics of a marriage, it was not always clear that informants meant exactly the same thing by them. For other questions analyzed for Chapter 6 I followed a simple inductive logic of axial coding.

I am quite confident that if other researchers attempted to replicate my analysis they would fail to do so. I doubt that they would come to different conclusions than I did, but I also doubt that they would agree with all of my coding decisions. This is the fundamental problem with the kind of interpretive epistemology and qualitative research methods that I use here. As many scholars have argued, however, qualitative interview methods and interpretive research should not strive to follow the logic of the empiricist and quantitative sciences.[5]

To strive for anything less than the deep, interpretive analysis of my informants' words would be a misrepresentation of them. Human communication resists positivist empirical analysis. Sometimes we say one thing but mean another—either intentionally through satire and irony or unintentionally because we all make mistakes. As with metaphors and analogies, sometimes there are hidden meanings in the things that we say, such that we often end up communicating more than we intend. Sometimes the smallest of words take on profound significance.

Communication is inherently interpretive, and the analysis of it must always return to its interpretive core. This is not to say that we cannot learn things by analyzing communication in other ways; simply counting the frequencies and appearances of words in bodies of text can be illuminating, but it is illuminating only when we take into account their meanings. If sociology is, as Weber defined it, "a science concerning itself with the interpretive understanding of social action and thereby with a causal explanation of its course and consequences," then the interpretive analysis of the meanings that actors communicate to us will always be essential to social research.[6]

TABLE A.2: Decomposition of Change in Opposition to Gay Marriage, 1988–2014: Cohort Replacement versus Intra-cohort Attitude Change

Observed change in opposition (2014–1988)	−1.3678
a. Cohort replacement	−0.4091
b. Intra-cohort attitude change	−0.919
Estimated change (a + b) / observed change	0.97

Note: This procedure follows Glenn Firebaugh's linear decomposition technique. See Firebaugh, "Methods for Estimating Cohort Replacement Effects"; Firebaugh and Davis, "Trends in Antiblack Prejudice." Cohort replacement (a) is calculated by multiplying the unstandardized OLS regression coefficient of opposition to gay marriage on cohort (controlling for year) by the change in the average birth year of people in 1988 versus 2014. Intra-cohort attitude change (b) is calculated by multiplying the unstandardized OLS regression coefficient of opposition to gay marriage on year (controlling for cohort) by 26 (the number of years elapsed).

TABLE A.3: Structural Equation Model Regressing Opposition to Gay Marriage on Intervening Variable (Moral Judgments of Homosexuality) and Covariates

Variable	Structural Model (DV = moral judgment of homosexuality)	Structural Model (DV = opposition to gay marriage)	Total Effects (Direct + Indirect)
Moral judgment[a]	—	0.551 (0.009)***	−0.551
Year	−0.148 (0.010)***	−0.106 (0.009)***	−0.188
Cohort (birth year)	−0.144 (0.010)***	−0.082 (0.009)***	−0.161
Male	0.106 (0.009)***	0.050 (0.008)***	0.109
White	−0.093 (0.010)***	−0.004 (0.008)	−0.055
Education	−0.190 (0.009)***	−0.038 (0.008)***	−0.143
Political conservatism	0.216 (0.010)***	0.151 (0.008)***	0.27
Religious attendance	0.211 (0.010)***	0.071 (0.009)***	0.187
Born-again	0.189 (0.010)***	0.047 (0.009)***	0.152
Constant	57.85 (2.51)***	38.67 (2.21)***	
Equation-level statistics			
Fitted	2.004	2.392	
Residual	1.301	1.09	
R^2	.351	.545	

Notes Analyses were performed in Stata 12.1. Standardized regression coefficients with OIM standard errors in parentheses. Covariance estimates not shown. Overall model statistics: N = 7,676; maximum likelihood estimation, log likelihood = −147666.07; RMSEA = 0.000; BIC = 295913.620; CFI and TLI = 1.000; R^2 = .418.
a. For this analysis, moral judgment of homosexuality was reverse coded to facilitate interpretation (1= *not wrong at all*, 4 = *always wrong*).
***$p < .001$.

TABLE A.4: Ordinal Regression of Opposition to Gay Marriage on Demographic and Attitudinal Variables, General Social Survey 1988–2014

Variable	Attribute	Demographic Model	Full Model
Male		1.641 (11.87)***	1.373 (7.05)***
White		0.772 (−5.12)***	0.967 (−0.63)
Education		0.894 (−15.93)***	0.953 (−6.34)***
Political conservatism		1.569 (28.29)***	1.385 (19.10)***
Religious attendance		1.162 (18.05)***	1.080 (8.43)***
Born-again		1.985 (14.75)***	1.342 (5.80)***
Cohort (3–18)	Illness (reference)	—	—
	Lifestyle	0.718 (−6.79)***	0.827 (−3.55)***
	Identity	0.394 (−15.63)***	0.510 (−10.59)***
Year	1988 (reference)	—	—
	2006	0.513 (−9.41)***	0.662 (−4.83)***
	2008	0.439 (−10.66)***	0.647 (−4.74)***
	2010	0.329 (−14.13)***	0.493 (−7.66)***
	2012	0.264 (−16.76)***	0.412 (−9.48)***
	2014	0.202 (−21.13)***	0.315 (−12.89)***
Morality of homosexuality	Always wrong (reference)		—
	Almost always wrong		0.314 (−10.94)***
	Sometimes wrong		0.167 (−20.66)***
	Not wrong at all		0.059 (−43.91)***
Log likelihood		−11380	−9218.6
Obs.		8,391	7,676
LR χ²		3556.15	5546.83
Pseudo-R²		.1351	.2313

Note: Analyses were performed in Stata 12.1. Odds ratios are reported here; z scores instead of standard errors are reported in parentheses to give a sense of the magnitude of statistical significance because the transformation of the coefficient to the odds ratio makes the relationship between the standard error and the odds ratio harder to eyeball. Use of robust standard errors makes no difference in results or interpretation. Because there are more than two categories of the dependent variable, the interpretation of the odds ratio assumes that the difference between any two categories of the dependent variable is the same. So in general each odds ratio can be interpreted as follows: a one-unit increase in the independent variable changes the odds that a person's opposition to gay marriage increases by one unit. Demographic variables that failed to achieve statistical significance are excluded from these models because they did not change the results or interpretation in any significant way. The cohort variable presented here (three categories, assuming eighteen-year coming of age) differs little from the results if other cohort variables are used.
***$p < .001$.

TABLE A.5: Multilevel Mixed Effects Linear Regression of Opposition to Gay Marriage on Age, Period, Cohort (Five Cohorts), and Demographic and Attitudinal Variables

Fixed effects	1	2	3	4	5
Intercept	2.26***	1.71***	3.35***	3.34***	3.33***
Age	0.02***	0.02**	0.02***	0.02***	0.02***
Age^2	0	0	−0.00**	−0.00**	−0.00**
Male		0.33***	0.15***	0.15***	0.15***
White		−0.18***	−0.01	−0.01	−0.01
Education		−0.07***	−0.02***	−0.02***	−0.02**
Political conservatism		0.28***	0.16***	0.16***	0.16***
Religious attendance		0.09***	0.04***	0.04***	0.04***
Born-again		0.45***	0.15***	0.15***	0.15***
Morality of homosexuality			−0.60***	−0.59***	−0.59***
Random effects					
Five cohorts	0.089	0.104	0.046	0.042	0.035
	(0.025)	(0.025)	(0.022)	(0.023)	(0.033)
Period (year)	0.476	0.449	0.252	0.176	0
	(0.14)	(0.132)	(0.075)	(0.058)	(0)
Morality of homosexuality slope				0.053	0.044
				(0.02)	(0.021)
Education slope					0.015
					(0.005)
Log likelihood	−15691	−13709	−11201	−11196	−11191
Obs.	8,840	8,391	7,676	7,676	7,676
LR χ^2	848***	906***	319***	329***	340***

Note: Analyses performed using Stata 12.1 *xtmixed* command on GSS data from 1988 to 2014. Maximum likelihood estimation method used, unweighted. Results in the top half of the table are unstandardized OLS regression coefficients; standard errors omitted for lack of space. Results in the bottom half of the table are estimates of the standard deviations for the intercepts of year and cohort and for the slopes of education and moral judgments about homosexuality by year (standard errors of the estimate in parentheses). The LR $\chi2$ test compares the mixed effects models in the table with a fixed effects OLS regression model.
**$p < .01$; ***$p < .001$.

TABLE A.6: Multilevel Mixed Effects Linear Regression of Opposition to Gay Marriage on Age, Period, Cohort (Identity Cohort versus Others), and Demographic and Attitudinal Variables

Fixed effects	1	2	3	4	5
Intercept	2.59***	2.04***	3.48***	3.46***	3.42***
Age	0.01	0	0.01**	0.01**	0.02**
Age²	0	0	0	−0.00*	−0.00*
Male		0.33***	0.15***	0.15***	0.15***
White		−0.18***	−0.02	−0.01	−0.02
Education		−0.07***	−0.02***	−0.02***	−0.02**
Political conservatism		0.28***	0.16***	0.16***	0.16***
Religious attendance		0.10***	0.04***	0.04***	0.04***
Born-again		0.45***	0.15***	0.15***	0.15***
Morality of homosexuality			−0.60***	−0.59***	−0.59***
Random effects					
Identity cohort	0.206	0.207	0.093	0.087	0.07
	(0.085)	(0.082)	(0.048)	(0.047)	(0.038)
Period (year)	0.431	0.397	0.24	0.166	0
	(0.154)	(0.147)	(0.08)	(0.067)	(0)
Morality of homosexuality slope				0.053	0.043
				(0.02)	(0.02)
Education slope					0.015
					(0.005)
Log likelihood	−15689	−13709	−11200	−11195	−11190
Obs.	8,840	8,391	7,676	7,676	7,676
LR χ²	853***	907***	322***	332***	342***

Note: All notes from Table A.5 apply here as well. Instead of five cohorts, these models compare only two cohorts: the Identity Cohort compared to all others.
*p < .05; **p < .01; ***p < .001.

TABLE A.7: Ordinal Regression of Opposition to Gay Marriage on Demographic and Attitudinal Variables, Pew Research Center 2003–2013

Variable	Attribute	Demographic Model	Full Model
Male		1.472 (4.52)***	1.124 (1.13)
White		0.933 (−0.64)	1.128 (0.94)
Education		0.876 (−4.98)***	1.013 (0.41)
Political conservatism		1.995 (13.67)***	1.345 (4.95)***
Religious attendance		1.353 (9.56)***	1.150 (3.69)***
Born-again		2.338 (9.15)***	1.187 (1.51)
Cohort (3–18)	Illness (reference)	—	
	Lifestyle	0.689 (−3.94)**	0.794 (−2.00)*
	Identity	0.497 (−5.57)***	0.716 (−2.23)*
Year	2003 (reference)	—	—
	2013	0.910 (−10.90)***	0.919 (−7.80)***
Sin	No (reference)		—
	Yes		7.138 (13.54)***
	Don't know/refused		4.229 (7.21)***
Gay/lesbian attitude			0.349 (−13.76)***
Personal contact			1.526 (3.14)**
Comfort	Uncomfortable (reference)		—
	Doesn't bother		0.488 (−4.65)***
	Don't know/refused		0.439 (−2.63)**
Attribution	Born gay (reference)		—
	Brought up		1.408 (1.92)
	Choice		1.365 (2.46)*
	Don't know/refused		1.404 (1.61)
Log likelihood		−2351.2	−1552.9
Obs.		2,069	1,660
LR χ^2		762.87	1329.75
Pseudo-R^2		.1396	.2998

Note: All notes from Table A.4 apply here as well. There are several reasons why the analysis here cannot be strictly compared with the analysis in Table A.4. First, the dependent variable here has only four categories, not five. Second, the baseline comparison year is 2003, not 1988. Third, many of the other independent variables are different: for example, political conservatism is on a 5-point rather than a 7-point scale. Finally, the bias due to nonresponse is greater in the Pew data than the GSS data. For making statistical inferences, then, the GSS data give us greater confidence, but the Pew data provide insights about how other variables affect people's attitudes about gay marriage.

*$p < .05$; **$p < .01$; ***$p < .001$.

NOTES

INTRODUCTION

1 Eilperin, "For Obama, Rainbow White House."

2 Graham, post on Facebook.

3 Rosenfeld, "Moving a Mountain."

4 At the time of the ruling, 57 to 60 percent of Americans supported gay marriage. McCarthy, "Record-High 60% of Americans"; Pew Research Center, "Changing Attitudes on Gay Marriage."

5 Newport, "Landing a Man on the Moon"; Jensen, "Democrats and Republicans Differ."

6 Gallup, "Congress and the Public."

7 Sullivan, "It Is Accomplished."

8 *Obergefell v. Hodges*, 576 US ___ (2015), 23–24.

9 Ibid., 7.

10 For an explanation of the multiple meanings of generation, see Kertzer, "Generation as a Sociological Problem."

11 Jaeger, "Generations in History."

12 Ryder, "Cohort as a Concept."

13 Durkheim, *Elementary Forms of Religious Life*.

14 There is no consensus definition of a schema; its use varies across disciplines. My use of the term here is influenced most by formulations from cognitive anthropology. D'Andrade, *Development of Cognitive Anthropology*; Strauss and Quinn, *Cognitive Theory of Cultural Meaning*; Shore, *Cognition, Culture, and the Problem of Meaning*.

15 Sometimes *cultural schema* is used synonymously with *cultural model* and *understanding*, though some authors prefer one term over others. Glaeser, *Political Epistemics*; Quinn, "Culture and Contradiction"; Quinn and Holland, "Culture and Cognition"; Sewell, "Theory of Structure"; Patterson, "Making Sense of Culture."

16 For illustrative examples on the relation between stereotypes and schemas, see Homan, Valentino, and Weed, "Being and Becoming Poor"; Hunzaker, "Making Sense of Misfortune"; Blair-Loy, "Cultural Constructions of Family Schemas"; Valentino, Hutchings, and White, "Cues That Matter."

17 Slusher and Anderson, "When Reality Monitoring Fails"; Blair, Ma, and Lenton, "Imagining Stereotypes Away."

CHAPTER 1. IMAGINING GENERATIONS AND SOCIAL CHANGE

1 Wikipedia, "Mendota Beacon."

2 For studies of attitudes about homosexuality, see Loftus, "America's Liberalization in Attitudes toward Homosexuality"; Wilcox and Wolpert, "Gay Rights in the Public Sphere"; Treas, "How Cohorts, Education, and Ideology Shaped a New Sexual Revolution"; Andersen and Fetner, "Cohort Differences in Tolerance of Homosexuality." For studies on gender ideology, see Brewster and Padavic, "Change in Gender Ideology"; Brooks and Bolzendahl, "Transformation of US Gender Role Attitudes"; Ciabattari, "Changes in Men's Conservative Gender Ideologies."

3 For example, Comte, *Auguste Comte and Positivism*; Ortega y Gasset, *Man and Crisis*.

4 Mannheim, "Problem of Generations."

5 This is not a case of Healy's "Actually Existing Nuance." Mannheim's generational theory is one example of a conceptual framework in which omitting its distinctions is fatal to empirical research, as this chapter shows. Healy, "Fuck Nuance."

6 The distinction between coevals and contemporaries is important here. A cohort is made of coevals—people who experience the same event during the same time of their life—while contemporaries are all people living at the same time. Ryder, "Cohort as a Concept."

7 Mannheim, "Problem of Generations," 304.

8 Elder, *Children of the Great Depression*.

9 Hart-Brinson, "Discourse of Generations."

10 Mannheim, "Problem of Generations," 304.

11 Unsurprisingly, blacks were more likely to name the Civil Rights Movement than whites, but among whites age had no relationship to memory of the Civil Rights Movement. Schuman and Scott, "Generations and Collective Memories."

12 Griffin, "'Generations and Collective Memory' Revisited."

13 Laufer and Bengtson, "Generations, Aging, and Social Stratification"; Larson and Lizardo, "Generations, Identities, and the Collective Memory"; Rintala, "Generation in Politics"; Klatch, *Generation Divided*.

14 Some scholars argue that a cohort is defined by objective location while a generation is defined by a combination of objective location and subjective identity. However, this distinction is inadequate because many people in an actual generation may not identify themselves as such. Mannheim argued that generation units (and their entelechies) can be either self-conscious or not ("Problem of Generations," 309). So while some generation units collectively identify themselves as generations by intentionally adopting new styles, languages, and behaviors, others will not consciously do so. One can be a member of a generation without knowing it. Alwin and McCammon, "Rethinking Generations"; White, "Succession and Generations"; Ryder, "Cohort as a Concept."

15 Ironically, Mannheim himself seemed to prophesy this development. I quote him at length, since he specifically rejects the social scientific approach to generational research that is exclusively demographic in perspective and centered on the

cohort concept. "A formal sociological clarification of the distinction between the categories 'generation location,' generation as actuality,' and 'generation unit,' is important and indeed indispensable for any deeper analysis, since we can never grasp the dominant factors in this field without making that distinction. If we speak simply of 'generations' without any further differentiation, we risk jumbling together purely biological phenomena and others which are the product of social and cultural forces: thus we arrive at a sort of sociology of chronological tables (*Geschichtstabellensoziologie*), which uses its bird's-eye perspective to 'discover' fictitious generation movements to correspond to the crucial turning-points in historical chronology." Mannheim, "Problem of Generations," 311.

16   Cutler and Bengtson, "Age and Political Alienation"; Roberts and Lang, "Generations and Ideological Change."

17   Bengtson, Furlong, and Laufer, "Time, Aging, and the Continuity of Social Structure."

18   Kertzer, "Generation as a Sociological Problem."

19   Among them are Schuman and Scott, "Generations and Collective Memories"; Schnittker, Freese, and Powell, "Who Are Feminists?"; Hout and Fischer, "Why More Americans Have No Religious Preference"; Weil, "Cohorts, Regimes, and the Legitimation of Democracy"; Demartini, "Change Agents and Generational Relationships."

20   Bauerlein's caricature of Millennials is a blame-the-victim narrative in which children are blamed for the world they were brought into. Twenge at least backs her conclusions with social scientific evidence. However, her analysis fails the basic test of demographic analysis in that she fails to disaggregate age, cohort, and period effects. Therefore, we cannot distinguish changes that are unique to the cohort from those that affect all of society. Twenge, *Generation Me*; Bauerlein, *Dumbest Generation*.

21   Howe and Strauss, *Millennials Rising*; Winograd and Hais, *Millennial Momentum*.

22   As I explain later, the problem with this literature is more fundamental: it builds upon a discredited theory of generations, called the pulse-rate paradigm, that falsely assumes that broad cohort groupings like the Millennials exist in the first place.

23   For quantitative researchers, interaction variables can be used to approximate the actual generation since the interaction of cohort with some other variable can help identify the subgroup of the cohort that experiences history in some unique way.

24   This book exemplifies this problem. Although I incorporate all three perspectives, my primary perspective is interpretive. Demographers, historians, and other specialists could justifiably find methodological and substantive flaws in Chapters 2 and 3.

25   Beyond sophisticated quantitative methods, historical and theoretical interpretation is still needed. Winship and Harding, "Mechanism-Based Approach"; Firebaugh, "Methods for Estimating Cohort Replacement Effects."

26 Alwin and Krosnick, "Aging, Cohorts, and the Stability of Sociopolitical Orientations"; Glenn, "Values, Attitudes, and Beliefs"; Jennings and Niemi, *Generations
and Politics*; Miller and Sears, "Stability and Change in Social Tolerance"; Sears
and Funk, "Evidence of the Long-Term Persistence"; Alwin, Cohen, and Newcomb, *Political Attitudes over the Life Span*.

27 Demartini, "Change Agents and Generational Relationships"; Schuman and Scott,
"Generations and Collective Memories."

28 Riley, Foner, and Riley, "Aging and Society Paradigm"; Alwin and McCammon,
"Rethinking Generations."

29 Eyerman and Turner, "Outline of a Theory of Generations"; Gilleard, "Cohorts and
Generations in the Study of Social Change"; Stevenson, Everingham, and Robinson,
"Choices and Life Chances"; Corsten, "Time of Generations"; Aboim and Vasconcelos, "From Political to Social Generations"; Cavalli, "Generations and Value Orientations"; McDaniel, "Generationing Gender"; Plummer, "Generational Sexualities."

30 Jaeger, "Generations in History," calls them hypotheses, but "paradigms" is more
accurate.

31 Strauss and Howe, *Generations*.

32 Ortega y Gasset, *Man and Crisis*.

33 Jaeger, "Generations in History," 282.

34 Strauss and Howe, *Generations*.

35 For one effort to name this group, see Twenge, *iGen*.

36 The Baby Boom cohort is defined empirically by the unusually high fertility rates
of American women in the post–World War II period.

37 For an example of how otherwise-valuable data are misrepresented because of
the influence of the pulse-rate paradigm, see Taylor, *Next America*. Research
organizations like the Pew Research Center also produce dozens of reports every
year on differences and similarities between cohorts on a wide array of issues. It is
important to document such age-related trends in society, but adopting the pulse-
rate paradigm and its labels mischaracterizes the significance of the findings and
constructs a distorted image of society.

38 Esler, "'Truest Community.'"

39 The collective mentality is a concept of the French *Annales* school of history—
similar to the notion of Zeitgeist (literally, "spirit of the times")—which denotes a
broadly shared cultural mind-set of a whole group in society at a particular time.

40 Pilcher, "Mannheim's Sociology of Generations."

41 The inspiration for this example comes from Gwin, "Strait of Malacca."

42 Connectionist and dual-process theories of cognition presuppose the existence
of such structures that facilitate information processing. Evans, "Dual-Processing
Accounts of Reasoning"; Vaisey, "Socrates, Skinner, and Aristotle"; Haidt, *Righteous Mind*; Strauss and Quinn, *Cognitive Theory of Cultural Meaning*; D'Andrade,
Development of Cognitive Anthropology.

43 I use "social imagination" rather than "social imaginary" because it is essential
to distinguish the process of imagination from its product and from the cultural

schemas upon which the imagination draws. Taylor's essay on "Modern Social Imaginaries," for all its merits, treats it as a thing that exists: "that common understanding that makes possible common practices," or the "background . . . within which particular features of our world become evident." A focus on the social imagination—the process whereby that social imaginary becomes constructed—can help explain both how the social imaginary exerts its influence over human action and how the social imaginary was created in the first place (not to mention how it can be changed). Taylor, "Modern Social Imaginaries," 106–107. Claudia Strauss also emphasizes the importance of the process in her critique. She argues "against attempts to turn culture into an abstraction and advocates instead that anthropologists study concrete material and symbolic conditions, on the one hand, and the understandings, emotions, and desires that individuals develop as they experience these conditions, on the other." Strauss, "Imaginary," 323.

44 On the imagination, see also Heidegger, *Kant and the Problem of Metaphysics.* On schemas, Kant called the "transcendental schema" a "mediating representation" between our categories of thought and the empirical objects that we perceive (181; Kant's second edition 177). On the relationship between schema and imagination, Kant writes: "The schema is in itself always a product of imagination" (182; Kant's second edition 179). Kant, *Critique of Pure Reason.*

45 Durkheim, *Elementary Forms of Religious Life*; Castoriadis, *Imaginary Institution of Society.*

46 For recent approaches to measuring dual-process cognition and cultural schemas in sociology, see Hunzaker, "Cultural Sentiments and Schema-Consistency Bias"; Moore, "Fast or Slow"; McDonnell, "Drawing Out Culture"; Boutyline, "Improving the Measurement of Shared Cultural Schemas"; Boutyline and Vaisey, "Belief Network Analysis."

47 Slusher and Anderson, "When Reality Monitoring Fails"; Blair, Ma, and Lenton, "Imagining Stereotypes Away."

48 Anderson, *Imagined Communities.*

49 Appadurai, *Modernity at Large.*

50 Taylor, "Modern Social Imaginaries."

51 Boltanski, *Distant Suffering*; Perrin, *Citizen Speak.* See also Baiocchi et al., *Civic Imagination.*

52 Orgad, *Media Representation and the Global Imagination.*

53 Olick, "Collective Memory."

54 My formulation of understanding differs somewhat from that of Andreas Glaeser, who talks about understanding as both process and outcome, though it is not clear how they are related. In one passage, he defines understanding as "a process of orientation from within a particular pursuit in a specific context, which orders relevant aspects of the world by simultaneously differentiating and integrating it, thus stipulating a practical ontology." By contrast, one page earlier, Glaeser characterizes understanding as the outcome and orientation as the process that leads to it: "Understanding is achieved in a process of orientation; it emerges in

the realization of what is what, and where located in relation to one another. This process is at once analytical and synthetic. It involves the differentiation of a totality into elements and simultaneously their qualitative integration." These passages are compatible with my own view of the social imagination, and since orientation is an unspecified concept here, I take the imagination to be the process that generates understandings. Glaeser, *Political Epistemics*, 9–10. On how framing works by altering belief importance, see Nelson, Clawson, and Oxley, "Media Framing of a Civil Liberties Conflict."

55 Pascoe, *Dude, You're a Fag.*

CHAPTER 2. CONTESTING HOMOSEXUALITY'S IMAGINATION, 1945–2015

1 Seinfeld Scripts, "The Outing."

2 Gable, "King of Pop."

3 As philosopher Wendy Brown observes, tolerance is not a noble virtue; it coexists with dislike and disgust, rather than challenging them directly. Although tolerance may be preferable to intolerance, Brown argues that discourses of tolerance can undermine challenges to the status quo by marginalized groups and preserve the power of dominant groups. Lesbians, gays, and all others who have been "tolerated" understand the difference between tolerance and affirmation or support. Brown, *Regulating Aversion.*

4 Becker, *Gay TV and Straight America.*

5 The power of fictional stories to generate attitudinal and behavior change is documented in studies of "entertainment-education." For theoretical explanations of the power of narratives, see Slater and Rouner, "Entertainment-Education and Elaboration Likelihood"; Moyer-Gusé, "Toward a Theory of Entertainment Persuasion." Shows with lesbian and gay protagonists like *Will & Grace* and *Ellen* may have had significant effects on public opinion, but even minor characters and storylines can affect audiences' attitudes if the narrative induces reactions like transportation, character identification, and parasocial interaction. Schiappa, Gregg, and Hewes, "Can One TV Show Make a Difference?"; Garretson, "Exposure to the Lives of Lesbians and Gays."

6 In his theory of time, Andrew Abbott conceptualizes turning points as events that, when viewed retrospectively (and they can be viewed *only* retrospectively), distinguish two separate periods of time that are characterized by qualitatively different and stable sets of social relations. The two periods on either side of a turning point have an "inertial quality" and a "coercive character" that stabilize the social relations that happen in them. By contrast, turning points may be experienced as unstable or "chaotic" (239) because they break with the previous period, and only when a sufficient amount of time has elapsed can one determine whether the discontinuity was a turning point or a temporary deviation from the norm. Additionally, Abbott is explicit that turning points have duration, so the fact that each of the turning points described in this chapter lasts many years is

not problematic theoretically; however, it does make the problem of identifying clear boundaries for cohorts intractable. Abbott, *Time Matters*, 239, 248, 249.

7 Peter Haas defines an epistemic community as "a network of professionals with recognized expertise and competence in a particular domain and an authoritative claim to policy-relevant knowledge within that domain or issue-area." Haas, "Introduction," 3; Ferree et al., *Shaping Abortion Discourse*; Danielian and Page, "Heavenly Chorus"; Gans, *Deciding What's News*.

8 Normatively speaking, Habermas deems it essential that interactions in the public sphere satisfy certain criteria: no one should be excluded; all ideas should be evaluated on the basis of merit, regardless of the speaker's status; and all communication should be insulated from the contaminating influences of wealth and power. In his later work, he recontextualized the concept of the public sphere in a broader theory of communicative action in the "lifeworld" of civil society that is oriented toward mutual understanding. Since power and money are contaminating influences in the operation of the public sphere, democracy suffers when public communication is shaped more by rational self-interest than by considerations of the common good. Habermas, *Structural Transformation of the Public Sphere*, 27, 181.

9 Conrad and Schneider, *Deviance and Medicalization*.

10 Stein, *Rethinking the Gay and Lesbian Movement*, 42.

11 *Newsweek*, "Homosexuals in Uniform."

12 Committee on Nomenclature and Statistics of the American Psychiatric Association, *Diagnostic and Statistical Manual of Mental Disorders*, 38–39. Homosexuality was also classified this way in the second edition of the *DSM*, published in 1968, except that the major category was called "Personality Disorders and Certain Other Non-Psychotic Mental Disorders."

13 This was not necessarily true in rural areas. John Howard's study of homosexuality in Mississippi from 1945 to 1985 shows both similarities to and differences from the prevailing narrative. Howard describes the 1940s and 1950s as a period of "quiet accommodation" (xvii): although considered deviant and immoral, homosexual encounters happened in daily life and were often willfully disregarded by political and religious authorities. In the South, at least, it was not until the 1960s that lesbians and gays became targets of police repression because of how homosexual deviance became semiotically linked with the Civil Rights Movement's threat to the social order. Howard, *Men Like That*.

14 The four main activities of the homophile movement between 1953 and 1961 were group meetings/discussions, service provision to individuals in need, education and communication, and direct political action. Stein, *Rethinking the Gay and Lesbian Movement*.

15 For an explanation of the process used by the Production Code Administration to review scripts and figures from 1946 regarding the outcomes, see Geoffrey Shurlock, "Motion Picture Production Code."

16 The code unraveled for various reasons: the weakening of Hollywood's monopoly on film production, the emergence of television and foreign films as competitors,

court decisions that extended First Amendment protections to filmmaking, and changes in Production Code Administration leadership. Russo, *Celluloid Closet*; Phillips, *Controversial Cinema*.

17 McCracken, "Regulating the Swish."

18 Murray, "Television Wipes Its Feet."

19 D'Emilio, *Sexual Politics, Sexual Communities*, 115.

20 Leavitt and Klassen, "Public Attitudes toward Homosexuality."

21 Sociologist Gaye Tuchman originally defined "symbolic annihilation" as the "condemnation, trivialization, or absence" of representations in the media. Tuchman, "Introduction."

22 For the story behind the elimination of the last remaining prohibition in the code, see Russo, *Celluloid Closet*, 119–122.

23 Doty, "Growth of Overt Homosexuality."

24 Welch, "Homosexuality in America"; Havemann, "Scientists Search for the Answers."

25 The video can be watched in full at https://www.youtube.com/watch?v =n2UNcDHa5ao.

26 For a discussion of these advances, see D'Emilio, *Sexual Politics, Sexual Communities*; Bernstein, "Identities and Politics."

27 Armstrong and Crage, "Movements and Memory."

28 Livingood, "National Institute of Mental Health Task Force on Homosexuality," 4.

29 Ibid., 5–6.

30 Socarides, "Homosexuality and Medicine," 1202.

31 There were three types of post-Stonewall organizations: liberationist groups, reformist liberal groups, and lesbian-feminist groups. Liberationist groups provided the spark, but lesbian-feminist groups and reformist liberal groups were the smoldering embers that sustained the movement. In her study of the movement in San Francisco, Elizabeth Armstrong found that the moment of gay liberation, as measured by organizational foundings, lasted only from 1969 to 1971: 12 of the 23 liberationist organizations in San Francisco between 1953 and 1994 were founded during those three years. By contrast, she identified 871 "gay identity" organizations in San Francisco during that same period, over 98 percent of which were founded after 1971. Armstrong, *Forging Gay Identities*; Stein, *Rethinking the Gay and Lesbian Movement*; Marotta, *Politics of Homosexuality*.

32 D'Emilio describes the coming out strategy this way: "The exhilaration and anger that surfaced when men and women stepped through the fear of discovery propelled them into political activity. . . . They relinquished their invisibility, made themselves vulnerable to attack, and acquired an investment in the success of the movement in a way that mere adherence to a political line could never accomplish. Visible lesbians and gay men also served as magnets that drew others to them. . . . Coming out provided gay liberation with an army of permanent enlistees." D'Emilio, *Sexual Politics, Sexual Communities*, 235–236. Coming out remained part of the movement's strategy throughout the 1990s because of an

additional benefit: it gave straight Americans personal contact with lesbians and gays, thereby reducing prejudice. Allport, *Nature of Prejudice*; Herek and Glunt, "Interpersonal Contact and Heterosexuals' Attitudes toward Gay Men." Zapping involved publicly disrupting events and demanding that public figures account for conditions that were oppressive of lesbians and gays. Two New York activists, Marty Robinson and Jim Owles, are credited with creating the "zapping" tactic when they confronted New York mayoral candidate Mario Procaccino: "Mr. Procaccino, what are you going to do about the oppression of the homosexual?" Marotta, *Politics of Homosexuality*, 137.

33 Bayer, *Homosexuality and American Psychiatry*, 102–107.

34 Ibid., 107–111.

35 Glass, "81 Words."

36 Bayer, *Homosexuality and American Psychiatry*, 137.

37 Marcus, *Making Gay History*, 179.

38 Lyons, "Psychiatrists, in a Shift, Declare Homosexuality No Mental Illness."

39 Marcus, *Making Gay History*, 180.

40 *Bowers v. Hardwick*, 478 US 186 (1986).

41 Fetner, *How the Religious Right Shaped Lesbian and Gay Activism*; Diamond, *Roads to Dominion*.

42 General Social Survey, "G.S.S. Data Explorer."

43 Fejes, *Gay Rights and Moral Panic*.

44 The New Right's emergence also affected the lesbian and gay movement's tactics and discourse. Tina Fetner shows that the frames and language used by prominent lesbian and gay organizations to talk about anti-discrimination issues from 1977 to 1981 differed substantially from those of previous years. Before 1977, the movement's language was inclusive and educational and emphasized justice and equality; after 1977, the movement adopted more combative language. Fetner, *How the Religious Right Shaped Lesbian and Gay Activism*, 30, 34–38.

45 Plummer, "Concept and Application of Life Style Segmentation."

46 Fejes, *Gay Rights and Moral Panic*, 50–51.

47 For accounts of the impact, see Shilts, *And the Band Played On*; Gould, *Moving Politics*; Epstein, *Impure Science*.

48 According to Gross, "Between January and June of 1985, the New York Times published fifty-two articles about AIDS; from July to December of 1985, the New York Times ran 323 articles about AIDS." Gross, *Up from Invisibility*, 98.

49 Ibid., 101.

50 Meyer, "Rock Hudson's Body," 261.

51 Ibid., 278.

52 Gross, *Up from Invisibility*, 102–103.

53 Clendinen and Nagourney, *Out for Good*.

54 Gould, *Moving Politics*, 141.

55 Clendinen and Nagourney, *Out for Good*, 538; Stein, *Rethinking the Gay and Lesbian Movement*, 165.

56 Gould, *Moving Politics*, 4–5.

57 Foucault's analysis of the confession as a mode of discourse captures the significance of witnessing one's coming out. He argues that the confession is so powerful because the witness to the speaker's self-disclosure retains the power to judge the speaker negatively for it. The confession "is corroborated by the obstacles and resistances it has had to surmount in order to be formulated" and "produces intrinsic modifications in the person who articulates it." Foucault, *History of Sexuality*, 61–62.

58 For Brock's full recollection of his experience, see Marcus, *Making Gay History*, 314–318.

59 Pierson, "Uptight on Gay News," 25.

60 Ibid., 32.

61 Fejes and Petrich, "Invisibility, Homophobia, and Heterosexism," 404.

62 Signorile, "Out at the New York Times"; Gross, *Up from Invisibility*.

63 Ghiglione et al., "Alternatives."

64 Gross, *Up from Invisibility*.

65 Ibid.

66 LeVay, "Difference in Hypothalmic Structure."

67 Suplee, "Brain May Determine Sexuality."

68 Maugh and Zamichow, "Study Ties Part of Brain to Men's Sexual Orientation."

69 Begley, "What Causes People to Be Homosexual?"

70 Hamer et al., "Linkage between DNA Markers."

71 Clinton, "Address Accepting the Presidential Nomination."

72 In the cover story, Jess Cagle attributes the new gay visibility in entertainment to the simple fact that it proved to be commercially lucrative. This begs the question of why Americans in the 1990s would approve of this when it would have been unpopular and controversial the previous decade. Cagle, "America Sees Shades of Gay."

73 Ghaziani, *Dividends of Dissent*, 155.

74 Becker, *Gay TV and Straight America*, 81.

75 Ibid., 165–166.

76 This was before the show's 2017 revival. Could it be a historical coincidence that the revival appeared two years after the nationwide legalization of gay marriage, whereas the original appeared two years after Congress passed the Defense of Marriage Act to prevent its legalization? The original series was unquestionably a product of its times, which makes its revival either deeply ironic or the ultimate proof of the distortion that nostalgia's rose-colored glasses introduce into our view of history.

77 Schiappa, Gregg, and Hewes, "Can One TV Show Make a Difference?"

78 Seidman, *Beyond the Closet*, 13.

79 Ibid., 160.

80 Walters, *All the Rage*.

81 Engel, *Fragmented Citizens.*

82 The first documented request for a same-sex marriage license came in 1970 from a Minneapolis couple, Michael McConnell and Jack Baker, and there were other isolated attempts by lesbians and gays to get marriage licenses in the 1970s (see Stein, *Rethinking the Gay and Lesbian Movement*, 105), but no sustained campaign. If anything, gay marriage in the 1970s was a weapon used against movements for equality. When two Yale law students published a note in the *Yale Law Journal* that the Equal Rights Amendment could make it illegal to deny a marriage license on the basis of sex, opponents of the ERA used the threat of gay marriage to build support for their cause. Fejes, *Gay Rights and Moral Panic.*

83 Quoted in Ghaziani, *Dividends of Dissent*, 110.

84 Gay marriage was never a consensus goal of the LGBTQ movement. In some ways, the fight over gay marriage symbolizes the triumph of the liberal-reformist wing of the movement over the liberationist and queer wings, which rejected the institution of marriage as heterosexist, patriarchal, and repressive of nonbinary sexualities. Rimmerman, "Beyond Political Mainstreaming"; Hull, *Same-Sex Marriage.*

85 Ghaziani, *Dividends of Dissent*, 120–122.

86 Sara Boesser, quoted in Marcus, *Making Gay History*, 300.

87 Ring, "8,100 Gay, Lesbian Couples Marry."

88 Goode and Ben-Yehuda, "Moral Panics."

89 Only 52 percent of voters approved of the constitutional amendments in South Dakota in 2006 and in California in 2008. Prior to 2012, the only defeat of a constitutional amendment occurred in Arizona in 2006, when voters were persuaded that the measure was written so broadly that it would apply to opposite-sex senior citizens as well. In 2008, 56 percent of Arizona voters approved a narrower constitutional ban on gay marriage.

90 Engel counts "sixteen state courts, twenty-nine federal district courts, and five federal appellate courts" that struck down bans on gay marriage. Engel, *Fragmented Citizens*, 272.

91 For a legal analysis of these rulings and their implications for lesbian and gay rights, see ibid.

92 For an authoritative account of the gay marriage movement after 2000 and how activists, lawyers, and social movement organizations laid the foundations for it during the twentieth century, see Frank, *Awakening.*

93 Taylor et al., "Culture and Mobilization."

94 For more on these events and others, see Frank, *Awakening.* Two documentary films that clearly underscore how much time, energy, talent, and resources were required to bring about the legalization of gay marriage through the courts are *The Case Against 8* (HBO Documentary Films, 2014), by Ben Cotner and Ryan White, and *The Freedom by Marry* (Eyepop Productions, 2016), by Eddie Rosenthal.

CHAPTER 3. THE EVOLUTION OF PUBLIC OPINION ABOUT GAY MARRIAGE

1 Centers for Disease Control and Prevention, "Births and Natality" and "Deaths and Mortality."

2 Since fewer than fifty thousand youth under age eighteen die each year, I treat the number of births and the number of youth turning eighteen as effectively equal. Among people who die between the ages of eighteen and sixty-five, I assume 50 percent oppose and 50 percent support gay marriage.

3 This calculation does not count immigration, either. Since 2003, the United States has gained just under one million people per year due to net immigration. To my knowledge, no studies exist about the attitudes of immigrants about gay marriage. It is likely that immigrants are less supportive of gay marriage than native-born whites, but even if all new immigrants opposed gay marriage, the number of new gay marriage supporters entering the population would continue to outpace the number of new gay marriage opponents by about one million annually.

4 Ryder, "Cohort as a Concept."

5 Danigelis, Hardy, and Cutler, "Population Aging."

6 Alwin and Krosnick, "Aging, Cohorts, and the Stability of Sociopolitical Orientations"; Sears and Funk, "Evidence of the Long-Term Persistence"; Glenn, "Aging and Conservatism."

7 The persistence hypothesis has also been called the aging-stability hypothesis. Both are well-supported in the literature. Schuman and Scott, "Generations and Collective Memories"; Alwin and Krosnick, "Aging, Cohorts, and the Stability of Sociopolitical Orientations"; Sears and Funk, "Evidence of the Long-Term Persistence"; Firebaugh and Chen, "Vote Turnout of Nineteenth Amendment Women."

8 Harding and Jencks, "Changing Attitudes toward Premarital Sex."

9 Weil, "Cohorts, Regimes, and the Legitimation of Democracy"; Alexander et al., Cultural Trauma and Collective Identity. One such gradual change is a society-wide increase in tolerance toward numerous stigmatized groups, like communists and atheists. The fact that all age groups are slowly becoming more tolerant of many minority groups suggests that we are currently living in a unique historical period that is distinguished more by cultural evolution than by cultural trauma. Schwadel and Garneau, "Age-Period-Cohort Analysis"; Danigelis, Hardy, and Cutler, "Population Aging."

10 There is no evidence that people's acceptance of homosexuality decreases with age; instead, tolerance of homosexuality has increased both because of cohort replacement and because people of all ages are becoming more tolerant. Loftus, "America's Liberalization in Attitudes toward Homosexuality"; Treas, "How Cohorts, Education, and Ideology Shaped a New Sexual Revolution."

11 General Social Survey, "Response Rate and Field Period."

12 Baunach, "Changing Same-Sex Marriage Attitudes"; Sherkat, de Vries, and Creek, "Race, Religion, and Opposition"; Sherkat et al., "Religion, Politics, and Support."

13 Response rates for these polling firms were consistently 30 to 40 percent during the 1990s, but they have now fallen below 10 percent. For the 2003 Pew study, the reported response rate was 27.3 percent. For the 2013 Pew study, the response rate for Americans contacted by landline was 10.2 percent, while the response rate for the cell phone sample was 5.7 percent.

14 Loftus, "America's Liberalization in Attitudes toward Homosexuality"; Treas, "How Cohorts, Education, and Ideology Shaped a New Sexual Revolution"; Ciabattari, "Changes in Men's Conservative Gender Ideologies"; Brewster and Padavic, "Change in Gender Ideology"; Brooks and Bolzendahl, "Transformation of US Gender Role Attitudes."

15 The slope of the linear regression for the 1988 data (.002, controlling for other demographic variables) is statistically no different from zero. Baunach, "Changing Same-Sex Marriage Attitudes."

16 In my own ordinal logistic regression analyses of these data, I compared six different measurements of age/cohort: two linear measures (age and birth year) and four categorical cohort measures (three- and five-category cohort measures, assuming sixteen- or eighteen-year coming-of-age moments). There were no substantive differences in the results that depended upon cohort measurement.

17 Comparing 1988 and 2008 data, Darren Sherkat and his colleagues write, "The most conservative cohorts were born before 1940, and these cohorts constituted only 14% of the sample by 2008—down from 38% of the sample in 1988. Further, the most liberal cohorts, those born after 1965, now comprise 43% of GSS respondents." Sherkat et al., "Religion, Politics, and Support," 177.

18 The choice to subtract eighteen years (rather than sixteen, seventeen, nineteen, or twenty) is somewhat arbitrary because it is a rough indicator of when individuals "come of age." However, eighteen years is more meaningful in the United States because that is the year when Americans are officially labeled adults and become eligible to vote. Because the boundaries of periods and cohorts are both fluid and partially determined by the idiosyncratic differences in individual experiences, the years used to define periods and cohorts should be interpreted as rough estimates, suggestive of a more complex phenomenon.

19 This is Firebaugh's linear decomposition technique. Firebaugh, "Methods for Estimating Cohort Replacement Effects"; Firebaugh and Davis, "Trends in Antiblack Prejudice."

20 See Table A.2 for details. If we exclude the 1988 data, about one-sixth of the total change in public opinion between 2006 and 2014 is due to cohort replacement, while five-sixths of the change is due to intra-cohort attitude change.

21 Baunach, "Changing Same-Sex Marriage Attitudes."

22 For more on the relation between religion, politics, and attitudes about gay marriage, see Sherkat et al., "Religion, Politics, and Support"; Olson, Cadge, and Harrison, "Religion and Public Opinion."

23 In my own ordinal regression analyses, opposition to gay marriage was statistically higher among men, whites, people with lower levels of educational attainment,

people with more conservative political beliefs, people who attend religious services more often, people who identify as born-again, and members of older cohorts. Additionally, opposition to gay marriage was statistically (and increasingly) lower with every passing year compared to 1988. Among the demographic variables that had no statistically significant association with gay marriage, controlling for other demographic variables, are religious identity, marital status, population size of the city/town of residence, and region of the country. See Table A.4 for the results of this analysis of GSS data.

24 Baunach, "Changing Same-Sex Marriage Attitudes," 376.

25 Among the likely contributing factors are increases in educational attainment, increasing personal contact with lesbians and gays, increasing visibility of lesbians and gays in the mass media, the rise of the "independent life stage," and expanding definitions of what counts as "family." Hull, "Same-Sex, Different Attitudes"; Powell et al., *Counted Out*; Ohlander, Batalova, and Treas, "Explaining Educational Influences"; Brewer, *Value War*; Herek and Glunt, "Interpersonal Contact and Heterosexuals' Attitudes toward Gay Men"; Rosenfeld, *Age of Independence*; Schiappa, Gregg, and Hewes, "Can One TV Show Make a Difference?"; Seidman, *Beyond the Closet*.

26 Powell, Quadlin, and Pizmony-Levy, "Public Opinion, the Courts, and Same-Sex Marriage."

27 See Table A.3 for estimates of the total effects (direct plus indirect) for each variable in the model.

28 See Table A.4.

29 Yang, "Social Inequalities in Happiness"; Yang and Land, "Mixed Models Approach." For an illustration of this method applied to tolerance for homosexuality, see Schwadel and Garneau, "Age-Period-Cohort Analysis."

30 See Table A.5. The first three models show that age is related to opinion about gay marriage, and that individuals in younger cohorts and in more recent years are more supportive than those in older cohorts and in earlier years. Models 4 and 5 allow for the effect of moral judgments of homosexuality and the effect of education on opinions about gay marriage to vary from year to year. These two models show that the effects of these two variables on public opinion—especially education—changed over time.

31 See Table A.6. Compared with Table A.5, each model performs slightly better with the Identity Cohort dummy variable, as measured by model fit statistics. The differences are quite small, but the results are consistent with an interpretation of history that those reaching adulthood after 1992 came of age in a unique historical period. In Models 1 and 2, an individual's age is unrelated to opinions about gay marriage, once cohort and year are taken into account.

32 For a scholarly analysis of the 2003 data, see Brewer, *Value War*. The Pew Research Center's descriptive reports of each survey are Dimock and Doherty, "In Gay Marriage Debate"; Pew Research Center, "Republicans Unified, Democrats Split."

33 The ordinal regression results of my analyses of the Pew data can be seen in Table A.7.

34 Pew's measure of relative discomfort about being "around homosexuals" is plausibly related to attitudes about lesbians and gays; however, it appears to have a small but statistically significant effect on opinion about gay marriage, apart from other variables.

35 Although these two numbers cannot be directly compared (they come from different questions), they suggest that the shift in Americans' attitudes had bigger policy implications.

36 The 2013 question is identical to a question from a 1993 NBC/*Wall Street Journal* poll, to which 61 percent replied that they knew someone who is gay or lesbian. Thus, over twenty years, the percentage of Americans saying they know someone who is gay or lesbian increased about 26 percentage points. Dimock, Doherty, and Kiley, "Growing Support for Gay Marriage."

37 It is possible that some of this change is attributable to a change in question wording. The 2003 question was phrased in terms of homosexuality, while the 2013 question was phrased in terms of gays and lesbians: "Which comes closer to your view: people are born gay or lesbian, being gay or lesbian is a result of a person's upbringing, or being gay or lesbian is just the way that some people choose to live?"

38 This question was not asked in the 2013 survey, so we don't know how much these beliefs may have changed.

CHAPTER 4. YOUNG AND OLD IN THE CROSS FIRE OF THE CULTURE WARS

1 This chapter draws on Mikhail Bakhtin's dialogic theory of language. He argues that each utterance or speech act cannot be interpreted purely on its own terms; it is always expressed in dialogue with other speech acts—past, present, and future—that compose the shared culture and language of a social group. Bakhtin, *Dialogic Imagination*. In other words, all statements must be analyzed in their broader sociohistorical context, not just the immediate context of interaction. From this perspective, people's answers to the questions of interviewers are not just expressions of inner belief, but interventions in a broader discursive field full of innumerable interlocutors.

2 Hunter, *Culture Wars*. "This election is about more than who gets what. It is about who we are. It is about what we believe and what we stand for as Americans. There is a religious war going on in this country. It is a cultural war as critical to the kind of nation we shall be as was the Cold War itself, for this war is for the soul of America." Buchanan, "Culture War Speech."

3 Evans, "Have Americans' Attitudes Become More Polarized?"; Fiorina, Abrams, and Pope, *Culture War?*; DiMaggio, Evans, and Bryson, "Have Americans' Social Attitudes Become More Polarized?"; Mouw and Sobel, "Culture Wars and Opinion Polarization."

4 Davis and Robinson, "Are the Rumors of War Exaggerated?" and "Religious Orthodoxy in American Society."

5 Evans, "'Culture Wars.'"

6 "Discourse" here refers to the patterns of talk that combine structurally related elements from a speaker's cultural repertoire in regular, repeating ways. My understanding of discourse combines Michel Foucault's more structural theory of discourse with Ann Swidler's analysis of how people creatively use the large, shared reservoir of culture to construct statements and interpret the world. Foucault, *Archaeology of Knowledge*; Swidler, *Talk of Love*.

7 Hunter, *Culture Wars*, 44–45. See also Hunter, "Response to Davis and Robinson."

8 Hunter, *Culture Wars*, 34.

9 Miller and Hoffmann show that religiously progressive and orthodox became increasingly likely to identify themselves as politically liberal and conservative, respectively, independent of any actual changes in belief. So people's collective identities changed, even when their beliefs didn't. Miller and Hoffmann, "Growing Divisiveness."

10 Baldassarri and Bearman describe culture war dynamics as "takeoff situations." Political polarization can happen around issues like abortion and gay marriage when it becomes a salient issue, when opinions are more polarized than other issues, and when people's social network structures are also more polarized. Baldassarri and Bearman, "Dynamics of Political Polarization."

11 I heard many varieties of middle-ground discourses in my interviews, and there were probably many more that I did not hear because of my sample demographics. All of the middle-ground discourses show some openness to the claims of both polar discourses. One will be discussed in Chapter 6 because the definition of marriage is central to it.

12 For more on how journalistic norms of objectivity and newsworthiness affect the appearance of elites in the news media, see Schudson, *Discovering the News*; Gans, *Deciding What's News*; Tuchman, *Making News*; Ferree et al., *Shaping Abortion Discourse*; Danielian and Page, "Heavenly Chorus."

13 Psychologist Jonathan Haidt has shown that this type of discourse is common in Western, individualistic societies like the United States. Haidt's interpretation would be that these informants' moral-emotional reactions to homosexuality are processed quickly and automatically, but that they use slow, deliberate cognition to evaluate whether or not the reaction is appropriate. Haidt, *Righteous Mind*.

14 Education could also explain this association, since young cohorts have higher rates of educational attainment, and education is positively associated with support for gay marriage. My research design makes it impossible to test this possibility with my data since my student informants have roughly equal (and incomplete) educational attainment.

15 Two more student-parent pairs appear to follow this pattern, but do not really because of a semantic disagreement. In these cases, the students fail to articulate

an unambiguously supportive discourse only because they insist that marriage is a religious institution and that all marriages should be called civil unions.

16 In a famous essay, Georg Simmel wrote, "The essence of the blasé attitude is an indifference toward the distinctions between things." It is not that young people do not notice a distinction between straight and gay, but that they attach very little significance to it. In my interviews, it was never clear whether people really *felt* that way or whether the blasé attitude—that we *should not* attach much significance to sexual orientation—was more normative. Simmel, "Metropolis and Mental Life," 329.

17 Schiappa, Gregg, and Hewes, "Can One TV Show Make a Difference?"

CHAPTER 5. THE IMAGINATION AND ATTRIBUTION OF HOMOSEXUALITY

1 Weiner, Perry, and Magnusson, "Attributional Analysis of Reactions to Stigmas."

2 Haider-Markel and Joslyn, "Beliefs about the Origins of Homosexuality"; Wilcox and Wolpert, "Gay Rights in the Public Sphere"; Wood and Bartkowski, "Attribution Style and Public Policy Attitudes."

3 LeVay, "Difference in Hypothalmic Structure."

4 Haider-Markel and Joslyn, "Beliefs about the Origins of Homosexuality"; Lewis, "Does Believing Homosexuality Is Innate Increase Support for Gay Rights?"; Powell et al., *Counted Out.*

5 For a very accessible discussion of this literature, see Haidt, *Righteous Mind.*

6 Boysen and Vogel, "Biased Assimilation and Attitude Polarization"; Gawronski, "Back to the Future of Dissonance Theory"; Skitka et al., "Dispositions, Scripts, or Motivated Correction?"

7 For a discussion of this, see Lewis, "Does Believing Homosexuality Is Innate Increase Support for Gay Rights?"; Whitehead, "Sacred Rites and Civil Rights."

8 This is a classic case of social desirability bias. If people do not already have knowledge or strong opinions about an issue, they are more likely to agree with a statement, and they are more likely to answer questions in ways that they think other people would approve of.

9 Haidt, *Righteous Mind*; Vaisey, "Motivation and Justification"; Evans, "'Culture Wars.'"

10 For one discussion of how ideology works both socially and cognitively, see Martin and Desmond, "Political Position and Social Knowledge."

11 Lakoff and Johnson, *Metaphors We Live By*, 5.

12 Ibid., 115.

13 More recently, psychologists and cognitive scientists have begun to argue that different theories of cognition—like dual process theories and embodied cognition theories—are consistent with this view of metaphors. In terms of dual process theories, people automatically, unconsciously process phenomena in terms of the schemas that structure our minds; any schema that is defined metaphorically will

cause us to process new experiences metaphorically, too. In terms of embodied (or grounded) cognition, metaphors redefine abstract concepts in terms that connect to our bodily existence in the world. Landau, Meier, and Keefer, "Metaphor-Enriched Social Cognition."

14 Ricoeur, *Rule of Metaphor*.

15 Berggren, "Use and Abuse of Metaphor, I," 247.

16 Ricoeur, *Rule of Metaphor*, 208.

17 Berggren, "Use and Abuse of Metaphor, I," 245–246.

18 The preceding discussion, as well as the analysis in this chapter, is a fusion of conceptual metaphor theory from the cognitive sciences with the tension theory of metaphor from the humanities. For the purpose of interpretive sociological analysis, I found the fusion necessary to capture the dynamics of structure and agency inherent in the work that metaphors do when actors articulate them. From conceptual metaphor theory, we learn how metaphors shape and constrain both human cognition and the cultural meanings that we take for granted. In tension theory, we see the agentic capacity of human communicators to construct new meanings from their poetic use of metaphors. Berggren, "Use and Abuse of Metaphor, I" and "Use and Abuse of Metaphor, II"; Ricoeur, *Rule of Metaphor*; Lakoff and Johnson, *Metaphors We Live By*; Gibbs, *Poetics of Mind*.

19 Schatzberg, *Political Legitimacy in Middle Africa*, 31.

20 For other studies that illustrate social significance of metaphor, see Burgers, "Conceptualizing Change in Communication"; Winchester, "Hunger for God"; Ignatow, "Speaking Together, Thinking Together?"; Merten and Schwartz, "Metaphor and Self."

21 Another prominent metaphor for talking about homosexuality is the closet, which has been thoroughly analyzed elsewhere. Seidman, Meeks, and Traschen, "Beyond the Closet?" An important difference between the metaphor of the closet and those discussed here is that the closet metaphor is still vital and poetic. It also has a very specific referent in discourse, unlike the metaphors of orientation and attraction. We will see, though, that the closet metaphor is nevertheless related to the larger invisibility metaphor that I discuss later in the chapter.

22 The *Oxford English Dictionary* dates the phrase *sexual orientation* to 1931, when James Lichtenberger used it to describe his society's awareness and preoccupation with sex. J. P. Lichtenberger, *Divorce*. Although it had attained its current meaning by the 1940s, the phrase was used only rarely in the sex research of the 1940s and did not even appear in indexes of major works on human sexuality (e.g., Seward, *Sex and the Social Order*; Kinsey, Pomeroy, and Martin, *Sexual Behavior in the Human Male*). In large-scale analyses of English literature, the use of "sexual orientation" increased gradually between 1970 and 1990, and then grew exponentially (about 300 percent) between 1991 and 1995. Michel et al., "Quantitative Analysis of Culture."

23 Lévi-Strauss, *Savage Mind*; Alexander and Smith, "Discourse of American Civil Society"; Gamson, *Freaks Talk Back*.

24 Thanks to the reviewer for pointing out this latter one.

25 There is an important substantive and phenomenological difference between formal rights and informal privileges. Public displays of affection between two individuals of the same sex—like holding hands and kissing—receive less public support than formal legal rights. Doan, Loehr, and Miller, "Formal Rights and Informal Privileges."

CHAPTER 6. THE IMAGINARY MARRIAGE CONSENSUS

1 For an extended analysis of how Americans talk about love and marriage, see Swidler, *Talk of Love.*

2 Habermas, *Theory of Communicative Action*, vols. 1 and 2.

3 Doan, Loehr, and Miller, "Formal Rights and Informal Privileges."

4 For more on what I am calling the social connotations of marriage, see Quinn's analysis of the "cultural model" of marriage. Quinn, "Culture and Contradiction."

5 On an impulse, I decided to see how easy it is to do this. It took me less than three minutes to do everything I needed on the Universal Life Church's website (the hardest part was choosing a password for my account). However, I declined to pay $29.99 for the "ordination package" that would provide me with the legal documentation that I am now a minister (along with some extra goodies, like an official-looking "Minister" parking permit—in both window-cling and rear-view-mirror-hanger forms).

6 On this latter point, see Boswell, *Same-Sex Unions.*

7 Illouz, *Consuming the Romantic Utopia*; Mintz and Kellogg, *Domestic Revolutions*; Cherlin, *Marriage-Go-Round*; Thornton and Young-DeMarco, "Four Decades of Trends."

8 See Smith's analysis of the Standard North American Family (SNAF) for a discussion of the ideological power of such discourses. Smith, "Standard North American Family."

9 Coontz, *Way We Never Were.*

10 Gamson, *Modern Families*; Stacey, *Brave New Families.*

11 "Catechism of the Catholic Church," paragraph 1603.

12 Thornton and Young-DeMarco, "Four Decades of Trends."

13 Powell et al., *Counted Out*; Gerson, *Unfinished Revolution*; Treas; Harding, and Jencks, "Changing Attitudes toward Premarital Sex"; Ciabattari, "Changes in Men's Conservative Gender Ideologies"; Brewster and Padavic, "Change in Gender Ideology"; Brooks and Bolzendahl, "Transformation of US Gender Role Attitudes."

14 That is not to say that no cultural values, beliefs, or ideals have changed. Karla Hackstaff argues that "marriage culture" has been replaced by "divorce culture" in the United States, such that we now believe that "marrying is an option, marriage is contingent, and divorce is a getaway." Her comparison of how two cohorts talked about marriage—couples who married in the 1950s versus those who married in the 1970s—shows both cohort differences and intra-cohort change. Hackstaff, *Marriage in a Culture of Divorce.*

15 Cherlin estimates that 84 percent of American women will marry by age forty, while 50 percent of US marriages will end in divorce. Cherlin, *Marriage-Go-Round*.

16 *Obergefell v. Hodges*, 576 US ___ (2015), 3.

17 Ibid., 17.

18 In effect, the US Supreme Court ruled in favor of gay marriage because of both the Due Process Clause and the Equal Protection Clause of the Fourteenth Amendment. Together, the two clauses read, "No state shall make or enforce any law which shall abridge the privileges or immunities of citizens of the United States; nor shall any State deprive any person of life, liberty, or property, without due process of law; nor deny to any person within its jurisdiction the equal protection of the laws." Although the Court could have legalized gay marriages throughout the United States on the basis of the Equal Protection Clause alone, the high cultural value that society places on marriage prompted the Court to classify marriage as one of those matters of "life, liberty, or property" that are so important that the government cannot deprive citizens of it. Ibid.

19 The efforts of American policy makers to promote marriage as part of the 1996 welfare reform bill are another illustration of how the social connotations of marriage can be deployed for political ends. In this case, they were put to work against the cause of gay marriage, not for it. Heath, *One Marriage under God*.

20 I was careful to never mention the topic of gay marriage to my participants before I had the opportunity to interview them about marriage and relationships in general.

21 Codes I considered to be religious were blessing, calling, chapel, church, covenant, faith, faithful, religious, God, sacred, and spiritual. Almost all informants eventually used some type of religious language after further probing and follow-up questions, so it is not that they don't see marriage as a religious institution. The point is that the contested definition of marriage is not something that people usually bring up in a nonpoliticized communication context.

22 For more on the cultural meanings of commitment in Americans' talk about marriage, see Quinn, "'Commitment' in American Marriage."

23 Back in 2002, Lisa Duggan defined "the new homonormativity" as "a politics that does not contest dominant heteronormative assumptions and institutions but upholds and sustains them while promising the possibility of a demobilized gay constituency and a privatized, depoliticized gay culture anchored in domesticity and consumption." Duggan, "New Homonormativity," 179. Although she is correct that gay marriage does not challenge the existing institution of marriage in a fundamental way, with the benefit of hindsight, I see no evidence to legitimate the fear that lesbians and gays will cease to be politically active after the battle is won. Quite the contrary: after the legalization of gay marriage, activists were quick to remind supporters that without equal protection in all fifty states, lesbians and gays could be "married on Sunday, but fired on Monday." Robinson, "State of LGBT Rights."

24 Cherlin, "Deinstitutionalization of American Marriage."

25 Studies that have analyzed the effects of gay marriage in European societies show that very little of consequence changed as a result of its legalization. M. V. Lee Badgett summarizes her findings thusly: "Marriage poses more of a challenge to gay people than gay people do to marriage." Badgett, *When Gay People Get Married*, 202; Eskridge and Spedale, *Gay Marriage*.

26 Recent studies suggest that marriage and family relationships that feature gender equality in educational attainment, earnings, and the household division of labor are more successful than they used to be—although not necessarily better than "traditional" male-dominated households. Schwartz and Han, "Reversal of the Gender Gap"; Carlson et al., "Gendered Division of Housework." Nancy Polikoff's work illustrates what it would mean legally and politically to value other family forms equally to marriage. Polikoff, *Beyond (Straight and Gay) Marriage*.

CHAPTER 7. NARRATIVES OF ATTITUDE CHANGE AND RESISTANT SUBCULTURES

1 This would also be a sound hypothesis: as mentioned earlier, there is plenty of evidence to support the contact hypothesis, which states that personal contact with particular members of an out-group can reduce prejudice toward the group as a whole under certain circumstances. In Taylor's case, though, those conditions were not present, so the tolerant attitudes never followed. Allport, *Nature of Prejudice*.

2 Alwin and Krosnick, "Aging, Cohorts, and the Stability of Sociopolitical Orientations"; Miller and Sears, "Stability and Change in Social Tolerance"; Sears and Funk, "Evidence of the Long-Term Persistence."

3 Danigelis, Hardy, and Cutler, "Population Aging."

4 Glaeser, *Political Epistemics*.

5 The concept of interpretive community comes originally from Stanley Fish and has been fruitfully applied in studies of culture to explain how different cultural artifacts—books, songs, etc.—come to mean different things to different people. Thinking about culture more broadly, the concept of interpretive communities describes real groups and networks of people who share a common framework or worldview for making sense of the world. Fish, *Is There a Text in This Class?*

6 Smith, *American Evangelicalism*.

CONCLUSION

1 When the Pew Research Center asked Americans if they thought the legal recognition of gay marriage was inevitable, 59 percent said yes in 2004, and 72 percent said yes in 2013. Dimock and Doherty, "In Gay Marriage Debate."

2 Although frequently attributed to King, it actually originated from a Unitarian minister named Theodore Parker, in a sermon called "Of Justice and the Conscience." Parker, *Ten Sermons of Religion*, 84–85.

3 For a discussion of the multiple, shifting legal rationales for challenging gay marriage bans as unconstitutional, see Engel, *Fragmented Citizens*.

4 *Masterpiece Cakeshop v. Colorado Civil Rights Commission*, no. 16-111 (2017).

5 North Carolina's "bathroom bill" (House Bill 2, signed into law in 2016) was the most infamous of these efforts. For a concise, accessible analysis of this particular form of backlash, see Schilt and Westbrook, "Bathroom Battlegrounds and Penis Panics."

6 McCarthy, "U.S. Support for Gay Marriage"; Pew Research Center, "Support for Same-Sex Marriage Grows."

7 Abramson and Inglehart, "Generational Replacement and Value Change"; Inglehart, Ponarin, and Inglehart, "Cultural Change, Slow and Fast"; Norris and Inglehart, *Sacred and Secular.*

8 As described in Chapter 1, the Baby Boom cohort is clearly defined and can be used as a meaningful cohort label. Absent this sort of evidence for the existence of other cohorts, we should reject the labels out of hand.

9 Twenge, *iGen.*

10 Hout and Fischer, "Explaining Why More Americans Have No Religious Preference"; Hout and Fischer, "Why More Americans Have No Religious Preference."

11 There is some suggestive evidence that support for gay marriage is associated with pornography consumption among men, for example. Wright and Randall, "Pornography Consumption, Education, and Support for Same-Sex Marriage." For evidence on the relation between gay marriage and marijuana legalization, see Schnabel and Sevell, "Should Mary and Jane Be Legal?"

12 Boutyline, "Improving the Measurement of Shared Cultural Schemas"; Boutyline and Vaisey, "Belief Network Analysis"; Goldberg, "Mapping Shared Understandings."

13 It is no coincidence that Mannheim has also written on the concept of worldviews. Mannheim, "On the Interpretation of the Weltanschauung."

14 On the social construction of time, see Berger and Luckmann, *Social Construction of Reality*; Zerubavel, *Social Mindscapes.*

15 Zerubavel, *Time Maps.*

16 Ortega y Gasset, *Man and Crisis*; Strauss and Howe, *Generations.*

17 Braudel, *On History.*

18 From vol. 4 of *Cours de Philosophie Positive*, quoted in Comte, *Auguste Comte and Positivism*, 256.

19 Comte himself had an evolutionary view of society and believed that progress was inevitable. Even though we now reject the idea of linear progress in history, it is nonetheless reasonable to imagine that the indefinite prolonging of life would dramatically decrease the pace of social change.

20 In Piotr Sztompka's rich analysis of theories of social change, neither is Mannheim cited nor is generational change discussed. "Generation" does not even appear in the index. Mannheim's theory is quite compatible with Sztompka's own model of "social becoming," so it would be incorrect to conclude that Sztompka's theory cannot account for generational change. However, it is striking that one of the most ubiquitous processes of social change, fundamental to every society, is never

mentioned. Generational change is in need of deeper theoretical and conceptual exegesis. Sztompka, *Sociology of Social Change*.

21 For influential sociological theories of time, structure, and change, see Abbott, *Time Matters*; Sztompka, *Sociology of Social Change*.

APPENDIX

1 My approach was guided by Glaser and Strauss's explanation of "theoretical sampling." Glaser and Strauss, *Discovery of Grounded Theory*.

2 The interview guide effectively made these "semistructured interviews," though I followed Rubin and Rubin's "responsive interviewing" approach before and during data collection. Rubin and Rubin, *Qualitative Interviewing*.

3 Glaser and Strauss, *Discovery of Grounded Theory*; Strauss, *Qualitative Analysis for Social Scientists*; Blumer, *Symbolic Interactionism*.

4 Listening to the audio recording while reading along with the transcript during the initial open coding phase not only served as a validity check on the accuracy of the transcriptions, but also helped generate a depth of insight into the interview that I would not have had otherwise. Being able to hear the interview helped me to remember it better and allowed me to hear tone, pacing, stutters, and emotion in the voice that would not otherwise have been evident in the written transcript alone.

5 For readings on the value of qualitative interview methods and interpretive studies, see Pugh, "What Good Are Interviews for Thinking about Culture?"; Reed, "Epistemology Contextualized" and "Justifying Sociological Knowledge"; Martin, *Explanation of Social Action*.

6 Weber, *Economy and Society*, 4.

BIBLIOGRAPHY

Abbott, Andrew. *Time Matters: On Theory and Method*. Chicago: University of Chicago Press, 2001.

Aboim, Sofia, and Pedro Vasconcelos. "From Political to Social Generations: A Critical Reappraisal of Mannheim's Classical Approach." *European Journal of Social Theory* 17, no. 2 (2013): 165–183.

Abramson, Paul R., and Ronald Inglehart. "Generational Replacement and Value Change in Six West European Societies." *American Journal of Political Science* 30, no. 1 (February 1986): 1–25.

Alexander, Jeffrey C., Ron Eyerman, Bernhard Giesen, Neil J. Smelser, and Piotr Sztompka. *Cultural Trauma and Collective Identity*. Berkeley: University of California Press, 2004.

Alexander, Jeffrey C., and Philip Smith. "The Discourse of American Civil Society: A New Proposal for Cultural Studies." *Theory and Society* 22, no. 2 (April 1993): 151–207.

Allport, Gordon W. *The Nature of Prejudice*. New York: Basic Books, 1954.

Alwin, Duane F., Ronald L. Cohen, and Theodore M. Newcomb. *Political Attitudes over the Life Span: The Bennington Women after Fifty Years*. Madison: University of Wisconsin Press, 1991.

Alwin, Duane F., and Jon A. Krosnick. "Aging, Cohorts, and the Stability of Sociopolitical Orientations over the Life Span." *American Journal of Sociology* 97, no. 1 (July 1991): 169–195.

Alwin, Duane F., and Ryan J. McCammon. "Rethinking Generations." *Research in Human Development* 4, nos. 3–4 (2007): 219–237.

Andersen, Robert, and Tina Fetner. "Cohort Differences in Tolerance of Homosexuality: Attitudinal Change in Canada and the United States, 1981–2000." *Public Opinion Quarterly* 72, no. 2 (Summer 2008): 311–330.

Anderson, Benedict R. *Imagined Communities: Reflections on the Origin and Spread of Nationalism*. New York: Verso, 1991.

Appadurai, Arjun. *Modernity at Large: Cultural Dimensions of Globalization*. Minneapolis: University of Minnesota Press, 1996.

Armstrong, Elizabeth A. *Forging Gay Identities: Organizing Sexuality in San Francisco, 1950–1994*. Chicago: University of Chicago Press, 2002.

Armstrong, Elizabeth A., and Suzanna M. Crage. "Movements and Memory: The Making of the Stonewall Myth." *American Sociological Review* 71, no. 5 (October 2006): 724–751.

Badgett, M. V. Lee. *When Gay People Get Married: What Happens When Societies Legalize Same-Sex Marriage*. New York: New York University Press, 2009.

Baiocchi, Gianpaolo, Elizabeth A. Bennett, Alissa Cordner, Peter Taylor Klein, and Stephanie Savell. *The Civic Imagination: Making a Difference in American Political Life*. Boulder, CO: Paradigm, 2014.

Bakhtin, Mikhail. *The Dialogic Imagination: Four Essays*. Translated by Caryl Emerson and Michael Holquist. Austin: University of Texas Press, 1981.

Baldassarri, Delia, and Peter Bearman. "Dynamics of Political Polarization." *American Sociological Review* 72, no. 5 (October 2007): 784–811.

Bauerlein, Mark. *The Dumbest Generation: How the Digital Age Stupefies Young Americans and Jeopardizes Our Future*. New York: Jeremy P. Tarcher/Penguin, 2008.

Baunach, Dawn Michelle. "Changing Same-Sex Marriage Attitudes in American from 1988 through 2010." *Public Opinion Quarterly* 76, no. 2 (June 2012): 364–378.

Bayer, Ronald. *Homosexuality and American Psychiatry: The Politics of Diagnosis*. New York: Basic Books, 1981.

Becker, Ron. *Gay TV and Straight America*. New Brunswick, NJ: Rutgers University Press, 2006.

Begley, Sharon. "What Causes People to Be Homosexual?" *Newsweek*, September 9, 1991.

Bengtson, Vern L., Michael J. Furlong, and Robert S. Laufer. "Time, Aging, and the Continuity of Social Structure: Themes and Issues in Generational Analysis." *Journal of Social Issues* 30, no. 2 (1974): 1–30.

Berger, Peter L., and Thomas Luckmann. *The Social Construction of Reality: A Treatise in the Sociology of Knowledge*. New York: Anchor Books, 1966.

Berggren, Douglas. "The Use and Abuse of Metaphor, I." *Review of Metaphysics* 16, no. 2 (December 1962): 237–258.

———. "The Use and Abuse of Metaphor, II." *Review of Metaphysics* 16, no. 3 (March 1963): 450–472.

Bernstein, Mary. "Identities and Politics: Toward a Historical Understanding of the Lesbian and Gay Movement." *Social Science History* 26, no. 3 (Fall 2002): 531–581.

Blair, Irene V., Jennifer E. Ma, and Alison P. Lenton. "Imagining Stereotypes Away: The Moderation of Implicit Stereotypes through Mental Imagery." *Journal of Personality and Social Psychology* 81, no. 5 (2001): 828–841.

Blair-Loy, Mary. "Cultural Constructions of Family Schemas: The Case of Women Finance Executives." *Gender & Society* 15, no. 5 (October 2001): 687–709.

Blumer, Herbert. *Symbolic Interactionism: Perspective and Method*. Berkeley: University of California Press, 1969.

Boltanski, Luc. *Distant Suffering: Morality, Media, and Politics*. Cambridge Cultural Social Studies. New York: Cambridge University Press, 1999.

Boswell, John. *Same-Sex Unions in Premodern Europe*. New York: Villard Books, 1994.

Boutyline, Andrei. "Improving the Measurement of Shared Cultural Schemas with Correlational Class Analysis: Theory and Method." *Sociological Science* 4 (2017): 353–393.

Boutyline, Andrei, and Stephen Vaisey. "Belief Network Analysis: A Relational Approach to Understanding the Structure of Attitudes." *American Journal of Sociology* 122, no. 5 (March 2017): 1371–1447.

Bowers v. Hardwick, 478 US 186 (1986).

Boysen, Guy A., and David L. Vogel. "Biased Assimilation and Attitude Polarization in Response to Learning about Biological Explanations of Homosexuality." *Sex Roles* 57 (2007): 755–762.

Braudel, Fernand. *On History*. Translated by Sarah Matthews. Chicago: University of Chicago Press, 1980.

Brewer, Paul R. *Value War: Public Opinion and the Politics of Gay Rights*. Lanham, MD: Rowman & Littlefield, 2008.

Brewster, Karin L., and Irene Padavic. "Change in Gender Ideology, 1977–1996: The Contributions of Intracohort Change and Population Turnover." *Journal of Marriage and Family* 62, no. 2 (May 2000): 477–487.

Brooks, Clem, and Catherine Bolzendahl. "The Transformation of US Gender Role Attitudes: Cohort Replacement, Social-Structural Change, and Ideological Learning." *Social Science Research* 33, no. 1 (2004): 106–133.

Brown, Wendy. *Regulating Aversion: Tolerance in the Age of Identity and Empire*. Princeton, NJ: Princeton University Press, 2006.

Buchanan, Patrick. "Culture War Speech: Address to the Republican National Convention." Voices of Democracy: The U.S. Oratory Project, 1992. http://voicesofdemocracy.umd.edu.

Burgers, Christian. "Conceptualizing Change in Communication through Metaphor." *Journal of Communication* 66, no. 2 (April 2016): 250–265.

Cagle, Jess. "America Sees Shades of Gay." *Entertainment Weekly*, September 8, 1995.

Carlson, Daniel L., Amanda J. Miller, Sharon Sassler, and Sarah Hanson. "The Gendered Division of Housework and Couples' Sexual Relationships: A Reexamination." *Journal of Marriage and Family* 78, no. 4 (August 2016): 975–995.

Castoriadis, Cornelius. *The Imaginary Institution of Society*. Translated by Kathleen Blamey. Cambridge, MA: MIT Press, 1987.

"Catechism of the Catholic Church." Libreria Editrice Vaticana, n.d. www.vatican.va.

Cavalli, Alessandro. "Generations and Value Orientations." *Social Compass* 51, no. 2 (2004): 155–168.

Centers for Disease Control and Prevention. "Births and Natality." US Department of Health and Human Services, 2017. www.cdc.gov.

———. "Deaths and Mortality." US Department of Health and Human Services, 2017. www.cdc.gov.

Cherlin, Andrew J. "The Deinstitutionalization of American Marriage." *Journal of Marriage and Family* 66, no. 4 (November 2004): 848–861.

———. *The Marriage-Go-Round: The State of Marriage and the Family in America Today*. New York: Knopf, 2009.

Ciabattari, Teresa. "Changes in Men's Conservative Gender Ideologies: Cohort and Period Influences." *Gender & Society* 15, no. 4 (August 2001): 574–591.

Clendinen, Dudley, and Adam Nagourney. *Out for Good: The Struggle to Build a Gay Rights Movement in America.* New York: Simon & Schuster, 1999.

Clinton, William J. "Address Accepting the Presidential Nomination at the Democratic National Convention in New York." American Presidency Project, 1992. www.presidency.ucsb.edu.

Committee on Nomenclature and Statistics of the American Psychiatric Association. *Diagnostic and Statistical Manual of Mental Disorders.* Washington, DC: American Psychiatric Association, 1952.

Comte, Auguste. *Auguste Comte and Positivism: The Essential Writings.* Chicago: University of Chicago Press, 1983.

Conrad, Peter, and Joseph W. Schneider. *Deviance and Medicalization: From Badness to Sickness.* Philadelphia: Temple University Press, 1992.

Coontz, Stephanie. *The Way We Never Were: American Families and the Nostalgia Trap.* New York: Basic Books, 1992.

Corsten, Michael. "The Time of Generations." *Time and Society* 8, no. 2 (1999): 249–272.

Cutler, Neal E., and Vern L. Bengtson. "Age and Political Alienation: Maturation, Generation, and Period Effects." *Annals of the American Academy of Political and Social Science* 415 (September 1974): 160–175.

D'Andrade, Roy. *The Development of Cognitive Anthropology.* New York: Cambridge University Press, 1995.

Danielian, Lucig H., and Benjamin I. Page. "The Heavenly Chorus: Interest Groups on TV News." *American Journal of Political Science* 38, no. 4 (November 1994): 1056–1078.

Danigelis, Nicholas L., Melissa Hardy, and Stephen J. Cutler. "Population Aging, Intracohort Aging, and Sociopolitical Attitudes." *American Sociological Review* 72, no. 5 (October 2007): 812–830.

Davis, Nancy J., and Robert V. Robinson. "Are the Rumors of War Exaggerated? Religious Orthodoxy and Moral Progressivism in America." *American Journal of Sociology* 102, no. 3 (November 1996): 756–787.

———. "Religious Orthodoxy in American Society: The Myth of a Monolithic Camp." *Journal for the Scientific Study of Religion* 35, no. 3 (September 1996): 229–245.

Demartini, Joseph R. "Change Agents and Generational Relationships: A Reevaluation of Mannheim's Problem of Generations." *Social Forces* 64, no. 1 (September 1985): 1–16.

D'Emilio, John. *Sexual Politics, Sexual Communities: The Making of a Homosexual Minority in the United States, 1940–1970.* Chicago: University of Chicago Press, 1983.

Diamond, Sara. *Roads to Dominion: Right-Wing Movements and Political Power in the United States.* New York: Guilford, 1995.

DiMaggio, Paul, John Evans, and Bethany Bryson. "Have Americans' Social Attitudes Become More Polarized?" *American Journal of Sociology* 102, no. 3 (November 1996): 690–755.

Dimock, Michael, and Carroll Doherty. "In Gay Marriage Debate, Both Supporters and Opponents See Legal Recognition as 'Inevitable.'" Washington, DC: Pew Research Center for the People and the Press, 2013.

Dimock, Michael, Carroll Doherty, and Jocelyn Kiley. "Growing Support for Gay Marriage: Changed Minds and Changing Demographics." Washington, DC: Pew Research Center for the People and the Press, 2013.

Doan, Long, Annalise Loehr, and Lisa R. Miller. "Formal Rights and Informal Privileges for Same-Sex Couples: Evidence from a National Survey Experiment." *American Sociological Review* 79, no. 6 (December 2014): 1172–1195.

Doty, Robert C. "Growth of Overt Homosexuality in City Provokes Wide Concern." *New York Times*, December 17, 1963, 1, 33.

Duggan, Lisa. "The New Homonormativity: The Sexual Politics of Neoliberalism." In *Materializing Democracy: Toward a Revitalized Cultural Politics*, edited by Russ Castronovo and Dana D. Nelson, 175–194. Durham, NC: Duke University Press, 2002.

Durkheim, Émile. *The Elementary Forms of Religious Life*. Translated by Karen E. Fields. New York: Free Press, 1995.

Eilperin, Juliet. "For Obama, Rainbow White House Was 'a Moment Worth Saving.'" *Washington Post*, June 30, 2015.

Elder, Glen H., Jr. *Children of the Great Depression: Social Change in Life Experience*. Chicago: University of Chicago Press, 1974.

Engel, Stephen M. *Fragmented Citizens: The Changing Landscape of Gay and Lesbian Lives*. New York: New York University Press, 2016.

Epstein, Steven. *Impure Science: AIDS, Activism, and the Politics of Knowledge*. Berkeley: University of California Press, 1996.

Eskridge, William N., Jr., and Darren R. Spedale. *Gay Marriage: For Better or for Worse?* Oxford: Oxford University Press, 2006.

Esler, Anthony. "'The Truest Community': Social Generations as Collective Mentalities." *Journal of Political and Military Sociology* 12, no. 1 (Spring 1984): 99–112.

Evans, John H. "'Culture Wars' or Status Group Ideology as the Basis of US Moral Politics." *International Journal of Sociology and Social Policy* 16, no. 1 (1996): 15–34.

———. "Have Americans' Attitudes Become More Polarized? An Update." *Social Science Quarterly* 84, no. 1 (March 2003): 71–90.

Evans, Jonathan St. B. T. "Dual-Processing Accounts of Reasoning, Judgment, and Social Cognition." *Annual Review of Psychology* 59 (2008): 255–278.

Eyerman, Ron, and Bryan S. Turner. "Outline of a Theory of Generations." *European Journal of Social Theory* 1, no. 1 (1998): 91–106.

Fejes, Fred. *Gay Rights and Moral Panic*. New York: Palgrave Macmillan, 2008.

Fejes, Fred, and Kevin Petrich. "Invisibility, Homophobia, and Heterosexism: Lesbians, Gays and the Media." *Critical Studies in Mass Communication* 10, no. 4 (December 1993): 396–422.

Ferree, Myra Marx, William A. Gamson, Jurgen Gerhards, and Dieter Rucht. *Shaping Abortion Discourse: Democracy and the Public Sphere in Germany and the United States*. New York: Cambridge University Press, 2002.

Fetner, Tina. *How the Religious Right Shaped Lesbian and Gay Activism*. Minneapolis: University of Minnesota Press, 2008.

Fiorina, Morris P., Samuel J. Abrams, and Jeremy C. Pope. *Culture War? The Myth of a Polarized America*. New York: Pearson, 2005.

Firebaugh, Glenn. "Methods for Estimating Cohort Replacement Effects." *Sociological Methodology* 19 (1989): 243–262.

Firebaugh, Glenn, and Kevin Chen. "Vote Turnout of Nineteenth Amendment Women: The Enduring Effect of Disenfranchisement." *American Journal of Sociology* 100, no. 4 (January 1995): 972–996.

Firebaugh, Glenn, and Kenneth E. Davis. "Trends in Antiblack Prejudice, 1972–1984: Region and Cohort Effects." *American Journal of Sociology* 94, no. 2 (September 1988): 251–272.

Fish, Stanley. *Is There a Text in This Class? The Authority of Interpretive Communities*. Cambridge, MA: Harvard University Press, 1980.

Foucault, Michel. *The Archaeology of Knowledge and the Discourse on Language*. New York: Pantheon, 1972.

———. *The History of Sexuality, Volume 1: An Introduction*. New York: Vintage, 1978.

Frank, Nathaniel. *Awakening: How Gays and Lesbians Brought Marriage Equality to America*. Cambridge, MA: Belknap, 2017.

Gable, Donna. "King of Pop and 'Queen' Rule the Ratings." *USA Today*, February 17, 1993, D3.

Gallup. "Congress and the Public." N.d. http://news.gallup.com.

Gamson, Joshua. *Freaks Talk Back: Tabloid Talk Shows and Sexual Nonconformity*. Chicago: University of Chicago Press, 1998.

———. *Modern Families: Stories of Extraordinary Journeys to Kinship*. New York: New York University Press, 2015.

Gans, Herbert J. *Deciding What's News: A Study of CBS Evening News, NBC Nightly News, Newsweek, and Time*. New York: Pantheon, 1979.

Garretson, Jeremiah J. "Exposure to the Lives of Lesbians and Gays and the Origin of Young People's Greater Support for Gay Rights." *International Journal of Public Opinion Research* 27, no. 2 (2015): 277–288.

Gawronski, Bertram. "Back to the Future of Dissonance Theory: Cognitive Consistency as a Core Motive." *Social Cognition* 30, no. 6 (2012): 652–668.

General Social Survey. "G.S.S. Data Explorer." National Opinion Research Center, 2018. https://gssdataexplorer.norc.org.

———. "Response Rate and Field Period." N.d. http://gss.norc.org.

Gerson, Kathleen. *The Unfinished Revolution: Coming of Age in a New Era of Gender, Work, and Family*. New York: Oxford University Press, 2010.

Ghaziani, Amin. *Dividends of Dissent: How Conflict and Culture Work in Lesbian and Gay Marches on Washington*. Chicago: University of Chicago Press, 2008.

Ghiglione, Loren, Reid MacCluggage, Leroy F. Aarons, and Lee Stinnett. "Alternatives: Gays and Lesbians in the Newsroom. American Society of Newspaper Editors Human Resources Committee Report." New London, CT: American Society of Newspaper Editors, 1990.

Gibbs, Raymond W., Jr. *The Poetics of Mind: Figurative Thought, Language, and Understanding*. New York: Cambridge University Press, 1994.

Gilleard, Chris. "Cohorts and Generations in the Study of Social Change." *Social Theory and Health* 2, no. 1 (2004): 106–119.

Glaeser, Andreas. *Political Epistemics: The Secret Police, the Opposition, and the End of East German Socialism*. Chicago: University of Chicago Press, 2011.

Glaser, Barney, and Anselm L. Strauss. *The Discovery of Grounded Theory: Strategies for Qualitative Research*. New York: Aldine de Gruyter, 1967.

Glass, Ira. "81 Words." In *This American Life*. Public Radio International, 2002.

Glenn, Norval D. "Aging and Conservatism." *Annals of the American Academy of Political and Social Science* 415 (September 1974): 176–186.

———. "Values, Attitudes, and Beliefs." In *Constancy and Change in Human Development*, edited by Orville G. Brim Jr. and Jerome Kagan, 596–640. Cambridge, MA: Harvard University Press, 1980.

Goldberg, Amir. "Mapping Shared Understandings Using Relational Class Analysis: The Case of the Cultural Omnivore Reexamined." *American Journal of Sociology* 116, no. 5 (March 2011): 1397–1436.

Goode, Erich, and Nachman Ben-Yehuda. "Moral Panics: Culture, Politics, and Social Construction." *Annual Review of Sociology* 20 (1994): 149–171.

Gould, Deborah B. *Moving Politics: Emotion and ACT UP's Fight Against AIDS*. Chicago: University of Chicago Press, 2009.

Graham, Franklin. Post on Facebook, June 29, 2015. www.facebook.com.

Griffin, Larry J. "'Generations and Collective Memory' Revisited: Race, Region, and Memory of Civil Rights." *American Sociological Review* 69, no. 4 (August 2004): 544–577.

Gross, Larry. *Up from Invisibility: Lesbians, Gay Men, and the Media in America*. New York: Columbia University Press, 2001.

Gwin, Peter. "The Strait of Malacca: Dark Passage." *National Geographic*, October 2007, 126–149.

Haas, Peter M. "Introduction: Epistemic Communities and International Policy Coordination." *International Organization* 46, no. 1 (Winter 1992): 1–35.

Habermas, Jürgen. *The Structural Transformation of the Public Sphere: An Inquiry into a Category of Bourgeois Society*. Studies in Contemporary German Social Thought. Cambridge, MA: MIT Press, 1989.

———. *The Theory of Communicative Action*. Vol. 1. Boston: Beacon, 1984.

———. *The Theory of Communicative Action*. Vol. 2. Boston: Beacon, 1987.

Hackstaff, Karla. *Marriage in a Culture of Divorce*. Philadelphia: Temple University Press, 1999.

Haider-Markel, Donald P., and Mark R. Joslyn. "Beliefs about the Origins of Homosexuality and Support for Gay Rights: An Empirical Test of Attribution Theory." *Public Opinion Quarterly* 72, no. 2 (Summer 2008): 291–310.

Haidt, Jonathan. *The Righteous Mind: Why Good People Are Divided by Politics and Religion*. New York: Vintage, 2012.

Hamer, Dean H., Stella Hu, Victoria Magnuson, Nan Hu, and Angela M. L. Pattatucci. "A Linkage between DNA Markers on the X Chromosome and Male Sexual Orientation." *Science* 261, no. 5119 (July 16, 1993): 321–327.

Harding, David J., and Christopher Jencks. "Changing Attitudes toward Premarital Sex: Cohort, Period, and Aging Effects." *Public Opinion Quarterly* 67, no. 2 (Summer 2003): 211–226.

Hart-Brinson, Peter. "Discourse of Generations: The Influence of Cohort, Period, and Ideology in Americans' Talk about Same-Sex Marriage." *American Journal of Cultural Sociology* 2, no. 2 (2014): 221–252.

Havemann, Ernest. "Scientists Search for the Answers to a Touchy and Puzzling Question: Why?" *Life Magazine*, June 26, 1964, 76.

Healy, Kieran. "Fuck Nuance." *Sociological Theory* 35, no. 2 (2017): 118–127.

Heath, Melanie. *One Marriage under God: The Campaign to Promote Marriage in America*. New York: New York University Press, 2012.

Heidegger, Martin. *Kant and the Problem of Metaphysics*. Translated by James S. Churchill. Bloomington: Indiana University Press, 1962.

Herek, Gregory M., and Eric K. Glunt. "Interpersonal Contact and Heterosexuals' Attitudes toward Gay Men: Results from a National Survey." *Journal of Sex Research* 30, no. 3 (August 1993): 239–244.

Homan, Patricia, Lauren Valentino, and Emi Weed. "Being and Becoming Poor: How Cultural Schemas Shape Beliefs about Poverty." *Social Forces* 95, no. 3 (March 2017): 1023–1048.

Hout, Michael, and Claude S. Fischer. "Explaining Why More Americans Have No Religious Preference: Political Backlash and Generational Succession, 1987–2012." *Sociological Science* 1 (2014): 423–447.

———. "Why More Americans Have No Religious Preference: Politics and Generations." *American Sociological Review* 67, no. 2 (April 2002): 165–190.

Howard, John. *Men Like That: A Southern Queer History*. Chicago: University of Chicago Press, 1999.

Howe, Neil, and William Strauss. *Millennials Rising: The Next Great Generation*. New York: Vintage, 2000.

Hull, Kathleen E. "Same-Sex, Different Attitudes." The Society Pages, March 27, 2014. http://thesocietypages.org.

———. *Same-Sex Marriage: The Cultural Politics of Love and Law*. New York: Cambridge University Press, 2006.

Hunter, James Davison. *Culture Wars: The Struggle to Define America*. New York: Basic Books, 1991.

———. "Response to Davis and Robinson: Remembering Durkheim." *Journal for the Scientific Study of Religion* 35, no. 3 (September 1996): 246–248.

Hunzaker, M. B. Fallin. "Cultural Sentiments and Schema-Consistency Bias in Information Transmission." *American Sociological Review* 81, no. 6 (December 2016): 1223–1250.

———. "Making Sense of Misfortune: Cultural Schemas, Victim Redefinition, and the Perpetuation of Stereotypes." *Social Psychology Quarterly* 77, no. 2 (2014): 166–184.

Ignatow, Gabriel. "Speaking Together, Thinking Together? Exploring Metaphor and Cognition in a Shipyard Union Dispute." *Sociological Forum* 19, no. 3 (September 2004): 405–433.

Illouz, Eva. *Consuming the Romantic Utopia: Love and the Cultural Contradictions of Capitalism*. Berkeley: University of California Press, 1997.

Inglehart, Ronald F., Eduard Ponarin, and Ronald C. Inglehart. "Cultural Change, Slow and Fast: The Distinctive Trajectory of Norms Governing Gender Equality and Sexual Orientation." *Social Forces* 95, no. 4 (June 2017): 1313–1340.

Jaeger, Hans. "Generations in History: Reflections on a Controversial Concept." *History and Theory* 24, no. 3 (October 1985): 273–292.

Jennings, M. Kent, and Richard G. Niemi. *Generations and Politics: A Panel Study of Young Adults and Their Parents*. Princeton, NJ: Princeton University Press, 1981.

Jensen, Tom. "Democrats and Republicans Differ on Conspiracy Theory Beliefs" Public Policy Polling, April 2, 2013. www.publicpolicypolling.com.

Kant, Immanuel. *Critique of Pure Reason*. Translated by Norman Kemp Smith. New York: St. Martin's, 1929.

Kecskemeti, Paul, ed. *Essays on the Sociology of Knowledge*. London: Routledge & Kegan Paul, 1952.

Kertzer, David I. "Generation as a Sociological Problem." *Annual Review of Sociology* 9 (1983): 125–149.

Kinsey, Alfred C., Wardell B. Pomeroy, and Clyde E. Martin. *Sexual Behavior in the Human Male*. Philadelphia: W.B. Saunders, 1948.

Klatch, Rebecca E. *A Generation Divided: The New Left, the New Right, and the 1960s*. Berkeley: University of California Press, 1999.

Lakoff, George, and Mark Johnson. *Metaphors We Live By*. Chicago: University of Chicago Press, 1980.

Landau, Mark J., Brian P. Meier, and Lucas A. Keefer. "A Metaphor-Enriched Social Cognition." *Psychological Bulletin* 136, no. 6 (2010): 1045–1067.

Larson, Jeff A., and Omar Lizardo. "Generations, Identities, and the Collective Memory of Che Guevara." *Sociological Forum* 22, no. 4 (December 2007): 425–451.

Laufer, Robert S., and Vern L. Bengtson. "Generations, Aging, and Social Stratification: On the Development of Generational Units." *Journal of Social Issues* 30, no. 3 (1974): 181–205.

Leavitt, Eugene, and Albert Klassen. "Public Attitudes toward Homosexuality: Part of the 1970 National Survey by the Institute for Sex Research." *Journal of Homosexuality* 1, no. 1 (1974): 29–43.

LeVay, Simon. "A Difference in Hypothalmic Structure between Heterosexual and Homosexual Men." *Science* 253, no. 5023 (August 30, 1991): 1034–1037.

Lévi-Strauss, Claude. *The Savage Mind.* Chicago: University of Chicago Press, 1966.

Lewis, Gregory B. "Does Believing Homosexuality Is Innate Increase Support for Gay Rights?" *Policy Studies Journal* 37, no. 4 (2009): 669–693.

Lichtenberger, J. P. *Divorce: A Social Interpretation.* New York: McGraw-Hill, 1931.

Livingood, John M. "National Institute of Mental Health Task Force on Homosexuality: Final Report and Background Papers." Rockville, MD: National Institute of Mental Health, 1972.

Loftus, Jeni. "America's Liberalization in Attitudes toward Homosexuality, 1973–1998." *American Sociological Review* 66, no. 5 (October 2001): 762–782.

Lyons, Richard D. "Psychiatrists, in a Shift, Declare Homosexuality No Mental Illness." *New York Times,* December 16, 1973.

Mannheim, Karl. "On the Interpretation of the Weltanschauung." 1923. In Kecskemeti, *Essays on the Sociology of Knowledge,* 33–83.

———. "The Problem of Generations." 1928. In Kecskemeti, *Essays on the Sociology of Knowledge,* 276–320.

Marcus, Eric. *Making Gay History: The Half-Century Fight for Lesbian and Gay Equal Rights.* New York: Perennial, 2002.

Marotta, Toby. *The Politics of Homosexuality.* Boston: Houghton Mifflin, 1981.

Martin, John Levi. *The Explanation of Social Action.* New York: Oxford University Press, 2011.

Martin, John Levi, and Matthew Desmond. "Political Position and Social Knowledge." *Sociological Forum* 25, no. 1 (March 2010): 1–26.

Masterpiece Cakeshop v. Colorado Civil Rights Commission, no. 16-111 (2017).

Maugh, Thomas H., II, and Nora Zamichow. "Study Ties Part of Brain to Men's Sexual Orientation: San Diego Researcher's Findings Offer First Evidence of a Biological Cause for Homosexuality." *Los Angeles Times,* August 30, 1991.

McCarthy, Justin. "Record-High 60% of Americans Support Same-Sex Marriage." *Gallup News,* May 19, 2015. http://news.gallup.com.

———. "U.S. Support for Gay Marriage Edges to New High." *Gallup News,* May 15, 2017. http://news.gallup.com.

McCracken, Chelsea. "Regulating the Swish: Early Television Censorship." *Media History* 19, no. 3 (2013): 354–368.

McDaniel, Susan A. "Generationing Gender: Justice and the Division of Welfare." *Journal of Aging Studies* 18, no. 1 (2004): 27–44.

McDonnell, Terence E. "Drawing Out Culture: Productive Methods to Measure Cognition and Resonance." *Theory and Society* 43 (2014): 247–274.

Merten, Don, and Gary Schwartz. "Metaphor and Self: Symbolic Process in Everyday Life." *American Anthropologist* 84, no. 4 (December 1982): 796–810.

Meyer, Richard. "Rock Hudson's Body." In *Inside/Out: Lesbian Theories, Gay Theories,* edited by Diana Fuss, 258–288. New York: Routledge, 1991.

Michel, Jean-Baptiste, Yuan Kui Shen, Aviva Presser Aiden, Adrian Veres, Matthew K. Gray, William Brockman, The Google Books Team, et al. "Quantitative Analysis of Culture Using Millions of Digitized Books." *Science* 331, no. 6014 (2010): 176–182.

Miller, Allan S., and John P. Hoffmann. "The Growing Divisiveness: Culture War or War of Words?" *Social Forces* 78, no. 2 (December 1999): 721–745.

Miller, Steven D., and David O. Sears. "Stability and Change in Social Tolerance: A Test of the Persistence Hypothesis." *American Journal of Political Science* 30, no. 1 (February 1986): 214–236.

Mintz, Steven, and Susan Kellogg. *Domestic Revolutions: A Social History of American Family Life.* New York: Free Press, 1988.

Moore, Rick. "Fast or Slow: Sociological Implications of Measuring Dual-Process Cognition." *Sociological Science* 4 (2017): 196–223.

Mouw, Ted, and Michael E. Sobel. "Culture Wars and Opinion Polarization: The Case of Abortion." *American Journal of Sociology* 106, no. 4 (January 2001): 913–943.

Moyer-Gusé, Emily. "Toward a Theory of Entertainment Persuasion: Explaining the Persuasive Effects of Entertainment-Education Messages." *Communication Theory* 18 (2008): 407–425.

Murray, Matthew. "Television Wipes Its Feet." *Journal of Popular Film and Television* 21, no. 3 (Fall 1993): 128–138.

Nelson, Thomas E., Rosalee A. Clawson, and Zoe M. Oxley. "Media Framing of a Civil Liberties Conflict and Its Effect on Tolerance." *American Political Science Review* 91, no. 3 (1997): 567–583.

Newport, Frank. "Landing a Man on the Moon: The Public's View." *Gallup News*, July 20, 1999. http://news.gallup.com.

Newsweek. "Homosexuals in Uniform." June 9, 1947, 54.

Norris, Pippa, and Ronald Inglehart. *Sacred and Secular: Religion and Politics Worldwide.* New York: Cambridge University Press, 2004.

Obergefell v. Hodges, 576 US ___ (2015).

Ohlander, Julianne, Jeanne Batalova, and Judith Treas. "Explaining Educational Influences on Attitudes toward Homosexual Relations." *Social Science Research* 34, no. 4 (2005): 781–799.

Olick, Jeffrey K. "Collective Memory: The Two Cultures." *Sociological Theory* 17, no. 3 (November 1999): 333–348.

Olson, Laura R., Wendy Cadge, and James T. Harrison. "Religion and Public Opinion about Same-Sex Marriage." *Social Science Quarterly* 87, no. 2 (June 2006): 340–360.

Orgad, Shani. *Media Representation and the Global Imagination.* Malden, MA: Polity, 2012.

Ortega y Gasset, José. *Man and Crisis.* Translated by Mildred Adams. New York: Norton, 1958.

Parker, Theodore. *Ten Sermons of Religion.* Boston: Crosby, Nichols, 1853.

Pascoe, C. J. *Dude, You're a Fag: Masculinity and Sexuality in High School.* Berkeley: University of California Press, 2007.

Patterson, Orlando. "Making Sense of Culture." *Annual Review of Sociology* 40 (2014): 1–30.

Perrin, Andrew J. *Citizen Speak: The Democratic Imagination in American Life.* Chicago: University of Chicago Press, 2006.

Pew Research Center. "Changing Attitudes on Gay Marriage." June 26, 2017. www. pewforum.org.

———. "Republicans Unified, Democrats Split on Gay Marriage; Religious Beliefs Underpin Opposition to Homosexuality." Washington, DC: Pew Forum on Religion and Public Life, 2003.

———. "Support for Same-Sex Marriage Grows, Even among Groups That Had Been Skeptical." Washington, DC: Pew Research Center, 2017.

Phillips, Kendall R. *Controversial Cinema: The Films That Outraged America.* Westport, CT: Praeger, 2008.

Pierson, Ransdell. "Uptight on Gay News: Can the Straight Press Get the Gay Story Straight? Is Anyone Even Trying?" *Columbia Journalism Review,* March/April 1982, 25–33.

Pilcher, Jane. "Mannheim's Sociology of Generations: An Undervalued Legacy." *British Journal of Sociology* 45, no. 3 (September 1994): 481–495.

Plummer, Joseph T. "The Concept and Application of Life Style Segmentation." *Journal of Marketing* 38 (January 1974): 33–37.

Plummer, Ken. "Generational Sexualities, Subterranean Traditions, and the Hauntings of the Sexual World: Some Preliminary Remarks." *Symbolic Interaction* 33, no. 2 (2010): 163–190.

Polikoff, Nancy D. *Beyond (Straight and Gay) Marriage: Valuing All Families under the Law.* Boston: Beacon, 2008.

Powell, Brian, Catherine Bolzendahl, Claudia Geist, and Lala Carr Steelman. *Counted Out: Same-Sex Relations and Americans' Definitions of Family.* ASA Rose Series. New York: Russell Sage Foundation, 2010.

Powell, Brian, Natasha Yurk Quadlin, and Oren Pizmony-Levy. "Public Opinion, the Courts, and Same-Sex Marriage: Four Lessons Learned." *Social Currents* 2, no. 1 (2015): 3–12.

Pugh, Allison J. "What Good Are Interviews for Thinking about Culture? Demystifying Interpretive Analysis." *American Journal of Cultural Sociology* 1, no. 1 (2012): 42–68.

Quinn, Naomi. "'Commitment' in American Marriage: A Cultural Analysis." *American Ethnologist* 9, no. 4 (November 1982): 775–798.

———. "Culture and Contradiction: The Case of Americans Reasoning about Marriage." *Ethos* 24, no. 3 (1996): 391–425.

Quinn, Naomi, and Dorothy Holland. "Culture and Cognition." In *Cultural Models in Language and Thought,* edited by Naomi Quinn and Dorothy Holland, 3–40. New York: Cambridge University Press, 1987.

Reed, Isaac Ariail. "Epistemology Contextualized: Social-Scientific Knowledge in a Postpositivist Era." *Sociological Theory* 28, no. 1 (March 2010): 20–39.

———. "Justifying Sociological Knowledge: From Realism to Interpretation." *Sociological Theory* 26, no. 2 (June 2008): 101–129.

Ricoeur, Paul. *The Rule of Metaphor: Multidisciplinary Studies of the Creation of Meaning in Language.* Toronto: University of Toronto Press, 1977.

Riley, Matilda White, Anne Foner, and John W. Riley Jr. "The Aging and Society Paradigm." In *Handbook of Theories of Aging,* edited by Vern L. Bengtson and K. Warner Schaie, 327–343. New York: Springer, 1999.

Rimmerman, Craig A. "Beyond Political Mainstreaming: Reflections on Lesbian and Gay Organizations and the Grassroots." In Rimmerman, Wald, and Wilcox, *Politics of Gay Rights,* 54–78.

Rimmerman, Craig A., Kenneth D. Wald, and Clyde Wilcox, eds. *The Politics of Gay Rights.* Chicago: University of Chicago Press, 2000.

Ring, Dan. "8,100 Gay, Lesbian Couples Marry after 2004 Decision." *Republican,* May 17, 2006.

Rintala, Marvin. "A Generation in Politics: A Definition." *Review of Politics* 25, no. 4 (October 1963): 509–522.

Roberts, Carl W., and Kurt Lang. "Generations and Ideological Change: Some Observations." *Public Opinion Quarterly* 49 (1985): 460–473.

Robinson, Gene. "State of LGBT Rights: Married on Sunday, but Fired on Monday." *Daily Beast,* December 14, 2014. www.thedailybeast.com.

Rosenfeld, Michael J. *The Age of Independence: Interracial Unions, Same-Sex Unions, and the Changing American Family.* Cambridge, MA: Harvard University Press, 2007.

———. "Moving a Mountain: The Extraordinary Trajectory of Same-Sex Marriage Approval in the United States." *Socius: Sociological Research for a Dynamic World* 3, no. 1 (2017): 1–22.

Rubin, Herbert J., and Irene S. Rubin. *Qualitative Interviewing: The Art of Hearing Data.* Thousand Oaks, CA: Sage, 2005.

Russo, Vito. *The Celluloid Closet: Homosexuality in the Movies.* New York: Harper & Row, 1981.

Ryder, Norman B. "The Cohort as a Concept in the Study of Social Change." *American Sociological Review* 30, no. 6 (December 1965): 843–861.

Schatzberg, Michael G. *Political Legitimacy in Middle Africa: Father, Family, Food.* Bloomington: Indiana University Press, 2001.

Schiappa, Edward, Peter B. Gregg, and Dean E. Hewes. "Can One TV Show Make a Difference? *Will & Grace* and the Parasocial Contact Hypothesis." *Journal of Homosexuality* 51, no. 4 (2006): 15–37.

Schilt, Kristen, and Laurel Westbrook. "Bathroom Battlegrounds and Penis Panics." *Contexts* 14, no. 3 (Summer 2015): 26–31.

Schnabel, Landon, and Eric Sevell. "Should Mary and Jane Be Legal? Americans' Attitudes toward Marijuana and Same-Sex Marriage Legalization, 1988–2014." *Public Opinion Quarterly* 81, no. 1 (2017): 157–172.

Schnittker, Jason, Jeremy Freese, and Brian Powell. "Who Are Feminists and What Do They Believe? The Role of Generations." *American Sociological Review* 68, no. 4 (August 2003): 607–622.

Schudson, Michael. *Discovering the News: A Social History of American Newspapers*. New York: Basic Books, 1978.

Schuman, Howard, and Jacqueline Scott. "Generations and Collective Memories." *American Sociological Review* 54, no. 3 (June 1989): 359–381.

Schwadel, Philip, and Christopher R. H. Garneau. "An Age-Period-Cohort Analysis of Political Tolerance in the United States." *Sociological Quarterly* 55, no. 2 (Spring 2014): 421–452.

Schwartz, Christine R., and Hongyun Han. "The Reversal of the Gender Gap in Education and Trends in Marital Dissolution." *American Sociological Review* 79, no. 4 (August 2014): 605–629.

Sears, David O., and Carolyn L. Funk. "Evidence of the Long-Term Persistence of Adults' Political Predispositions." *Journal of Politics* 61, no. 1 (February 1999): 1–28.

Seidman, Steven. *Beyond the Closet: The Transformation of Gay and Lesbian Life*. New York: Routledge, 2004.

Seidman, Steven, Chet Meeks, and Francie Traschen. "Beyond the Closet? The Changing Social Meaning of Homosexuality in the United States." *Sexualities* 2, no. 1 (1999): 9–34.

Seinfeld Scripts. "The Outing." N.d. www.seinfeldscripts.com.

Seward, Georgene H. *Sex and the Social Order*. New York: McGraw-Hill, 1948.

Sewell, William H., Jr. "A Theory of Structure: Duality, Agency, and Transformation." *American Journal of Sociology* 98, no. 1 (July 1992): 1–29.

Sherkat, Darren E., Kylan Mattias de Vries, and Stacia Creek. "Race, Religion, and Opposition to Same-Sex Marriage." *Social Science Quarterly* 91, no. 1 (March 2010): 80–98.

Sherkat, Darren E., Melissa Powell-Williams, Gregory Maddox, and Kylan Mattias de Vries. "Religion, Politics, and Support for Same-Sex Marriage in the United States, 1988–2008." *Social Science Research* 40, no. 1 (2011): 167–180.

Shilts, Randy. *And the Band Played On: Politics, People, and the AIDS Epidemic*. New York: Penguin, 1988.

Shore, Bradd. *Cognition, Culture, and the Problem of Meaning*. New York: Oxford University Press, 1996.

Shurlock, Geoffrey. "The Motion Picture Production Code." *Annals of the American Academy of Political and Social Science* 254 (November 1947): 140–146.

Signorile, Michelangelo. "Out at the New York Times: Gays, Lesbians, AIDS, and Homophobia Inside America's Paper of Record." *Advocate*, May 5, 1992.

Simmel, Georg. "The Metropolis and Mental Life." In *On Individuality and Social Forms: Selected Writings*, edited by Donald N. Levine, 324–339. Chicago: University of Chicago Press, 1971.

Skitka, Linda J., Elizabeth Mullen, Thomas Griffin, Susan Hutchinson, and Brian Chamberlin. "Dispositions, Scripts, or Motivated Correction? Understanding Ideological Differences in Explanations for Social Problems." *Journal of Personality and Social Psychology* 83, no. 2 (2002): 470–487.

Slater, Michael D., and Donna Rouner. "Entertainment-Education and Elaboration Likelihood: Understanding the Processing of Narrative Persuasion." *Communication Theory* 12, no. 2 (May 2002): 173–191.

Slusher, Morgan P., and Craig A. Anderson. "When Reality Monitoring Fails: The Role of Imagination in Stereotype Maintenance." *Journal of Personality and Social Psychology* 52, no. 4 (1987): 653–662.

Smith, Christian. *American Evangelicalism: Embattled and Thriving.* Chicago: University of Chicago Press, 1998.

Smith, Dorothy E. "The Standard North American Family: SNAF as an Ideological Code." In *Writing the Social: Critique, Theory, and Investigations*, edited by Dorothy E. Smith, 157–171. Toronto: University of Toronto Press, 1999.

Socarides, Charles W. "Homosexuality and Medicine." *Journal of the American Medical Association* 212, no. 7 (May 18, 1970): 1199–1202.

Stacey, Judith. *Brave New Families: Stories of Domestic Upheaval in Late-Twentieth Century America.* Berkeley: University of California Press, 1990.

Stein, Marc. *Rethinking the Gay and Lesbian Movement.* New York: Routledge, 2012.

Stevenson, Deborah, Christine Everingham, and Penelope Robinson. "Choices and Life Chances: Feminism and the Politics of Generational Change." *Social Politics* 18, no. 1 (Spring 2011): 125–145.

Strauss, Anselm L. *Qualitative Analysis for Social Scientists.* New York: Cambridge University Press, 1987.

Strauss, Claudia. "The Imaginary." *Anthropological Theory* 6, no. 3 (2006): 322–344.

Strauss, Claudia, and Naomi Quinn. *A Cognitive Theory of Cultural Meaning.* New York: Cambridge University Press, 1997.

Strauss, William, and Neil Howe. *Generations: The History of America's Future, 1584 to 2069.* New York: Harper, 1991.

Sullivan, Andrew. "It Is Accomplished." *Daily Dish*, June 26, 2015. http://dish.andrewsullivan.com.

Suplee, Curt. "Brain May Determine Sexuality." *Washington Post*, August 30, 1991.

Swidler, Ann. *Talk of Love: How Culture Matters.* Chicago: University of Chicago Press, 2001.

Sztompka, Piotr. *The Sociology of Social Change.* Malden, MA: Blackwell, 1993.

Taylor, Charles. "Modern Social Imaginaries." *Public Culture* 14, no. 1 (2002): 91–124.

Taylor, Paul. *The Next America: Boomers, Millennials, and the Looming Generational Showdown.* New York: Public Affairs, 2014.

Taylor, Verta, Katrina Kimport, Nella Van Dyke, and Ellen Ann Andersen. "Culture and Mobilization: Tactical Repertoires, Same-Sex Weddings, and the Impact on Gay Activism." *American Sociological Review* 74, no. 6 (December 2009): 865–890.

Thornton, Arland, and Linda Young-DeMarco. "Four Decades of Trends in Attitudes toward Family Issues in the United States: The 1960s through the 1990s." *Journal of Marriage and Family* 63, no. 4 (November 2001): 1009–1037.

Treas, Judith. "How Cohorts, Education, and Ideology Shaped a New Sexual Revolution on American Attitudes toward Nonmarital Sex, 1972–1998." *Sociological Perspectives* 45, no. 3 (Autumn 2002): 267–283.

Tuchman, Gaye. "Introduction: The Symbolic Annihilation of Women by the Mass Media." In *Hearth and Home: Images of Women in the Mass Media*, edited by Gaye Tuchman, Arlene Kaplan Daniels, and James Benét, 3–38. New York: Oxford University Press, 1978.

———. *Making News: A Study in the Construction of Reality*. New York: Free Press, 1978.

Twenge, Jean M. *Generation Me: Why Today's Young Americans Are More Confident, Assertive, Entitled—and More Miserable Than Ever Before*. New York: Free Press, 2006.

———. *iGen: Why Today's Super-Connected Kids Are Growing Up Less Rebellious, More Tolerant, Less Happy—and Completely Unprepared for Adulthood*. New York: Atria Books, 2017.

Vaisey, Stephen. "Motivation and Justification: A Dual-Process Model of Culture in Action." *American Journal of Sociology* 114, no. 6 (May 2009): 1675–1715.

———. "Socrates, Skinner, and Aristotle: Three Ways of Thinking about Culture in Action." *Sociological Forum* 23, no. 3 (September 2008): 603–613.

Valentino, Nicholas A., Vincent L. Hutchings, and Ismail K. White. "Cues That Matter: How Political Ads Prime Racial Attitudes during Campaigns." *American Political Science Review* 96, no. 1 (March 2002): 75–90.

Walters, Suzanna Danuta. *All the Rage: The Story of Gay Visibility in America*. Chicago: University of Chicago Press, 2001.

Weber, Max. *Economy and Society: An Outline of Interpretive Sociology*. Berkeley: University of California Press, 1978.

Weil, Frederick D. "Cohorts, Regimes, and the Legitimation of Democracy: West Germany since 1945." *American Sociological Review* 52, no. 3 (June 1987): 308–324.

Weiner, Bernard, Raymond P. Perry, and Jamie Magnusson. "An Attributional Analysis of Reactions to Stigmas." *Journal of Personality and Social Psychology* 55, no. 5 (1988): 738–748.

Welch, Paul. "Homosexuality in America." *Life*, June 26, 1964, 66–80.

White, Harrison C. "Succession and Generations: Looking Back on Chains of Opportunity." In *Dynamics of Cohort and Generations Research*, edited by Henk A. Becker, 31–51. Amsterdam: Thesis, 1992.

Whitehead, Andrew L. "Sacred Rites and Civil Rights: Religion's Effect on Attitudes toward Same-Sex Unions and the Perceived Cause of Homosexuality." *Social Science Quarterly* 91, no. 1 (March 2010): 63–79.

Wikipedia. "The Mendota Beacon." https://en.wikipedia.org.

Wilcox, Clyde, and Robin Wolpert. "Gay Rights in the Public Sphere: Public Opinion on Gay and Lesbian Equality." In Rimmerman, Wald, and Wilcox, *Politics of Gay Rights*, 409–432.

Winchester, Daniel. "A Hunger for God: Embodied Metaphor as Cultural Cognition in Action." *Social Forces* 95, no. 2 (December 2016): 585–606.

Winograd, Morley, and Michael D. Hais. *Millennial Momentum: How a New Generation Is Remaking America*. New Brunswick, NJ: Rutgers University Press, 2011.

Winship, Christopher, and David J. Harding. "A Mechanism-Based Approach to the Identification of Age-Period-Cohort Models." *Sociological Methods and Research* 36, no. 3 (February 2008): 362–401.

Wood, Peter B., and John P. Bartkowski. "Attribution Style and Public Policy Attitudes toward Gay Rights." *Social Science Quarterly* 85, no. 1 (March 2004): 58–74.

Wright, Paul J., and Ashley K. Randall. "Pornography Consumption, Education, and Support for Same-Sex Marriage among Adult U.S. Males." *Communication Research* 41, no. 5 (2014): 665–689.

Yang, Yang. "Social Inequalities in Happiness in the United States, 1974–2004." *American Sociological Review* 73, no. 2 (April 2008): 204–226.

Yang, Yang, and Kenneth C. Land. "A Mixed Models Approach to the Age-Period-Cohort Analysis of Repeated Cross-Section Surveys, with an Application to Data on Trends in Verbal Test Scores." *Sociological Methodology* 36 (2006): 75–97.

Zerubavel, Eviatar. *Social Mindscapes: An Invitation to Cognitive Sociology*. Cambridge, MA: Harvard University Press, 1997.

———. *Time Maps: Collective Memory and the Social Shape of the Past*. Chicago: University of Chicago Press, 2003.

INDEX

Aarons, Leroy, 58

Actual generation. *See* Generation: as an actuality

Adolescence and early adulthood, 5, 14, 18, 24, 27, 223, 232

Adoption, 120

Advocate (magazine), 51

Age effect, 74–77, 83, 179–180, 192, 207, 254n10

Agency, 24–25, 95, 143, 223–227, 260n18

Aging, 73–74, 206–207, 227–228. *See also* Life course

Aging-stability hypothesis. *See* Persistence hypothesis

AIDS Coalition to Unleash Power (ACT UP), 54–57

AIDS Memorial Quilt, 54

American Psychiatric Association (APA), 41–42, 47–49, 69, 249n12

American Society of Newspaper Editors, 57–58

Analogy. *See* Metaphor

As Good as It Gets (movie), 63

Attitude change: analysis in public opinion data, 74–77; intra-cohort, 73–74, 83–84, 88, 94–95, 162, 192–195, 203–208, 209–211. *See also* Period: effect

Attitude stability, 73–74, 75. *See also* Persistence hypothesis

Attribution theory, 131–134, 162. *See also* Homosexuality: attribution of

Baby Boom: cohort, 4, 14, 26, 127, 153, 158, 161, 169, 246n36, 264n8

Baehr v. Lewin, 65

Ballot initiative, 50–51, 66–67, 253n89

Basic Instinct (movie), 58

Bible, 112, 114–115, 163

Binary oppositions, 141–142, 143, 147, 186, 217

Biography: 5, 13, 34, 100, 103

Bird Cage, The (movie), 62–63

Bisexuality, 141–142, 217

Boundaries: between cohorts, 14, 23, 25, 27–28, 81, 94, 220–221, 223–223, 248n6, 255n18; between periods, 23, 25, 27–28, 223–224, 248n6, 255n18; of substantive scope, 25, 28, 221–222

Bourdieuian theory, 24

Braudel, Fernand, 225–226

Brock, Greg, 55

Brokeback Mountain (movie), 68

Bryant, Anita, 50

Buchanan, Patrick, 71, 99, 257n2

Bush, George W., 64, 66

Castoriadias, Cornelius, 32

CBS Reports (television show), 45

Celebrities, influence of, 39. *See also* Media representation: in entertainment

Chasing Amy (movie), 63

Civil Rights Movement, 14, 17–19, 148, 201, 207, 210, 244n11, 249n13

Civil unions, 66, 97, 148, 164–165, 258n15

Clinton, Bill, 1, 59–61, 65, 82

Cohabitation, 122, 123, 129, 163, 187

Cognition: dual-process, 31, 33–34, 130–131, 133, 135–136, 159–160, 246n42, 259n13; relation to culture, 31–34, 138–140, 228, 260n18

Cognitive dissonance, 133

Cohort(s): analysis, 20–21, 29, 81–82, 255n16; defined, 4, 244n6; effect, 74–77, 78–88, 91, 94–95, 162, 192–193, 211; effect on discourse, 98, 102–105, 111–112, 120–128, 131, 144, 161–162; Identity, 70, 73, 81–82, 87–88, 94, 97, 104, 140, 160–161, 232; Illness, 69–70, 73, 81–82, 87, 89, 104, 232; Lifestyle, 69–70, 82, 87–88, 104, 232; vs. generation, 15–22, 29, 193, 209, 211, 218–221, 244n14, 244n15

Cohort norm formation, 24

Cohort replacement: demographic metabolism, 4, 5, 64, 68, 70, 72–73, 128, 214, 215–216, 224–227; in public opinion, 5, 72, 76, 81–83, 94–95, 99, 192–193, 196, 254n10, 255n17; vs. generational change, 4, 72–73, 95, 218, 224

Collective identity. See Status group identities

Collective mentality, 29, 246n39

Collective representation, 6, 32–33

Coming of age, 5, 8, 13–15, 23, 27, 29, 69–71, 73, 94, 126–128, 139–140, 161–162, 192–193, 211, 214, 223–224, 255n18

Coming out, 39, 47, 55–58, 157, 197–199, 204, 225, 250n32, 252n57. See also Metaphor: the closet; National Coming Out Day

Commitment, 165, 173, 176–179, 187, 216

Common sense, 2, 6, 129, 139, 210

Communicative action, 100, 103, 165–166, 249n8, 262n21. See also Habermas, Jürgen

Comte, Auguste, 227, 264n19

Conjuncture, 226

Constitutional amendment, 66–67, 253n89

Contact hypothesis, 125, 250n32, 263n1

Corroboration, 194–196, 199, 203, 207, 208

Cultural trauma, 76, 254n9

Culture, 100, 127, 193, 203, 209, 227, 228

Culture industries, 39, 58–59, 64, 70–71, 249n16. See also Media representation: in entertainment

Culture war, 35, 68, 71, 96–102, 107–108, 111, 126–128, 174, 257n2, 258n10; middle ground, 98, 102–103, 111–112, 120–121, 126–127, 207, 258n11

Daughters of Bilitis, 42–43

Defense of Marriage Act, 1, 63, 65–66, 79, 89, 225, 252n76

Degeneres, Ellen, 61–62, 248n5

Demedicalization, 45–49, 51, 69

Democratic Party, 59–60, 64, 70, 99, 114

Demographic perspective, 23, 72–77, 217–218, 226–227, 244n15, 245n20

Demographics: related to discourse, 103; of informants, 232–233; related to public opinion, 84–86, 91, 93–94, 96, 255n23

Deviance, tolerance of, 200–203

Diagnostic and Statistical Manual of Mental Disorders (DSM). See American Psychiatric Association

Dialogic: antagonism, 105–11, 127, 173–174; culture wars, 99–102; discourse, 98, 102–103, 136, 202, 257n1

Digital Natives, 14–15, 220–221

Discourse, 6, 8, 70, 77, 97–128, 130, 136–137, 160, 224, 252n57, 258n11; defined, 100, 258n6; immoral inclusivity, 98, 102–104, 112–116, 123–126, 191, 196, 219; libertarian pragmatism, 96–98, 102–104, 116–119, 121–123, 125–126, 152, 158, 191, 219, 258n13; unambiguous opposition, 98, 102–111, 120–121, 123–127, 136, 158, 173–174, 191, 196–200; unambiguous support, 98, 102–111, 120–123, 126, 136, 152, 173–174, 191, 200–203

Discursive field, 99–103, 126–127, 257n1

Divorce, 169, 171–172, 187, 262n15; attitudes, 122, 123, 163, 180–181; as sin, 115
Doan, Long, 166–167
Don't Ask Don't Tell. *See* Military, gays in the
Durkheim, Emile, 32–33

Early adulthood. *See* Adolescence
Education: predictor of public opinion, 84, 91, 93, 95, 255n23, 256n25, 258n14
Elder, Glen, Jr., 16, 22
Election of 2008, 96–97, 149
Ellen (television show). *See* Degeneres, Ellen
Entertainment Weekly (magazine), 60
Epistemic community, 39–41, 46–47, 69–71, 249n7
Equal Rights Amendment, 50, 253n82
Esler, Anthony, 29
Essentialist language, 149–151, 153

Family, 163, 168–169, 171, 187, 256n25, 263n26
Fourteenth Amendment, 1, 172–173, 262n18
Fox Network, 61
Framing, 10, 33, 44, 51, 69–70, 248n54
Fresh contact, 25, 223, 227
Freud, Sigmund, 41

Gay and Lesbian Alliance Against Defamation (GLAAD), 58, 61
Gay marriage: as inevitable, 77, 213–214, 263n1; effects of legalizing, 107, 150–151, 186–188, 189, 202, 215–217, 262n23, 263n25, 264n5; future of, 215–218; how much controversy is about marriage or homosexuality, 163–165, 166, 175, 186
Gay marriage generation, 3, 6, 27, 28, 29, 35, 87, 224
Gay rights. *See* Politics: of gay rights
Gender: attitudes in public opinion, 12, 81; binary, 143–144; equality, 101, 169, 171,

173, 187, 263n26; in marriage, 104, 106, 109–110, 113–115, 168–170, 175, 184–186; predictor of public opinion, 84, 91, 93
General Social Survey, 2, 63, 78–88
Generation: as an actuality, 16–22, 28, 193, 209, 210, 218–221, 245n23; -as-group vs. -as-process, 23–25, 211, 217, 219; cycles, 26, 223–224; defined, 3–4, 21, 29; imprint paradigm, 14, 23, 27–28, 220–221; kinship descent meaning, 4, 6, 12, 21, 29, 120–126, 231; pulse-rate paradigm, 14, 23–27, 220, 224, 245n22, 246n37; vs. cohort, 15–22, 29, 193, 209, 211, 218–221, 224, 244n14, 244n15
Generational change: and history, 223–228; processes, 23–25, 68, 193, 196; in public opinion data, 2, 5, 12, 76–77, 88, 93–95, 144, 208–209, 222; in social imagination, 8, 120, 161–162, 166, 186, 188, 200; vs. cohort replacement, 4, 72–73, 83–84, 95, 214, 218. *See also* Generation; Social change
Generational mythology, 27, 218–225, 228
Generational theory, 5, 13–19, 21, 34–35, 76, 139–140, 191–195, 209–211, 217–228, 244n5; common sense view, 13–14
Generational triggers, 218–221, 227
Generation entelechy, 17–19, 22, 219, 244n14
Generationism, 220
Generation location, 16, 19, 193. *See also* Cohort(s); Cohort replacement
Generation unit, 17–22, 218–221, 244n14
Generation X, 4, 5, 12, 14, 26–27
Generation Z. *See* iGen
Gittings, Barbara, 48–49
Glaeser, Andreas, 194–195, 210, 247n54
Glee (television show), 68
Gold, Ronald, 48
Goodridge v. Department of Public Health, 66, 89
Graham, Franklin, 1
Great Depression, 4, 16–17, 24

Griffin, Larry, 18–19, 22
Grounded theory, 235–236

Habermas, Jürgen, theory of public
sphere, 39–40, 165–166, 249n8
Heteronormativity, 41, 62, 186
Historical participation, 24; HIV/AIDS,
51–57, 69–70, 251n48
History: and biography, 5, 6, 34, 74;
perspective on generations, 23
Hollywood. *See* Media representation: in
entertainment
Homonormativity, 186–187, 262n23
Homophile movement. *See* Social movement: homophile
Homophobia, 36–37, 62–63, 118, 158,
189–190
Homosexuality: attitudes expressed in
discourse, 98, 104, 116–119, 121–128,
155–156, 259n16; attribution of, 44–45,
79, 90, 92, 93, 104, 106–109, 115, 128,
130–137, 142–144, 155, 159–162, 204,
257n37; as behavior, 37, 49–54, 63, 64,
69–70, 125, 127, 131, 140, 144–145,
152–158, 160–161, 191, 194, 196; as deviant, 33–34, 41–45, 49–54, 64, 69–70, 96,
116, 121, 123, 125, 127, 144, 160–161, 194,
196, 207, 249n13; gendered masculine,
119; as identity, 37, 59, 60–64, 69–70,
131, 140, 144–152, 155, 157, 159–161, 191,
197–198, 217; as illegal, 42, 46, 49,
53–54; imagination of, 6, 8, 28, 33–34,
37–38, 41, 46, 49, 58–59, 69–71, 73, 126,
128, 131, 137, 139–140, 144–146, 152–153,
158–162, 186, 191, 193, 196, 200, 203,
216, 221–222; as lifestyle, 43, 49–54,
60, 69–70, 96, 121, 127, 128, 152–155; as
mental illness, 41–45, 46–49, 51, 64,
69, 127, 249n12; moral judgment of, 79,
85–88, 90–95, 104–107, 110–111, 116–119,
121–126, 135, 144, 147, 161, 205–206,
221; public opinion of, 12, 43, 50, 58,
62, 70, 76, 81, 89–93, 126, 132–133, 144,

210, 254n10; scientific research on
attribution, 59, 132; as sin, 52, 90–91,
96, 108–109, 112–114, 117, 123–127, 152,
153–155, 158, 160, 161, 196–199
Hooker, Evelyn, 44, 47
Howe, Neil, and William Strauss, 21–22,
26
Hudson, Rock, 52–53
Hunter, James Davison, 99–101

Ideology: explicit belief vs. implicit
schema, 129–131, 136–137, 159–161,
165–167, 171, 173, 194–195; influence on
discourse, 98, 102–126, 131, 136, 152, 158,
159–162, 191; influence on public opinion, 84–88, 89, 93–95, 131; political, 75,
133, 146, 158, 161; religious, 129–130, 133,
153–155, 160, 170, 196–200, 201,
205–206, 210–211, 216
iGen, 26, 219–220
Illinois, 5, 97, 232
Imagination: common sense view, 30;
and metaphor, 137–140; in psychology, 7, 30, 32; social, 6–8, 13, 28, 30–34;
38–41, 68, 71, 130–131, 137, 159–162, 166,
194, 216, 224, 246n43, 247n54. *See also*
Homosexuality: imagination of; Marriage: social connotations
Impressionable years hypothesis, 24, 75,
192, 222
Interpretive: community, 195–200, 203,
263n5; perspective, 23, 29, 34–35,
192–193, 236–237; processes, 100–101,
194–200, 210
Interview methods, 10, 107, 133, 135, 175,
185, 213, 231–237, 265n2, 265n4

Jaeger, Hans, 26

Kameny, Frank, 48
Kant, Immanuel, 32, 247n44
Kennedy, Anthony, 3, 5, 166, 172–173
Kennedy, John, assassination of, 5

Kertzer, David, 21, 29
Kinsey, Alfred, 41

Labeling, 10, 27, 205
Lesbian and gay movement. *See* Social
    movement: lesbian and gay
Lesbians and gays: attitudes toward, 79,
    90–95, 109–112, 115, 122–127, 156, 190,
    206–207, 257n34; equal rights for, 107,
    112–114, 116–119, 122, 126–127, 156–158,
    164; personal contact with, 79, 90, 92,
    93, 108–110, 122–125, 163, 189–190, 195,
    196–199, 201–205, 207, 210, 250n32,
    256n25, 257n36; as protected class, 133
LeVay, Simon, 59, 132
LGBTQ movement. *See* Social movement:
    LGBTQ
Liberation: sexual, 47, 49–50, 250n31,
    253n84
Libertarianism, 222
Life (magazine), 58–59
Life course: phases of, 24, 25, 73–74, 75,
    192–193, 210–211, 223–224, 228; and pulse-
    rate paradigm, 14. *See also* Adolescence
    and early adulthood; Coming of age
Longue durée, 226
Los Angeles Times (newspaper), 59
Love, 110–111, 165, 173, 176–178, 187, 216

Mannheim, Karl, 15–19, 27, 34, 193, 219–
    220, 227, 244n5, 244n15, 264n13, 264n20
March on Washington: Second National,
    54–55, 64–65, 78; Third National, 60–
    61, 65
Marijuana legalization, 222
Marriage: Catholic/Christian definition,
    96, 112–115, 163–164, 168; cohort-related
    similarities and differences, 166, 171,
    176–186, 216, 261n14; companionate,
    169, 171, 183, 187; deinstitutionaliza-
    tion of, 187; evolutionary view, 170;
    individualized, 169, 171; institution, 1, 8,
    11, 125, 161, 162–188, 216, 253n84; laws in
the US, 165, 167–168, 172–173, 262n18;
    media representation, 172, 181–182; as
    privilege, 166–167, 261n25; religious vs.
    secular/legal definition, 112–115, 162,
    164–175, 216, 236, 262n21; role of gov-
    ernment and religion in, 104, 167–168;
    social connotations, 3, 165–167, 171–173,
    175–188, 216, 236, 261n4, 262n19; sym-
    bolic validation of relationship, 1, 165,
    173, 187; traditional, 168–170, 175
Marx, Karl, and problem of class con-
    sciousness, 15
Massachusetts, 6, 11, 66, 89, 225
Mass media: defined, 39; effect on culture
    wars, 100–101, 105, 111, 127; and the
    public sphere, 40–41, 224
Mattachine Society, 42–43, 45
McCain, John, 96–97
Media representation, 7, 8, 33, 70; censor-
    ship of, 42–44, 249n15, 249n16; in
    entertainment, 36–38, 42–44, 52–53,
    58–59, 61–64, 68–69, 125, 248n5,
    252n72, 256n25; in news media, 38,
    44–45, 45–46, 52–53, 54–59
Mental health professionals, 41, 46–47, 69
Mental image, 30, 32, 53, 137, 139
Memory, 7, 18, 30, 228; collective, 18–19, 33
Metaphor, 103, 131, 217, 221, 235–237; attrac-
    tion, 140, 142–145, 160; business, 145,
    157–158; the closet, 150–151, 157, 260n21;
    conceptual, 137–138, 140–144, 161, 259n13,
    260n18; in discourse, 138–162; explore or
    experiment, 142, 145, 198; to heterosexu-
    ality, 145–149; invisibility, 122, 145, 152,
    155, 156–158, 161; lifestyle, 145, 152–155,
    158, 161; living vs. dead, 138–139, 140, 143;
    to major acts of deviance, 125, 145, 152,
    154; no big deal, 145, 151–152; orientation,
    140–145; to race, 119, 131, 145–149, 160;
    tension theory, 138–139, 260n18; theory,
    137–140; unnatural, 121, 145, 152, 155–156,
    158, 161. *See also* Homosexuality: as
    behavior; as identity

Midnight Caller (television show), 58

Military, gays in the, 41–42, 61, 63

Milk (movie), 68

Millennials, 4, 5, 12, 14–15, 26–27, 219–221, 245n20, 245n22

Modern Family (television show), 68

Morality of non-discrimination, 111, 200–203, 210

Moral panic, 66

Motion Picture Production Code, 42–44, 249n15, 249n16

Narrative, 33, 59, 248n5; of attitude change, 203–208, 210–211; progress, 148–149, 223

National Association of Radio and Television Broadcasters, 43

National Coming Out Day, 55–56, 225

National Institute of Mental Health, 46

National Lesbian and Gay Journalists Association, 58

National Opinion Research Center. *See* General Social Survey

New Right movement. *See* Social movement: conservative opposition

News media, 38, 40, 56–59, 64, 70–71, 101; as gatekeepers, 38, 39–41, 56–59, 258n12

Newsom, Gavin, 68

Newsweek (magazine), 41, 59

New York Times (newspaper), 44, 48, 56, 57, 59, 251n48

Nightline (television show), 59

Nonsense, 2, 6, 64, 78, 159, 216

Obama, Barack, 1, 66–67, 149

Oprah Winfrey Show (television show), 55

Ortega y Gasset, José, 26

Palin, Sarah, 96–97

Parent-child relationship. *See* Generation: kinship descent meaning

Peer personalities, 25

Period: effect, 74–77, 78–88, 89, 91, 94–95, 162, 192–193, 195, 209–211; Gay Rights, 60–64, 70–71, 78, 88, 94–95, 126, 132, 146, 217; Homophile, 41–45, 69, 78, 127; in history, 14, 23, 29, 69–71, 76, 194–195, 221, 226, 254n9; Resistance, 49–54, 69–70, 78, 127

Persistence hypothesis, 24, 75, 192, 210, 254n7

Pew Research Center, 27, 78–79, 89–92, 246n37

Philadelphia (movie), 62

Pilcher, Jane, 29

Pirate: schema, 30–31

Politics, 8, 67; effect on culture wars, 100–103, 111; of gay marriage, 64–67, 70–71, 215–218, 225, 253n82, 253n84, 253n89, 253n90; of gay rights, 36–37, 49–51, 60–61, 63–64, 70, 82, 86, 93, 101, 126–127, 158, 163, 165, 166–167, 200–202, 208, 215, 217, 224, 262n23

Post-materialist values, 217

Premarital sex attitudes, 75, 122, 129, 169, 171

Pride marches and celebrations, 47, 53

Problems of generational analysis, 19–28; of boundaries, 25–28; of intra-cohort variation, 19–22; of measurement, 22; of perspective, 22–23; of reification, 23–25

Procreation, 163–164, 170, 173, 182–183, 186, 187, 216

Proposition 8 (California), 67, 68

Prototype, 7, 30–32

Psychiatry, 41–42, 46–49, 69. *See also* American Psychiatric Association; Mental health professionals

Public opinion: on gay marriage, 1–3, 5, 66–67, 71, 72, 74, 76, 77–95, 132–133, 140, 162, 195–196, 208–209, 211; theory of, 39–41. *See also* Homosexuality: public opinion of

Public sphere, 38–41, 51, 165–166, 249n8; privileged communicators in, 38, 39–41, 105

Queer: identity, 186, 217, 253n84; theory, 25

Radio and Television News Directors Foundation, 58
Recognition, 194–196, 199, 203, 208
Red scare, 42
Religion, 4, 105, 129–130; atheism, 164–165, 222; freedom laws, 215; generational change in, 222; orthodox, 99–102, 196–200, 210, 216; secular, 99, 196, 199–200, 211, 216
Republican Party, 60, 70, 99, 114
Resonance, 194–196, 199, 203, 208
Rhetorical questions, 106–107
Ryder, Norman, 4, 20, 72

"Same Love" (song), 68–69
Schema: cultural, 7–8, 30–34, 131, 234, 243n15, 246n43; of homosexuality, 37, 70, 73, 131, 137, 139–140, 216, 221; mental, 7, 31, 221, 228, 243n14, 247n44, 259n13. See also Homosexuality: imagination of; Ideology: explicit belief vs. implicit schema
Script, 33, 36, 56
Seinfeld (television show), 36–37, 60
Sexual attraction: metaphor, 140, 142–145, 160; role in marriage, 173, 182–186, 216
Sexual orientation, 45, 63, 92, 123, 141, 156, 198, 260n22. See also Metaphor: orientation
Shepard, Matthew, 63
Silence of the Lambs (movie), 58
Sixties Generation, 14–15, 17–22, 24
Socarides, Charles, 46–47
Social change, 2, 5, 27, 97, 220, 223–228, 264n20; causes of, 67–68, 225; pace of, 67–68, 72, 94, 225–226, 264n19
Social desirability bias, 135, 234, 259n8

Social generation: defined, 29; social generational processes, 16–17, 23, 28, 29–30
Social imagination. See Imagination: social
Social imaginary, 33, 38–41, 246n43
Socialization, 4, 6, 7, 24, 120, 126, 128, 227, 231; resocialization, 204
Social media, 14–15, 28, 211, 221
Social movement, 39–40, 224; conservative opposition, 37, 49–51, 60, 61, 63–64, 66, 69, 101, 251n44; feminist, 50, 250n31; homophile, 41–45, 47, 69, 249n14; lesbian and gay, 37, 40–41, 45–49, 50–51, 69–70, 225, 250n31, 251n44, 253n82; LGBTQ, 37, 40–41, 64–65, 68–69, 70–71, 225, 253n84
Social networks, 101, 103, 112, 160, 193, 194–196, 199–200, 210–211
Social reproduction, 72, 227–228
Sodomy laws. See Homosexuality: as illegal
Spitzer, Robert, 48
Status group identities, 15, 99–103, 127, 136–137, 192, 244n14
Stereotype: generational, 5, 12, 14–15, 17, 21–22, 28, 191, 208–209, 219–220; of lesbians and gays, 39, 52, 55, 56–58, 62; of old age, 73, 75; as schema, 7–8, 30, 32
Stigma, 49, 51–53, 55–56, 119, 121, 132, 225
Stonewall Rebellion, 40, 45–47, 82, 250n31
Strauss, William. See Howe, Neil, and William Strauss
Subculture, 192–196, 200–203, 209–211, 216
Sullivan, Andrew, 2
Symbolic annihilation, 43–44, 69, 219, 250n21

Time, 3, 27, 74, 223–227, 248n6; long-term vs. short-term, 67–68, 225–226
Time (magazine), 59

Tolerance, 12, 37, 62–63, 112–113, 123, 125–126, 132, 156, 200, 202–204, 210, 217, 248n3, 254n9, 254n10

Transgender: identity, 186, 217; politics, 215, 264n5

Turning point, 23, 38, 40–41, 52, 64, 68–71, 82, 226, 248n6; demedicalization, 45–49, 69, 250n31; legitimation, 54–60, 70, 132, 225

Understanding, 33, 160, 180, 216, 222, 234, 243n15; of marriage, 3, 165–167, 171–173, 175–188; theory of, 194–196, 210, 247n54

US Supreme Court: *Bowers v. Hardwick*, 40, 49, 53–54, 58, 69; *Obergefell v. Hodges*, 1–3, 67, 89, 172–173, 215, 262n18; protests, 54; *Roe v. Wade*, 50; *United States v. Windsor*, 67, 89

Vietnam War, 4, 14, 17, 20

Washington Post (newspaper), 59

Wedding protest, 54, 65

Will & Grace (television show), 62, 125, 248n5

Worldview, 2, 5, 6, 10, 13–14, 23, 29, 68, 73, 75, 76–77, 83, 114, 136–137, 191–200, 202–206, 210–211, 214, 221–222, 227, 234, 264n13; measured in public opinion, 79, 81, 89–92; orthodox vs. progressive, 100–103, 258n9

World War II, 41–42

Youth rebellion, 5, 228

Zapping, 47, 251n32

Zeitgeist, 37, 193, 210, 246n39

ABOUT THE AUTHOR

Peter Hart-Brinson is Associate Professor of Sociology and Communication/Journalism at the University of Wisconsin–Eau Claire. A graduate of the University of Wisconsin–Madison and the New College of Florida, he teaches courses on cultural sociology, political sociology, research methods, media, diversity, and communication.